UFO HUNTERS

ALSO BY WILLIAM J. BIRNES

UFO Hunters: Book One

UFO HUNTERS

BOOK TWO

WILLIAM J. BIRNES

A TOM DOHERTY ASSOCIATES BOOK
NEW YORK

UFO HUNTERS: BOOK TWO

A Tor Book
Published by Tom Doherty Associates, LLC
175 Fifth Avenue
New York, NY 10010

www.tor-forge.com

Tor® is a registered trademark of Tom Doherty Associates, LLC.

The Library of Congress Cataloging-in-Publication Data is available upon request.

ISBN 978-0-7653-2521-1 (hardcover)
ISBN 978-1-4299-5396-2 (e-book)

Our books may be purchased in bulk for promotional, educational, or busi-
ness use. Please contact your local bookseller or the Macmillan Corporate and
Premium Sales Department at 1-800-221-7945, extension 5442, or by e-mail at
MacmillanSpecialMarkets@macmillan.com.

First Edition: January 2016

Printed in the United States of America

10 9 8 7 6 5 4 3 2 1

TO THE MEMORY OF LEONARD NIMOY, whose series *In Search Of . . .* was the inspiration for *UFO Hunters.* In the *Star Trek* episode "The Gamesters of Triskelion," Spock's Sherlock Holmesian argument that the *Enterprise* had to follow the mysterious and unexplainable ion trail to find the missing Kirk was the basis of how we pursued the mystery of the unexplainable on *UFO Hunters.* You are, and always will be, our friend. LLAP.

CONTENTS

ACKNOWLEDGMENTS

First to Pat Uskert, Ted Acworth, and Jeff Tomlinson, the cast of *UFO Hunters*, who put their own lives and jobs aside to join the search for UFOs. We all came from different backgrounds, had different belief systems and life experiences, but had to mesh together in front of a camera, where we argued cogently and intelligently about how facts can support speculation and what happens when two and two doesn't equal four.

Next, of course, to Jon Alon Walz, our executive producer and head of the production company Motion Picture Productions, whose vision about a unique show with four guys from different backgrounds on an impossible quest that ultimately paid off made the show possible. Our senior producer Dave Pavoni, who was the beating-heart center of the setup for each episode by turning the impossible into reality, and our coexec producers, show runners, and directors Alan LaGarde and Steve Nigg, both of whom were unflappable in the face of unimaginable difficulties with schedules and travel and last-minute conflicts. Both Alan and Steve had very special talents that went way beyond telling the camera which way to shoot. Both individuals knew how to harmonize a crew, get the best out of everyone, and all the while deal with daily demands from the production office and the network. When we almost missed our flight in Mexico City and had to get all the way across the airport while carrying our bags, it was Alan LaGarde who commandeered an electric golf cart, piled us all on top, leaned on the horn, and, in a scene from *The Great Race,* got us to the jetway just in time for the flight, while proclaiming to all, "This is what makes us a family."

Jeff Tober, the coexecutive producer and later executive producer, was in charge of all the editing and postproduction. You can watch hundreds of other UFO- and paranormal-themed reality shows, but you won't find one that even comes close to the look, feel, continuity, and intelligence of *UFO Hunters.* And that's because of Jeff Tober, one of the most skilled heads of editing and postproduction in the business.

Our line producers were John Duffy and Jeremy Gardiner, assisted by coproducer and field coordinator Dan Zarenkiewicz, all of whom kept the daily production schedule flowing and coordinated the production office with the field crew.

Our writer/producers for individual episodes in Season 1 were Kevin Cummins, Tracy Chaplin, Autumn Humphreys, and Chad Horning, and also Stu Chait. Stu also served as story editor and was probably single-handedly responsible for our getting picked up for Season 2 when he was in the editing bay at the Santa Monica production office, saw my "you are a hybrid" conversation with Terrell Copeland—that was only a suggestion, by the way, not an accusation—and just as the film editor was about to cut that scene out, told him to leave it in. Stu's instincts were that good. When our new exec at History, Mike Stiller, saw the scene, he said that was the reason for the Season 2 pickup. Thanks, Stu.

In the second season we were joined by Kevin Barry, Rob Bluemthal, John Greenwald, Scott Goldie, and Dave Story, all of whom pushed us to do better, think harder, and not to cop out.

John Tindall was our FX producer, the guy who set off explosions in his lab, demonstrated what type of electrical failure brought down the B-25 over Kelso, Washington, and, with Ted Acworth, debunked the debunkers of the Rendlesham forest story by proving with his magical GPS equations that the light the U.S. Air Force personnel saw floating above the forest floor could not have been the lighthouse at Orford Ness. So much for the debunkers.

Our director of photography was Kevin Graves, probably one of the most gifted DPs in the business, who had the ability to size up a shot in an instant and pull it off quickly even as the sun was uncooperatively sneaking behind a cloud. Our B-camera operator was Brian Garrity, who could hang upside down from a rock overlooking the North Sea one day, wiggle himself into a crevasse outside of Roswell on another day, go caving while still wielding a large Varicam on another day, and still go back to L.A. to compete in a triathlon and keep up with the best and the fastest. Finally, our assistant camera, Linh Nguyen, was the support that kept the cameras rolling. He could take apart a camera and reassemble it in 110-degree Arizona desert heat and do it so quickly that the sun didn't have time to set.

Our sound mixer was my friend Shah Martinez for season 1, who worked with electrician, gaffer, and swing man Stan Eng, who never met an Asian fusion buffet he didn't like. While Shah could get sound out of a rock, Stan had the ability to create and strike a set in minutes, even as the vans were getting loaded. During season 1, on our way back to the United States from the UK after the Bentwaters episode, we discovered at the airport, to our chagrin, that the British airport baggage handlers wouldn't move our equipment because it was overweight. Brian Garrity, Kevin Graves, Linh Nguyen, Shah Martinez, and Stan Eng broke down all the equipment and repacked it while Alan LaGarde and Dan Zarenkiewicz negotiated with the airline to allow our equipment to fly home with us. It was an amazing display of competence.

I have to acknowledge all our associate producers and production assistants, our editors and assistant editors, and all the help we received on the road.

Finally, of course, to Dolores Gavin at History, who picked us up as a series after our pilot episode and never stopped prodding us to do better, and to our exec at History, Mike Stiller, who inspired us and stood up for us the entire time.

It would be churlish and ungrateful of me not to thank my most patient publisher, Tom Doherty, and even more patient editor, Bob

Gleason, as well as editor Eric Raab and assistant editors Whitney Ross and Kelly Quinn for steering this manuscript through.

Thanks, guys, thanks to everyone, the best crew and best editors ever, for making *UFO Hunters* one of the top reality shows on television and a piece of our cultural zeitgeist. We hunted for, and eventually found and caught on camera, a UFO. It was a magnificent experience, the best three seasons of my life.

I have gret wonder, be this lighte.

—Geoffrey Chaucer, *The Book of the Duchess*

UFO HUNTERS

"A FUNNY THING"

Afunny thing happened to me on the way to the California bar exam. It wasn't the LAPD unit that followed me all the way from Lincoln Boulevard toward LAX and into the parking lot of the Radisson Hotel, turning on its lights and a burst of siren when I pulled into the parking space. I was already late, and now this. The officer was cautious, but aggressive in his glare as he raised his sunglasses and approached the back of my SUV, his one hand resting on his gun and the other motioning me to open the back gate.

"I have to get my canoe paddle out of the back," I told him, trying to explain that the pneumatic struts that held open the top tail window were broken. "I have to prop it up." I could see the officer's suspicions increase as I reached inside, holding the tail window open with one hand while I extracted the canoe paddle with the other. I finally propped the thing open and the officer approached.

"What's in the boxes?" he asked.

"Magazines," I told him. With his left index finger he motioned for me to open one of the boxes. A warrantless search? But with the exam attendance registration only minutes away and an impending impound of my car, containing my typewriter, if I demanded a warrant, I acceded and opened one of the boxes. "Magazines," I said, holding one of them up so he could see it.

I am sure over the course of this officer's professional law enforcement career there were others whose behavior elicited the same look of utter derision on his face that I saw as he examined the magazine cover and slowly, but almost inaudibly, sighed the letters, "U-F-O" as he traced them with his left hand. His right hand was no longer resting on his gun handle, and waves of disdain were rising off him that were so thick, you could almost see them shimmering in the warm morning Southern California sun.

"These all the same?"

"Yes, our latest edition. Want one? Want a box for the guys at the station house?"

"What are you doing here?"

"Bar exam," I said.

"You're late. Get inside," he ordered, jerking his thumb toward the hotel entrance. "And don't carry so many boxes in your car. Makes us nervous."

With that he turned around, walked back to his car, turned his light bar off, and drove away, his tires screeching as he wheeled out of the parking lot and busted a U-turn to get back to LAX. My cell phone began to vibrate, but I didn't pick it up until the black-and-white had spun onto the airport on-ramp.

That wasn't the funniest thing that happened to me that morning, however. I caught my BlackBerry on the last ring. It was the executive producer of the motion picture company where Nancy, Pat Uskert, and I had pitched a television series called *UFO Road Trip*.

"Dude, you got game," the exec said. "History gave us the pilot order. Saddle up."

My first TV series. And so much for the California bar exam where the proctors would immediately throw out my old clattering typewriter whose keystrokes reverberated throughout the entire test hall so loudly that they drew menacingly vicious looks of hatred, reminiscent of the fierce glares of martial arts acolytes in a Chuck Norris film.

These were the young Ivy League Bar candidates, who would eventually flock to the honey-money spigots of Mitt Romney's presidential campaign, where they would lap at the heavy flow like thirsty kittens and then inhabit the high-storied glass-walled offices of Wall Street, Century City, or Silicon Valley law firms.

B ut I had a pilot order, and the smog never smelled so sweet.
That pilot order would ultimately turn into the first season of the television series, *UFO Hunters*. And that was how we wound up in Boston on an unseasonably cold and blustery night, perched at our tables, watching the huge sports monitor on the wall of a bar called Cheers.

At first, when the opening credits come up on the television screen, you can only hope that what you've done will be a success. You're sitting with an audience at a bar, watching their reactions, hoping they will take their eyes off their dates, even if only for a minute, to watch what's happening on the large monitor hanging on the wall. Our field coordinator Dan Zarenkiewicz had asked the bartender if he could turn the channel from whatever game was being played—Celtics or Bruins—to History. He did. And it was the first time anyone in the cast saw what the final cut of the first episode looked like.

Because we'd been on the road, with only a few days off, from September 2007 through January 2008, we never saw the editing process taking place in the postproduction bays at the MPPI production offices in Santa Monica. Therefore, when the first episode aired, we also got a chance to see what an audience—albeit a small audience of young Lochinvars hoisting their Sam Adams or Harpoon lagers and more interested in wooing the girls at their tables than watching what was playing on the huge wall monitor—thought of the show.

The credits came up, the music played, our images in black and white slowly appeared and then dissolved on the screen and the deep voiceover announced that this was "the UFO before Roswell." A couple of heads at the table perked up from the pitchers in front of them when they heard the word, "Roswell."

"They're watching it," someone on the crew said.

Indeed they were, intermittently, as if allowing their collective gaze to float to the monitor to see what this was all about. No, it wasn't a Bruins game nor was it the Celtics playing the Lakers, nor was it a shapely starlet hyping the girl-magnet features of a new car, but folks were looking up nevertheless. As the episode, covering the bizarre story of the Maury Island UFO incident and the subsequent crash of a B-25 Mitchell bomber in Kelso, ostensibly carrying UFO debris from the Maury Island, Washington, beach played out, it seemed as if everyone enjoying the January evening at Cheers suddenly knew our name. We were the "UFO Hunters," and our season had just begun.

I believe one of the attractions of *UFO Hunters* was the difference between our series and prior specials and documentaries about UFOs. First of all, and believe it or not, *UFO Hunters* was not about proving that UFOs were real. It was about the evidence-based assertions concerning UFO encounters, sightings, and other UFO-related incidents and the arguments of debunkers. Our process was to focus on whatever real evidence could be gleaned from an incident and to put it through the filters of scientific testing and logical evaluation.

For example, if a debunker argued that the Rex Heflin photos from our episode on James McDonald's lost UFO files were totally hoaxed because Heflin couldn't have snapped off three photos of a flying disk in twenty seconds because of the time it took his Polaroid 101 camera to process the prints, we proved that wrong by having a Polaroid expert shoot three photos in under twenty seconds. If debunkers said that the photos were hoaxed because everything in the frame was in focus at the same instant, a "depth of field" issue, our expert showed, again, that by setting his camera lens to infinity, Heflin would have kept items both in the foreground and background in sharp focus.

Prior UFO series, whether on cable or conventional network channels, including the old *UFO Files,* were focused on asserting unconventional explanations of strange events and then presenting the debunker arguments so as to keep the episodes balanced. From the outset *UFO Hunters* was different. Our premise was to focus on real people telling real stories of what they perceived to be real UFO encounters. Real witnesses telling their stories with a sense of awe made our episodes truly dramatic and conveyed a sense of urgency to the show's theme. In addition, particularly in seasons two and three, the series took an entirely different tack, combining organic interaction among the principal investigators with onscreen expert scientific analysis and demonstrations to evaluate the conventional arguments against unconventional events. The result was an almost Sherlock Holmesian pursuit of theories that stood up to the tests of logic and science. That approach is what differentiated us from the UFO shows that had come before us and set the model for those UFO shows that would come after us.

◆ We also realized that rather than stalwartly pounding the table with assertions that UFOs were real, we were going up against the biology of underlying belief systems. Studies have shown that people's core belief systems may be neurologically wired. In ultrasound and MRI procedures, when test subjects were presented with statements that comported with their core beliefs, certain parts of their brains lit up. When the same subjects were presented with statements that challenged their belief systems, different parts of their brains lit up. Thus for certain individuals holding fast to their core beliefs, no amount of logic or rational argument could change their opinions because there is a neurological filter, a physiological sluice gate, determining what gets through and what doesn't. Their actual biology predetermines their reactions so that the outcome of the interaction is also predetermined. This helps to explain why some individuals, especially hard-core UFO debunkers refuse to entertain evidence about UFO encounters even when their counterarguments are completely implausible. It explains why debunkers in general cling desperately to the Stanton Friedman maxim of "anything but alien" in order to dismiss real evidence about UFO encounters even when their counter arguments fly directly into the face of established evidence. Thus *UFO*

Hunters took the tack of focusing on the debunker arguments and, like Sherlock Holmes, using evidence to eliminate them one after the other.

Our episodes were successful as we traveled to Washington State to unravel the mysteries of the Maury Island and Kelso incidents; to New England to interview Betty Hill's niece Kathy Marden about her aunt's description of her abduction and subsequent recovered memories about what happened onboard what she described as a spacecraft. We also went to places like Catalina Island in Santa Monica Bay to explore the stories of unidentified submerged objects and their interaction with human beings. We hit a high point with our trip to England where we investigated the case of the strange object United States Air Force personnel saw in Rendlesham Forest right outside RAF Bentwaters, a NATO nuclear weapons base that was staffed and managed by the USAF. And as we pursued these investigations, we emphasized that our mission was to peel away the known from the unknown to get to what we could not identify as conventional.

This peeling away, this process of eliminating what we could explain dispositively from what we could not explain became the primary focus of each episode. Our scientific demonstrations, separating and eliminating the known from the unknown, enabled us to pinpoint what was unidentifiable when it came to an event. We hunted for the unidentifiable by documenting the identifiable. And it worked.

By the time we were midway into the 2008 season, there were preliminary rumblings from the network. Our ratings, over a million households, were good, but were they good enough to get us a second season? We'd had conversations with our executive at History, who told us that the decision was still up in the air. More numbers had to come in. And then, in early spring, we landed in Suffolk, Virginia, for what would be a fateful encounter with Terrell Copeland, whose videos of UFOs and his story of following a giant triangle floating across the sky captured our attention as well as that of a number of folks on YouTube. Copeland had been a Marine, but had left the service for medical reasons. He told me privately—although our show runner and coexecutive producer, Al LaGarde, had a camera on us the whole time and could hear our conversation through my open mike—about his experiences with a strange woman who had contacted him and urged him to connect with his "star seed."

As the conversation progressed, Terrell described an incident in which he had heard a sound at the door of his apartment and heard someone trying to turn the doorknob. Thinking someone was trying to break in, Terrell, who had been napping on his couch, reached for his handgun, but realized with a shock that he was completely paralyzed. He could move his eyes, could think, but his hands and feet were frozen. Then he heard a voice resonate in his mind, telling him not to go for his gun, that all would be well if he just relaxed. Then, whoever or whatever was at his door simply disappeared and Terrell was able to move again.

Pat Uskert and I walked Terrell back into his parents' house where we continued the conversation. Terrell told us about his strange ability to know exactly when the phone would ring and who was on the other end. It was uncanny, but it was only one of a number of strange, seemingly psychic, abilities that Terrell described. But he kept on returning to his questions about his "star seed." What was it? How did he get it? And what was he supposed to do about it?

I had heard this same line of inquiry many times before from other individuals during the course of my tenure at *UFO Magazine,* and I had also heard Phil Corso talk about it, so I suggested to Terrell that maybe he was a hybrid ET-human who was contacted by others who wanted to show him how to manifest his abilities.

Pat Uskert was freaked out to the point of near apoplexy and chastised me—and that's putting it mildly—for making that suggestion. Al LaGarde, seeing the makings of an organic TV moment, rushed the two of us outside where we continued our debate, with Pat saying that I shouldn't jump to an unprovable conclusion and my saying that it was just a suggestion. The conversation was recorded, of course, and made its way to the editing room where our newly hired story editor, Stu Chait, was reviewing the raw footage before the first gross cuts of material. But that afternoon, visiting the editing bay in the postproduction suite was our new network executive, Mike Stiller, who was watching the editing process.

When the first editor went to cut the Terrell Copeland "you are a hybrid" conversation and Pat's response, Stu Chait told him to put it back in, saying it was the kind of spontaneous television moment that the network might like. We could always cut it out in a later round. However, as the fate of our second season of *UFO Hunters* was hanging in the balance—up or down—Mike Stiller saw the scene and instantly saw the promise of that interaction. He later told me that it was at that moment he decided the show should go into a second season. Stu Chait's instincts had saved the day, and that's how *UFO Hunters* was renewed for its second season.

And that's where we start this book.

"THE REAL ROSWELL"

on't you love it when the debunkers start to howl about UFO cases being simply delusions of a conspiratorial mind? Ask about a specific case and they demand proof, hard evidence, photographs, UFOs at the White House, and the like. And you, being a good UFO researcher, begin to mention a specific case, regardless of what it is, and the debunker responds, as if you've tripped his gag button, "Roswell." They'll tell you with the voice of empty authority that the case had been totally debunked over sixty-five years ago and any idiot who would still be talking about it should not pass Go, but head directly to an asylum for a long needed rest, multiple shock treatments, and a lobotomy to boot. But you know better. And so do we.

There are many people who claim we've been over-Roswelled to the point where it's simply boring. How many times do we have to hear the story, get into the same arguments, knock heads with the same detractors, and trot out the arguments of the Roswell historians? After a while, one would say we've already heard all there is to hear about Roswell and still have no definitive answer to the real mystery and the real story. But they would be wrong because new information still surfaces even after sixty years.

We know that something did happen at Roswell because of all the fuss. There was that press release saying the Army had captured a flying disk outside of town. Then there was that story the next day featuring a smiling Major Jesse Marcel in front of a weather balloon under a headline saying that the Army had retracted its initial statement because it was really just a standard off-the-shelf balloon. Sorry, folks, nothing doing here. You can all go home. Move along now.

But then there was Jesse Marcel himself, popping up almost thirty years later, saying something did happen at Roswell. And then, years after that, the Air Force came out with another statement saying that it really wasn't a weather balloon after all. It was a super secret Project Mogul balloon made of exotic material and that's why it fooled people at the time. Project Mogul was a high-altitude device designed to sniff the atmosphere for evidence of Soviet atom bomb testing. But that didn't satisfy the curious people researching the Roswell story because there were all those pesky witnesses who said they remembered exactly what they were doing in Roswell during those weeks in July 1947, and what the Army Air Force told them. Many of these were eyewitnesses who even said they saw strange-looking little creatures being transported to the Army Air Force base at Walker Field on the edge of the city of Roswell.

Then, fifty years to the month of the reported Roswell incident, the Air Force released yet another report saying that the entire incident was really a case of crash dummies that landed in the desert outside of Roswell. Case closed. Just a bunch of dummies that other dummies thought were alien creatures. Too bad the crash dummies were so burned up in the crash. They were great-looking dummies, photos of which would have resolved the whole problem. The crash dummy explanation might have had some traction had there not been a tiny problem: not only were the crash dummies too small and not adult sized, but the crash dummies weren't used until the early 1950s. The Roswell incident took place in 1947. The Air Force would have had to have sent the dummies back in a time machine.

Moreover, the crash dummy story didn't really satisfy anyone researching the case because of all those reported government documents doing what documents do, documenting the entire affair. The documents, called the MJ-12 documents, purportedly revealed the truth about the crash, saying it was actually an alien spacecraft that contained real ETs—extraterrestrial biological entities, or EBEs, as they called them—and the whole event really happened the way the researchers said it happened. The documents even contained briefing information for the incoming president, Dwight Eisenhower.

Then, as expected, there was another dispute over the documents. "They were planted," debunkers said, "simply to throw researchers off the trail. They were hoaxes." But researchers were undeterred and investigated the documents and said they corroborated statements made by Army Air Force and government officials at the time, matched the style and presentation of documents at the time, and were real, not hoaxes.

Next came the claims of retired Army Lieutenant Colonel Philip Corso, who said that he actually saw the Roswell alien at Fort Riley in 1947 and the Roswell crash debris at the Pentagon in 1961. Then the debunkers jumped on him. They jumped on me, too, because I wrote that book with Corso (*The Day After Roswell*, 1997). Then in 2008, Jesse Marcel, Jr., wrote a book: *The Roswell Legacy: The Untold Story of the First Military Officer at the 1947 Crash Site* about the experiences of the Marcel family and the Roswell story. In the book he talked about the crash itself, his father's experience retrieving debris from the crash site, and his own recollections handling the strange crash debris when his father stopped off at the Marcel house on his way back to the base. Jesse, Jr., eleven years old at the time, remembers that his father said to him and his mother to look carefully at the material he had brought back from the crash site because it was something that the family—or most people on earth, for that matter—had never seen before and would likely never see again. Jesse Marcel, Jr.'s retelling of the Roswell incident, particularly in light of his family's experiences, was the coup de grâce to the military's Project Mogul theory in which they argued that what really fell out of the sky was a top-secret balloon device to sniff out the remnants of Soviet nuclear testing in the atmosphere.

Perhaps one of the most revealing books about Roswell was Thomas Carey and Donald Schmitt's *Witness to Roswell* (2009) in which, as the book title indicates, the authors go back to the very beginning of the case and interview all the witnesses, including Lieutenant Walter Haut, the public information officer at the Roswell Army Airfield in 1947, about what he was and was not told to do. They reprinted an affidavit Haut made in contemplation of his death in which Haut affirms that he was at the debris field; saw the bodies of aliens on stretchers; saw the craft under a tarp on a flatbed truck; held a piece of the strange debris from the crashed object in his own hands; and was part of a conference of officers at the Roswell Army Airfield in which the mechanism of the cover-up was discussed and put into place.

The statement, dated December 26, 2002, first identifies Haut and his military posting to the Roswell Army Airfield and says that he became aware of reports of a "downed vehicle" when he returned to the base after the July 4 holiday and that the base commanding officer, his boss, Colonel William Blanchard had ordered the base's head of intelligence, Major Jesse Marcel to investigate those reports. Haut said he learned that more civilian reports were coming in regarding a second crash site outside of Roswell.

The next day, Haut stated, he attended a regularly scheduled staff meeting also attended by Blanchard and Jesse Marcel as well as Captain Sheridan Cavitt, Colonel James I. Hopkins, Lieutenant Colonel Ulysses S. Nero, "and from Carswell AAF in Fort Worth, Texas, Blanchard's boss, Brig. Gen. Roger Ramey and his chief of staff, Col. Thomas J. Dubose." At the conference, the attendees discussed the two air crashes that Marcel and Cavitt had reported: one, seventy-five miles northwest of Roswell, and the other, forty miles north of the city. As evidence of the crash report and of the recovery of the resulting debris, Haut stated, "Samples of wreckage were passed around the table. It was unlike any material I had or have ever seen in my life. Pieces which resembled metal foil, paper thin yet extremely strong, and pieces with unusual markings along their length were handled from man to man, each voicing their opinion. No one was able to identify the crash debris."

The issue put before the assembled officers concerned whether the Army should or should not make a public statement regarding crashes and the recovery of the debris. Haut said that General Ramey offered a plan, which Haut said he believed was handed down to him from higher-ups, "his bosses at the Pentagon," that the Army couldn't just deny the reports that were coming in from civilians because too many people were already involved and the press was on top of the story.

A couple of hours after the meeting, Colonel Blanchard dictated a statement to Lieutenant Haut over the phone, ordering him to tell the press as well as local radio stations in an official news release that the Army had in its possession, "a flying disk, coming from a ranch northwest of Roswell," which Marcel would be flying up to command headquarters. Haut, who was the base public information officer, said that even as the press release was reported by the wire services, he began getting phone calls from "around the world," and as messages asking for a response came pouring in, Blanchard told Haut to take a break and get out of the office.

Haut said that Blanchard accompanied him to witness the assembly of the recovered debris at Hangar 84 where Haut said he noticed that the facility was under heavy guard both within and around the perimeter of the building. And from a distance, Haut saw with his own eyes the recovered vehicle that had crashed. Although he was seeing it in poor light, he could tell that the object seemed to be metallic and had no windows, no tail assembly, nor any visible landing gear. The object was about "twelve to fifteen feet in length, not quite as wide, about six feet high, and more of an egg shape."

Haut said that he was also able to see what appeared to be two bodies under a canvas covering, but he could see that a head, extending outside the covering, from one of the bodies that, although otherwise featureless, appeared to be abnormally large. Days later, Blanchard, in describing the bodies to Haut when the two of them were in his office, extended his arm "about four feet above the floor to indicate the height" of the bodies under the canvas.

Haut said that, as agreed, Major Marcel flew with the debris to Fort Worth, command headquarters, but upon his return described to Haut what had taken place there after his return to the wreckage from a map room. The wreckage had been replaced; Haut said Marcel told him, replaced with the debris from a weather balloon that had been substituted for the Roswell debris when Marcel was out of the room. Marcel was very upset about this, he told Haut, and the two of them would never discuss it again.

Since the publication of *Witness to Roswell,* Carey and Schmitt, as well as one of the original Roswell incident researchers, Kevin Randle, Ph.D., have decided to review all the information about the case again, including what might have happened to pieces of the craft.

Recently, Annie Jacobsen, a *Los Angeles Times* editor, in her book *Area 51: An Uncensored History* (2010), taken seriously by news commentators anxious to debunk anything UFO even though she actually misstated the date of the base's inception as a secret air base, which wasn't 1951 as a simple fact-check would have shown, repeated in her book the same Roswell debunking, which doesn't even match the government's official line. She explained that a Horten brothers flying wing, or a disk, was responsible for all the confusion about what had actually landed. She said that the Army had tracked down the Horten brothers after 1947, who admitted they were working with the Russians. The theory was that the Horten brothers craft, which in the years prior to World War II was actually a flying wing, a type of craft depicted in the H. G. Wells 1936 motion picture *Things to Come,* had been dispatched to Roswell by Josef Stalin to frighten America. The craft—and the original Horten flying wings were made of wood, not some exotic compound—even had Cyrillic markings on it. Imagine a base intelligence officer, who'd been at radar school shortly before the crash, not recognizing Cyrillic or confusing wood with another material, or not knowing what a jet engine was. Imagine further that while Josef

Mengele was on the run through South America to avoid capture by both American and Soviet Nazi hunters he stopped to provide Stalin with deformed children who would burn up in the crash and be confused with extraterrestrials. If that latter theory sounds implausible, now imagine the pundit heads—who embraced this Mengele theory because it sounded rational and provided the standard "anything but aliens" answer to stories of UFOs—covering the flying wing theory without inviting anyone with solid evidence of what happened to give an alternate opinion. Almost sounds like a cover-up.

If you want a real cover-up of what might have been a concern when the Army detected the crash debris, consider this: During the latter years of World War II, from 1944 to 1945, the Japanese launched what they called "fire balloons" or fusen bakuden, hydrogen-filled balloons carrying an incendiary device laced with shrapnel over the Pacific to northwestern U.S. cities. Some of these actually landed and caused damage. However, for war censorship purposes and so as not to give the Japanese military information about their success or any propaganda advantage, the U.S. military did not allow reports of these balloon crash landings to appear in the press. It was a successful censorship operation that is still taught in CIA training today. Thus, upon coming upon debris in New Mexico, perhaps a first thought was that it was a Japanese balloon bomb that had drifted over the Pacific years after the war ended or maybe even a doomsday weapon launched by remnants of the Japanese military. Best to cover it up until they knew what it was. But the Jesse Marcel and Walter Haut stories themselves convincingly contradict the balloon bomb theory as well as the Annie Jacobsen story in her book about Area 51.

For the UFO Hunters, all of this research indicated that the story of Roswell was not just a mass of confusion or some concocted story to explain the crash of a test aircraft, a Russian secret weapon, or a Japanese balloon bomb. It was a real event about the crash of something truly anomalous or otherworldly, the result of which was nothing less than a change in the course of human history. No television series about UFOs would be complete if that series did not include a trip to

Roswell, New Mexico, to interview living witnesses and retrace the story. And that's exactly what we did.

"The Real Roswell" episode took us back to New Mexico in the second season right during the town's sixty-first anniversary celebration of the 1947 Roswell incident. We joined up with researchers and authors Stan Friedman, Tom Carey, and Don Schmitt and a new, heretofore, unknown eyewitness to events at Walker Field, the 509th Army Air Force base, both before and after the incident. I had been to Roswell before with Philip Corso to promote *The Day After Roswell*, and then later with a motion picture company interviewing witnesses, interviews that would become part of *UFO Magazine*'s 1998 "Children of Roswell" issue.

Debunkers point to the military's continuing re-explanations of the Roswell incident, such as the weather balloon story, the Project Mogul story, and the crash dummy story as examples of the need to hide what was happening in the interests of national security. However, as Stanton Friedman has pointed out on *UFO Hunters*, in July 1947, just days after the collection of crash debris from the Foster Ranch, the Army Air Force authorized a release of information to the national news in a statement written by Lieutenant Walter Haut, now deceased, admitting that it had retrieved a crashed disk outside of Roswell. That statement, later retracted publicly by Major Jesse Marcel after the debris arrived at Fort Worth, headquarters of the Eighth Air Force, was probably the truest public statement about Roswell that the military ever made. Why?

In 1995, years before I would visit Roswell with Lieutenant Colonel Corso, I had written a book about Ted Bundy and the Green River Killer with Detective Robert Keppel, the chief criminal investigator for the Washington State attorney general (*The Riverman*, 1995; reprint 2003). In that book about serial murderers, Bob Keppel, who was on the Ted Bundy task force back in the 1970s, investigating what were then referred to as the "Ted Murders," explained that when investigators are presented with a serial murder case, their best approach is to take a hard look at the earliest occurrences of the murders, the first cases. There, he said, investigators would find the best clues because serial killers become more accomplished at manipulating the police and hiding evidence as they pursue their crimes. Thus, Keppel demonstrated by evaluating the Lynda Healy case in Seattle, Ted's first murder in the University of Washington district, all the clues were present that pointed to Bundy's presence as he stalked his first victim. Therefore, the earlier the case in a series, the more likely it would be for investigators to discover important clues to solving the mystery.

Applied to the Roswell story, this means that because what happened at Roswell was one of the earliest occurrences of what witnesses described as a UFO crash in the twentieth century, the beginning of the modern era of ufology history, investigating it thoroughly should provide clues to not only what happened at Roswell, but the nature of what ufologists say was the beginning of a sixty-five year cover-up of a UFO presence on Earth. And when looking at the events as they unfolded in Roswell in July 1947, interviewing the stories of the last living witnesses, a picture emerges that even the most die-hard skeptic would have a tough time debunking.

We wanted to present as unvarnished a history of Roswell as we could during our second season on *UFO Hunters*, complete with testimony from eyewitnesses, who had little to gain from telling their stories. We wanted to go back to what witnesses said was the original debris field, to the 509th Army Air Force base at Walker Field in Roswell where we would stand on the spots where our eyewitness, retired Army Air Force Staff Sergeant Earl Fulford, now deceased, told us he and some of his fellow service personnel saw a formation of UFOs days before the crash. We wanted to do this because we hoped that people watching the show would judge for themselves the soundness of this testimony and the logic behind our contention that whatever happened at Roswell, it wasn't a weather balloon, Project Mogul, or a set of crash dummies. As Stan Friedman told us, you would have had to have had a time machine to get a Project Mogul balloon back to 1947 and an even more powerful time machine to bring miniature crash dummies back to 1947 from 1953. And why would you want miniature crash dummies when the whole purpose of crash dummies is to resemble adult human beings who fly planes? The government's cover story simply doesn't wash.

THE CASE

In the earliest hours of an incident that presented a perceived threat to national security, our government and military generally throw a blanket over it so as to investigate it thoroughly. It makes sense because many times the nature of the ensuing investigation may compromise the very classified methods our national security agencies employ to get to the truth. Thus, whatever happened at Roswell during the first week of July 1947, the military's first response might have been to keep it covered up. But that's not what happened. In fact, the government's first response, according to a sworn affidavit by former Army Air Force base public information officer Lieutenant Walter Haut, made in contemplation of his death, was to disclose the crash to the local newspapers. It was only a day or so later that the Army debunked itself and changed the story. Given that disclosure and retraction and subsequent cover-up, what really happened at Roswell that got everybody so worked up?

Army Staff Sergeant Earl Fulford, working at the 509th Army Air Force at Walker Field in Roswell, New Mexico, remembered that one night in late June or very early July, he and other NCOs at the base were sitting out by the runways for an evening cigarette, when they noticed silvery disklike craft flying in formation above the end of the runway. But these were not planes, at least not any airplanes that the Army Air Force personnel recognized. They were nothing like craft they had seen before, but they were more of a curiosity than anything else.

During this period in early summer, severe summer thunderstorm weather moved into the area, marked by powerful lightning strikes. Some UFO researchers have speculated that the electrical storm might have either compromised the navigation systems of the objects that Fulford and the other Army personnel saw flying over the runway or that one of the objects was actually struck by lightning, thereby causing its pilots to lose control of the craft, which then collided with another UFO, causing both of them to crash. According to Tom Carey, coauthor of *Witness to Roswell,* the two craft came down in different locations near Roswell, one approximately forty miles north of the city, and another seventy-five miles northwest of Roswell. The pilots of one of the crafts seemed to have ejected themselves from the craft in a kind of pod and came down in a different location. One of the crafts might have come down nose first into the side of a mesa and cracked open. Reportedly, the bodies of strange-looking creatures, at least one or two of whom were still alive, were disgorged from the craft and were discovered lying amid the wreckage strewn among the sagebrush.

Dates vary. In the Army version, the material on the Foster Ranch was discovered in early July. According to Mac Brazel, the person who reportedly discovered the debris field, the date was June 14, 1947. According to the Army press release, on July 8, 1947, the Army announced that it had recovered a crashed disk from the desert outside of Roswell. The announcement was authorized by the 509th base commander, Colonel William Blanchard, a World War II pilot, who was the backup pilot for Colonel Paul Tibbets, the B-29 pilot who dropped the first atomic bomb over Japan. Blanchard eventually made it up the ladder to Air Force general and Air Force vice chief of staff. The newspaper announcement of the retrieval of the flying disk got into the afternoon editions of newspapers, especially on the West Coast and was important because it demonstrated that in the early hours of the military's decision-making over the crash of the object outside of Roswell, it was disclosing what it believed to be the truth.

However, the very next day, when Major Jesse Marcel, the 509th base intelligence officer, flew to the Fort Worth headquarters of the Eighth Army Air Force, later the Eighth Air Force after the armed services separated in August 1947, with the debris from the Roswell crash, Eighth Air Force commandant General Roger Ramey—according to both Walter Haut and later Jesse Marcel himself—switched out the debris with material from a weather balloon and told Marcel to pose for a photo in front of it. Marcel had accompanied the crash debris from Roswell to Carswell Army Air Force Base under orders from General Ramey, but upon his arrival, Ramey ordered the major to take a look at some maps in the map room. When Marcel returned to Ramey's office, the Roswell debris had been replaced with a weather balloon and Marcel was ordered to pose with it. The Army Air Force then claimed that Marcel and others at the 509th had mistaken the weather balloon for a flying saucer. Everyone had a big laugh, Marcel was made to look like a fool, but the story, now reported in subsequent editions of newspapers, officially died. No flying saucer. The poor befuddled major couldn't tell a balloon from a spacecraft. Must have been all that cactus juice.

The story of Roswell, which had caused another blip in the 1950s after a reported UFO invasion in the skies over Washington, D.C., seemed to die away until 1978 when Jesse Marcel, who had left the Air Force before the start of the Korean War and moved to Houma, Louisiana, to open an electronics and television repair business, finally went public and talked about the Roswell incident and his part in it. Nuclear physicist Stanton Friedman, who had been researching the Roswell incident, was linked up with Marcel by a Louisiana radio talk show host, and the modern age of Roswell research began with Jesse Marcel's sharing of his experience with Stan Friedman. Friedman, who brought to the Marcel interview his own experience working as a nuclear physicist in highly classified research, understood how the government might have been so concerned about the nature of what had crashed at Roswell—a secret Soviet weapon, a Japanese balloon bomb that finally floated across the Pacific and that had been kept secret after World War II, a German weapon that the Russians had retooled, or an actual alien spaceship that might have been the precursor to an invasion of planet Earth—that their first response was to cover it up.

With Jesse Marcel coming forward to dispute the weather balloon story of the Roswell crash that had been promulgated at Fort Worth per General Ramey's orders and perhaps orders he received from higher-ups in Washington, the weather balloon story was easy to dispute. Not only was it manifestly untrue, even the physical description of the balloon itself belied the witness descriptions of the material on the debris field and didn't comport with what Major Jesse Marcel said he had seen.

The Marcel revelations and the research by UFO historians such as Stanton Friedman, Donald Schmitt, Tom Carey, and Kevin Randle discovered that there were many more witnesses than just Marcel and his son, Jesse, Jr. The Roswell witness stories were so precise that researchers were able to figure out a timeline of events of not just one crash, but of multiple crash sites from a craft that broke up, jettisoned an ejection pod, and came to rest at the foot of an arroyo. What researchers learned was that even before the personnel at the Roswell Army Airfield realized that something had crashed out in the desert, Mac Brazel, the foreman of the Foster Ranch, had discovered the debris field. And before the Army realized that there was a debris field, the sheriff of Chaves County, George Wilcox, had been alerted that something had gone down in the desert over thirty miles out of Roswell and that the local fire department was on its way to the site. Sheriff Wilcox also went out to the site where fire and safety personnel discovered that whatever had gone down, it was nothing that they recognized. They discovered strange debris, a metallic substance that one could squeeze or fold but snapped right back into shape. They also discovered humanoid creatures that looked remarkably human, but clearly were not. As one Roswell firefighter would tell his daughter, the creature looked like an insect with a humanlike face called "child of the desert." Another witness, a repairman at Walker Field, was present when the retrieval team brought back the living alien to Hangar 84. He was standing outside the hangar smoking a cigarette when he saw a group of soldiers carrying a small body on a stretcher right past him and into the hangar. He looked down at the figure on the stretcher and saw something that looked human, but, again, clearly was not. Moreover, the entity on the stretcher looked at him and he experienced an

intense emotion of sadness because the creature was dying. The maintenance man was taken aside by officers, threatened, physically pushed
around, and then rescued by another set of officers who vouched for
him as someone trustworthy who would not breach a national security secret.

Other people from Roswell became involved with the event as well,
from the local mortician who was asked to supply small child-sized
coffins to the air base to a nurse who was asked to provide health care
triage to one of the entities. Then, of course, there was Mac Brazel
himself, who, by the time the Army took him into temporary custody,
had already told Sheriff Wilcox and Frank Joyce, the local radio station
owner. Wilcox himself had taken possession of a box of the debris,
which he stored inside a jail cell while he contacted the Roswell Army
Airfield to come get it. We know this because the sheriff's wife, Inez
Wilcox, wrote about the incident in her diary even before Jesse Marcel's story became widely publicized. Accordingly, by the time the
military had recovered any of the debris and sought to keep the crash
secret, it was already too late and they had to play catch up. But the
story becomes even more convoluted.

One of the keys to the mystery of the goings-on at Roswell in July
1947, is Walter Haut, then a lieutenant and ad hoc aide to base commander Colonel William Blanchard. It was Walter Haut who copied
the press announcement from Blanchard revealing that the Army had
retrieved a flying saucer from the desert outside of Roswell. And it was
Walter Haut who steadfastly maintained his silence about the cover
story of the weather balloon and then the Project Mogul balloon as the
explanations for the debris the Army had actually retrieved. But as Don
Schmitt and Tom Carey explain in Witness to Roswell, there was much
more to the Walter Haut story that started coming out in bits and pieces
as he got older. In two instances, Haut—who stayed in Roswell after
the war and became an insurance agent and ultimately helped establish the International UFO Museum and Research Center—told a group
of veterans and then members of the foreign press that he was at the
crash debris field and that it was an anomalous object that had crashed

in the desert, not a balloon. He then told Dennis Balthaser, a columnist for *UFO Magazine,* and Wendy Connors in a video interview that he was at the crash site and that the events described by Major Jesse Marcel actually happened.

Haut's comments prompted his friend, Donald Schmitt, who had been urging Walter Haut to come clean about the crash for years, to suggest that Haut could keep his promise of silence to William Blanchard and reveal the truth at the same time. He could answer questions that would then be drafted into an affidavit to affirm or ratify with his attorney and swear to its veracity in the presence of a notary public. The affidavit would then be sequestered until after his death, leaving it up to his family to release it or continue to keep it secret. Thus, Haut would not reveal the secret of Roswell, keeping his promise of silence to Blanchard, but leave it to his family to decide about releasing the true story. Haut agreed to Schmitt's suggestion and in December 2002, signed an affidavit based on questions posed to him by Schmitt and coauthor Tom Carey.

If we believe that what Walter Haut swore to is the truth, then his affidavit just about says it all. Not only does Haut confirm the existence of a strange otherworldly craft that crashed outside of Roswell, he confirms two crash sites, the involvement of civilian public safety services at one of the sites, the recovery of strange bodies at the site, the recovery of anomalous debris, and the creation of a cover-up by General Ramey, probably upon orders from his bosses at the Pentagon. He also confirms what can only be described as a double-cross by General Ramey with Colonel Blanchard's complicity that compromised the credibility of Major Jesse Marcel. The affidavit is a stunning document that outlines not only what happened out in the desert, but confirms two crash sites, and details the course of the cover-up in such a way that it involved the entire officer staff at Walker Field. It also indicates that General Ramey was not concocting the cover-up on his own, but upon orders from those above him.

Both Haut, in his affidavit, and Jesse Marcel, Jr., who actually handled the debris from the crash site when his father brought it back to the house before taking it to the base, told stories that confirmed Major Marcel's reaction to what happened at Carswell Army Air Force Base. Upon his return to the 509th, Marcel said that he would never speak of the Roswell incident again. He said the same thing to his wife and son, telling them when he returned that the entire event was over and that the family should never bring it up again. Marcel was clearly disturbed by what he was forced to do at Carswell in Fort Worth, feeling that he had not only been deceived by the commanding officer, but that his own military career had been compromised. By 1948, Marcel left the service, a bitter man, to open a television repair business in Louisiana.

After the Marcel photo in Ramey's office at Fort Worth, the Roswell debris material was transported from Fort Worth to Wright Field, later to be called Wright-Patterson, where it was stored under the control of General Nathan Twining of the Air Materiel Command. For Nikola Tesla conspiracy aficionados, Nathan Twining also came into possession of Tesla's antigravity notes after the Office of Alien Properties seized Tesla's files after he was found dead in his room in the New Yorker Hotel in January, 1943. Thus, some UFO historians believe, by the time the Roswell debris reached Wright Field and came into the possession of the Air Force Materiel Command, General Twining had already been apprised of Tesla's antigravity research and well might have understood the importance of the Army Air Force discovery at Roswell. If this is so, it means that as early as July 1947, the military could have understood the nature of what it had and needed to formulate policy about what it might well have considered to be a hostile entity's ability to penetrate U.S. classified military airspace with complete impunity.

Are there any clues to what the military might have done to assess the nature of what they deemed to be a threat to national security after the Roswell crash material, including whatever still-living entities reached Wright Field? If we give credence to the testimony of the children of the late Marine fighter pilot and squadron commander Lieutenant Colonel Marion "Black Mac" Magruder, the answer is yes. In telephone interviews and a June 2006 interview with *UFO Magazine,* Mark Magruder said that his father belonged to the National Air War College class of 1948, which, in April 1948, was dispatched to Wright Field outside of Dayton, Ohio, on a special assignment. Lieutenant Colonel Magruder's military records confirm that his class was on an unspecified assignment during that month. At Wright Field, Mark revealed, his father was not only shown debris from the crash at Roswell—which Black Mac Magruder described as strange and anomalous and made of a type of material he had never seen before—but that he encountered a live alien creature face-to-face.

Magruder told his children that the creature was eerie because it looked more human than not, with a grayish flesh-colored face, larger than normal eyes with deep black centers, and a larger than normal skull shaped vaguely like a lightbulb. The strangest aspect of the creature, Magruder said, was that it had long spindly arms that were constantly waving as the creature itself seemed to sway in a wavelike motion. Magruder referred to the creature as "squiggly" because of the way it kept swinging its long arms. The creature, Magruder told his children, communicated with him, but not with words or by any method Magruder understood. Instead, Magruder explained that he received impressions from the creature, impressions that told him the creature was being experimented on by the military, experiments that were killing it.

"They were killing it," Magruder told his children. "It was one of God's creatures and they were killing it slowly and deliberately. It was a sin, what they were doing," Magruder said.

To be sure, this is a sensational story, backed up by only personal testimony from the Magruder children and the circumstantial evidence of Magruder's military records. However, when one considers Magruder's background and his service during World War II, fighting in the South Pacific, his credibility plays a large part in the veracity of his statements to his children. Magruder was one of the very early pilots to receive training in radar-guided air-to-air nighttime combat from the RAF in the early years of the war. He brought his training in the tactics of night fighting to his Hellcat squadron, VMFA(AW)-533, dubbed "Black Mac's Killers," at the battle of Okinawa. There, using radar-guided nighttime tactics, Magruder's squadron registered over thirty kills of incoming Japanese warplanes, many of them Kamikaze fighters bent on destroying the United States fleet supporting the invasion of Okinawa. Magruder's ground crew also staved off an attack by Japanese ground troop suicide bombers that attacked the squadron's airfield, defending the aircraft in bloody hand-to-hand combat. In July 1952, according to his youngest child, who was still living at home, Magruder was one of the few personnel taken to the Pentagon where he monitored aircraft transmissions during the UFO incursion into Washington, D.C., airspace. Thus, Magruder's statements to his children about his knowledge of what happened at Roswell and his eyewitness account of meeting one of the ET pilots of the crashed UFO has, at least in my estimation, a high credibility.

There is another intriguing post-Roswell story from 1947 that prompted us to revisit Roswell in our second season on *UFO Hunters*. The April 1998 issue of *UFO Magazine* describes how President Harry Truman, having been informed of the crash at Roswell, asked his military advisers to find the "lowest common denominator" of technology retrieved from that crash debris and to hand it over to a R&D laboratory working on something similar in order to determine the function of that technology and how to harvest it for American industry. (This is the story Philip Corso also told in the book he and I wrote, *The Day After Roswell*.) The technology, one of many delivered to Bell Laboratories, ultimately became the model for the transistor, which Bell patented in its own name. According to the story, the Army became furious that the patent went to an American corporation and not to the government and shut down the program conveying technology to American companies until the late 1950s. At that time Lieutenant General Arthur Trudeau was posted to Army R&D, discovered a cache of Roswell crash debris files at the Pentagon, and sought a budget from the Senate, specifically Senator Strom Thurmond, to develop that technology. Senator Thurmond laid down the gauntlet. He said that unless the technology to be reverse engineered was ultimately patented by United States defense contractors in their own name, he would not argue for a budget for any development. Thus began the plan to reverse engineer the Roswell technology, a plan that would soon involve Lieutenant Colonel Philip Corso, who was posted to Army R&D in 1961. According to Corso he was shown the Roswell debris and ordered to filter it into the research departments of American defense contracts. If this story is true, it means that we can actually track the physical debris retrieved from the crash at Roswell from New Mexico to Fort Worth to Wright Field and thence to the Pentagon and into American industry. It is a compelling story.

But what's the evidence that a crash at Roswell of an otherworldly craft ever took place? How were the government's own cover stories so shot full of holes that simple investigations into the evidence of those cover stories showed how hollow and false they were? That was the premise of our second season episode on *UFO Hunters*, "The Real Roswell."

THE EPISODE

The purpose of this episode was to visit the city of Roswell during the crash anniversary events sponsored by the town and the International Roswell UFO Museum and reinterview as many of the witnesses as we could, including crash researcher Art Campbell and our *UFO Magazine* columnist Dennis Balthaser. We were investigating the stories of UFO historians who said there were actually two separate crashes in the Roswell area, one traditionally referred to as Roswell and the other referred to as the crash on the Plains of San Agustin.

Our second season of *UFO Hunters* also marked a different approach to covering stories, an approach we first developed in the Stephenville, Texas, lights episode. Instead of Ted, Pat, and I—Jeff was no longer a part of the cast—covering the same story, we split the team up into three different investigations so that in the Roswell episode, Pat followed a clue that some of the Roswell debris was buried deep in a cave on one of the neighboring ranches, Ted visited the San Agustin crash site with Art Campbell to look for any debris that might still remain there, and I interviewed Dennis Balthaser and former Army Staff Sergeant and Roswell witness from 1947, Earl Fulford.

After we arrived in Roswell, I met with Dennis Balthaser at the offices of the *Roswell Daily Record,* the newspaper that received the first briefing about the crash in July 1947, from Lieutenant Walter Haut. In our interview, Dennis advocated for continued searches and interviews with Roswell witnesses, many of whom are in their eighties and most whom have already died.

"There is an urgency about this," Balthaser asserted. "The urgency is to find witnesses and search for physical evidence both at the Roswell crash site and at the Plains of San Agustin." Balthaser said he believed that there still might be pieces of debris, shards or fragments of anomalous materials still embedded in the soil at both sites.

I next interviewed my good friend, the celebrated UFO scholar and author, Stanton Friedman, who was one of the first investigators of the Roswell incident and a proponent of the second crash site theory. The theory makes sense, Friedman asserts, because if the pilots of the craft that crash-landed were looking for a safe spot to bring their damaged craft down, San Agustin would have been ideal because it is a flat area, surrounded by high hills, and isolated. According to this theory, a man named Barney Barnett, who was working in the area, discovered the downed craft, including alien bodies, but said that the military arrived soon after he made the discovery and was ordered to leave the site and keep quiet about what he found. Why would Barnett have been so willing to keep an astonishing discovery quiet?

"You have to remember," Friedman told me, "Barnett was a World War I veteran, who was working for the Soil Conservation Service. It would be ridiculous for him to keep talking about his discovery when he was ordered to shut up about it." But Barney was not alone. There were people there, including an archeologist and some students. All were present when the military showed up and told them to keep quiet about what they saw, and, Friedman says, "They meant it." It was 1947. Friedman points out, and in the wake of World War II and the growing "Red Scare" in the United States, people did what they were told, especially when they were told something by the military.

Stan Friedman's descriptions of what might have happened at the San Agustin site prompted Ted Acworth and Pat Uskert to speculate over the nature of a site two hundred miles away from the Roswell debris field. Could it have been a single craft that broke up or ejected some sort of safety pod that landed two hundred miles away from Roswell? Or, Ted suggested, might the San Agustin site have been the result of an entirely different crashed craft, perhaps one that collided with the Roswell craft? Pat agreed and described what he called a "cue ball effect" in which one of the UFOs bounced off another causing it to carom to a distant crash site. Meanwhile, while Ted and Pat journeyed to the second site, I met up with UFO researcher and author Tom Carey, who had brought a new witness to Roswell for the anniversary festivities. His name was Earl Fulford, a staff sergeant at the 509th in 1947.

Tom explained to us that part of his research into potential witnesses involved his combing the 509th base yearbook, looking for veterans that were still alive, calling them up, and asking whether they remembered anything about the events of July 1947. To his surprise, Carey said, Fulford's wife answered the phone, put her husband on the line, and Fulford told Carey he was glad for the phone call and was ready to talk. Carey had struck gold. Carey and I interviewed Fulford on the grounds of the base itself, Walker Field in Roswell.

"What happened to get you involved in this incident?" I asked, referring to the events surrounding the crash, the cleanup of the debris field, and the aftermath.

"It happened," Fulford said. "A week or so before the incident happened, folks here on the base and even in town started seeing objects flying in the sky." Fulford indicated that the objects were not conventional aircraft, which, because he worked at an Army Air Force base, he would have been able to identify. Pointing to the edge of the runway behind one of the hangars, Fulford said that he and others at the base had seen them hovering in the distance over the runway. He described the objects as things he had never seen before.

"We looked up and there were three up there. They were circular and hung motionless. We watched them for two or three minutes and they suddenly disappeared," Fulford said. "It was maybe a week later that the crash occurred."

Fulford's description of circular objects hanging motionlessly and low over the runway does not comport with the military's Project Mogul explanation for the Roswell incident. First of all, Mogul balloons had long trains trailing behind them and flew very high in the sky. The entire purpose of the Project Mogul balloon experiment was to get to an altitude high enough where the upper air currents would have carried radioactive debris from nuclear tests. What Fulford described were objects well below the altitude of even a weather balloon. It was also clear that he would not have been able to spot a Project Mogul balloon because it would have been flying too high.

"One day, one of the days after we had seen the objects, Sergeant Rosenberg came into the mess hall, picked out twelve or fifteen of us, and loaded us onto trucks. We were driven to a field about seventy miles out of Roswell."

"And what did you do there?" I asked Fulford.

"We were unloaded and picked up some debris from the field," he said. "The debris was of a very unusual shape and feel." He said that he had never seen material of this type before. It was metallic, a shiny silver like foil, and you couldn't cut it or tear it with your hands. The strange thing, he said, was that it was very malleable, flexible, but if you crushed it in your hand, it snapped right back into shape.

Pat, Tom Carey, and I, brought Earl Fulford to the original crash site he described while Ted Acworth went to the second crash site with Art Campbell to search for debris there. The original site, to which Fulford directed us, was on high ground about three hours outside of Roswell. He said that the debris on this site was spread out like a fan. At the site, the vehicles from the base formed a circular perimeter around the debris and the soldiers got out, formed into a grid search pattern, and started walking from one end of the field to the other, picking up debris as they went. The soldiers walked about ten to fifteen feet apart, each covering the area directly in front of him but also cross-covering one another. "That way," Fulford said, "I could see what you could see and you could see what I could see." And what did Fulford see?

"I saw strips of metal like aluminum foil spread across the ground." But when he picked it up to stuff the pieces into the gunnysack he was carrying, it did a strange thing. Earl said, "I was surprised. I picked up the piece and crunched it to get it into the bag but before I could stuff it in, it popped back into its original shape. I wadded it up again and same thing."

Many other witnesses described this strange metal, but Earl Fulford was our first witness who actually described collecting the material off the ground. This was a first in terms of eyewitnesses to the crash debris and the nature of its qualities.

"How many pieces did you collect?" I asked him.

"Ten, twelve, maybe fifteen pieces," he said. "But once I put it in the bag, I never saw it again." And who took possession of the bags when they had been filled up with collected debris? "They were military police," Fulford said. It would be the last time Fulford or anyone else in that collection effort would ever see the debris. "They told me that if I showed anyone or told anyone, I would be in deep trouble," he revealed.

This was a first for us on *UFO Hunters*: an eyewitness and a participant to the debris collection at the Roswell crash site. Pat Uskert, however, was intrigued by another possibility suggested by Tom Carey. What if the first witnesses who had gotten to the crash site before the military, particularly Mac Brazel, took some of the debris for themselves and secreted it away in other locations? Might that debris still be found by searching suspect locations? Pat was on it.

We know, from Inez Wilcox's diary, that Mac Brazel had brought some of the debris to the local sheriff's office where Sheriff George Wilcox put it in a jail cell while they waited for personnel from the Army base to pick it up. We know from other witnesses, particularly Frankie

Rowe, whose father was a local Roswell firefighter, that public safety officials reached one of the sites before the military and that her father described the strange life-forms they discovered amid the wreckage and the metal that Fulford described. Frankie herself told us she'd handled the metal at the local firehouse, remarking about the same qualities Fulford described: when you wadded up the metal strip, it bounced right back into shape. What if some of that metal, called "memory metal" by Roswell researchers, still exists in caves where it had been stashed by some of the first visitors to the site back in July 1947?

Pat sought out the help of local rancher Sue Mannis whose grandfather, she believed, was one of the first people to reach the crash site Fulford took us to. Pat asked her whether she thought her grandfather or other early witnesses might have stashed some of the debris away in caves. Sue pointed Pat toward a cave where her uncle often visited. It was a cave Pat would explore to see whether he might uncover a piece of debris that had been stashed away in there.

The cave, Pat found, was probably a drainage cave that captured runoff from storms. Although there was no identifiable artificial material in the silt that covered the cave floor, Pat was able to ascertain that these types of hidden caves exist, they were accessible to anyone with the right kind of apparatus, and because they permeated the desert floor, an organized and meticulous search might well, someday, uncover debris that had originally been stashed there.

Ted Acworth speculated that if we could not find any material at the first crash site closer to Roswell, perhaps he, Pat, and Art Campbell might find material at the San Agustin crash site that might be valuable evidence supporting the UFO crash account. Campbell told them that he first explored the San Agustin site in 1995 and, finding debris and artificial material there, cross-referenced the coordinates of the site with the description given by Barney Barnett, who said that he was driven off the site by an Army team after discovering a crashed craft. Campbell described Barnett in the same way Friedman did, a soil conservation engineer who was helping farmers protect the land they were cultivating, particularly with cattle farming. The San Agustin area was in the district he was responsible for.

Barnett was at the site in early July 1947, Campbell explained and "he saw an object glinting in the sun." At first Barnett thought it might have been an airplane crash. So he drove over to where he saw it, drove over the top of a ridge, and there it was, not an airplane at all, but a strange craft, he later said, the likes of which he had never seen before. At the site, Barney was met by a team of archeology students coming from a different direction. Hence, Barney said, there were multiple witnesses to what he saw. All of this would have been simply the testimony of one man, Campbell said, had it not been for his discovery of corroborating evidence in the form of a letter by archeologist Herbert Dick, who had written in a letter to Harvard University that he was working at a site called "Bat Cave" on the Plains of San Agustin. Dick confirmed that he and his team were chased out of the area by an Army unit, thus corroborating Barnett's story of a military presence in the area.

Ted asserted that if a vehicle had crashed at the San Agustin site, regardless of what the nature of the vehicle was, any crash would have had to have left a gouge along the desert floor. Probably the nature of the gouge might indicate the force of the crash and even the size of the object that had crashed. There might even be crash debris still present if the site had not been cleaned up by recovery teams. Campbell agreed, saying that "whatever it was that crashed into the sagebrush, it left a swath through it."

The site, Campbell explained, had numerous artifacts that he recovered, artifacts, he believes, indicate that something did crash there. He rode with Ted and Pat back to the site to show them where he recovered debris. It was the first time he'd been back to the site in five years. The exploration of the site excited Pat because it was the first time its existence had been revealed on television (the exact location was still not revealed for privacy reasons).

Ted asked, "From what direction did the craft enter the site?"

"From the northeast on a flat trajectory," Campbell answered, thus giving Ted an indication of what any crash swath along the ground might look like and the direction it should have. Campbell had taken aerial photographs of the site and noticed two sets of gouges, one of which, toward the southwest, was a draw cut by water runoff. But the other was a track of parallel lines running in the opposite direction. He referred to the second set of gouge tracks as a trench, which he verified, in response to Ted's question, because the soil samples he took from the trench were different from the soil in the surrounding area. Ted also said that he could see what he described as an "alley through the sage," still visible after over sixty years, although, Ted explained, there could be multiple conventional explanations for the apparent trench. "It may be completely natural," Ted suggested. "I can't tell either way."

But Campbell had another piece of evidence, an artifact he uncovered from the same site that he, Ted, and Pat were exploring, an artifact that Ted suggested looked organic. It was smooth, lightweight, and appeared to have melted or collapsed in on itself. Campbell said he didn't know what it was at first, but thought it might be some organic material from a cow. He took the artifact to cattle experts, who told him that as far as they were concerned, whatever this thing was, it didn't come from a cow. With that expert opinion, and because he had found the object in the trench he believed was made by a UFO crash, Campbell said, "I was off and running."

"What I want to do," Ted said, "is get this thing back to the lab and test it. The first thing I want to know is what's it made of. Is it organic, inorganic, or is it something completely unidentifiable?" So we sent Art Campbell's artifact off for chemical testing.

*After visiting Roswell, New Mexico, the team headed back to California where Pat met with Michael Keane, a United States intelligence expert and lecturer at the University of Southern California in Los Angeles, to see if the Air Force Project Mogul explanation for the crash had any independent validity. Keane explained that in 1947 the United States believed that it had the monopoly on atomic weapons. "But," he qualified, "what if, unknown to the United States, the Soviets had acquired an atomic bomb? What we feared was a nuclear Pearl Harbor. So we developed a top-secret surveillance to sniff the upper air currents for evidence of Soviet nuclear testing."

"Just exactly what was Project Mogul?" Pat asked.

"It was a string of balloons," Keane explained. "It contained listening devices to listen for sound waves from nuclear testing." The string of weather balloons, connected in a series and also had radar detectors to find evidence of missile or bomb tests. The device was close to seven hundred feet long, about half the height of the Eiffel Tower.

"Pieces of the balloon might fall off," Keane explained. "The falling pieces might be spread over a large area. Or the balloon itself could come down and it would look as if it had been spread over multiple sites or over one large debris field." Keane said it would be easy for the military to have confused it with something else, especially if Jesse Marcel could not identify the Mylar material used in the radar reflectors. However, as logical as Keane's explanation was, there are, as Stan Friedman points out, a number of real issues that belie the possibility of Marcel's confusing a Mogul balloon with something anomalous.

First, in 1947, Project Mogul was simply a string of weather balloons, as Keane admitted, and not just one big balloon. Weather balloons had been used for years and were easily recognizable. Also, far from sporting any exotic material, weather balloons were made of neoprene rubber, the same type of rubber used in World War II and also familiar to anyone who worked with machinery, from fan belts to aircraft, at the 509th. Earl Fulford pointed out that the weather balloon facility was right across the street from the base, meaning that anyone who worked at the base would have seen regular weather balloons, even those strung together for attaining greater altitude.

And what about the radar reflectors? Records indicate that Major Jesse Marcel, the base intelligence officer, had been at radar school less than a month before the Roswell incident. It's inconceivable that someone of his rank at radar school would have been unable to recognize a standard radar reflector device. Also, the radar reflectors had an easily recognizable shape. The strange metallic material that Earl Fulford and others gathered from the debris field was in irregular strips, some longer than others. Simply stated, the shapes were all wrong for radar reflectors, which Earl also would have recognized had they been part of the debris that he recovered. Therefore, Michael Keane's explanation to Pat Uskert, while logical, didn't comport with the actual facts of the Roswell debris recovery. Stanton Friedman put it very succinctly: For the Roswell crash to be the Project Mogul that the Air Force described, he said, "you would have needed a time machine to have brought Project Mogul from 1949 back to 1947."

But what about the strange memory metal that all the witnesses who handled it described? Was it something as basic as Mylar? To test this out, we set up a materials test back in Los Angeles with Brick Price, our effects producer who built special effects devices for the motion picture industry. I brought two witnesses to Brick's lab, Earl Fulford, who collected the material at the Roswell debris field in 1947, and Jesse Marcel, Jr., whose father, Major Marcel, brought some of the material home for his son and his wife to handle before he returned it to the base. Both Fulford and Marcel, Jr., are not only eyewitnesses to this material, they handled it and manipulated it and described its unique qualities. Could they identify it now?

Ted was in charge of the actual testing, and he explained that he and Brick Price assembled a number of materials he believed would mimic some of the qualities of what witnesses described as "memory metal." We would bring in Earl Fulford and Jesse Marcel, Jr., independently to see if either one of them could identify any of the materials as something similar, or identical, to what they handled back in July 1947. The materials were aluminum, magnesium, steel, cardboard, silver-painted acetate, and Mylar. I was particularly interested in the Mylar because that was one of the "exotic" materials mentioned by the Air Force as something that would have confused witnesses, especially Jesse Marcel, Jr. Now, over sixty years after he first handled the material, assuming it was the Mylar from a Mogul balloon, Jesse Marcel, Jr., would handle it again.

Earl Fulford was the first one in the lab and he methodically went through each piece. He dubbed the steel "too thick" and too rigid. The aluminum, he said, was too heavy. The original memory metal was so light, it almost floated, "almost weightless," Fulford said, and seemed so flimsy you could tear it into pieces. But it was so strong, it stood up to all kinds of handling. The Mylar was too stiff, Fulford said, and didn't fold the way the memory metal did in his hands when he stuffed it into his sack. Then he came to the acetate, which, he said, had about the right thickness and was flexible enough that he could have wadded it up. But it sprang back into shape. Okay, I thought, time for my own test and scrunched it. It snapped back into shape. Earl said as he handled it again, "It makes chills run up and down my back." Ted pushed it further, reminding Fulford what he said about crumpling up the material from the debris field and watching it snap back. "Can you crumple this material?" Ted asked about the acetate.

Earl wadded up the material as if he were trying to stuff it into a sack, let it go, and it snapped right back into its original shape. "You got something there," he said. "It's as close as anything I've seen."

The acetate, although developed in the 1930s, according to the official 1994 Air Force report on Project Mogul, was not used in the construction of the balloon or any parts of the apparatus. Time for our next witness. Ted reminded us that this was a blind test and that we should not in any way suggest what Earl had chosen as the closest material. We were starting from scratch, Ted told us.

We brought Jesse Marcel, Jr., to Brick Price's shop. "My dad laid the debris out on the floor," Marcel told us. "And he said that he was showing us this because 'you'll probably never see this again.'" Jesse Marcel, Jr., who died of a heart attack in August 2013, served in the military, like his father and Earl Fulford, but was a physician, who was not given to speculation or flights of fancy in any way. Jesse, along with Earl Fulford, was one of the last members of a generation of Roswell witnesses who handled the material from the debris field and went public about what they saw and felt. He wrote a book about it called *The Roswell Legacy: The Untold Story of the First Military Officer at the 1947 Crash Site* with Linda Marcel and Stanton Friedman (New Page, 2008).

＊ Jesse Marcel, Jr.'s experience with the Roswell debris was unique because it was book-ended by his father's reactions to it in the days after the crash. First, Major Marcel seemed enthusiastic about the exotic nature of the material and encouraged his wife and son to handle it, get the feel of it, because he knew that once he put it into the Army's possession, his family would never see it again. Thus, the younger Marcel got a chance to explore the qualities of the different pieces of debris in a way that few, if any, people ever had. And he remembered his excitement over inspecting the debris for the rest of his life. Second, Jesse, Jr., said he remembered well when his father returned from Fort Worth in an entirely different mood, almost sullen and bitter about the experience. What Jesse, Jr., remembered about his father's attitude was confirmed independently by Walter Haut's description of the elder Marcel upon his return from Fort Worth in Haut's affidavit sworn out in contemplation of his death. The elder Marcel told his son and his wife that they should never speak of the debris or what happened outside of Roswell ever again. The matter was over. Walter Haut wrote that Marcel said the same thing to the other officers at the base upon his return.

Because of Jesse, Jr.'s experience, we saw him as one of our most important witnesses when it came to testing the material that Brick Price had fabricated for our Roswell episode. Marcel described the flexible metal as more like foil than a stiff metal skin. Handling the steel and aluminum, he said that both samples were too stiff and not malleable enough in his hand for him to identify them as similar to what he handled in 1947. The sheet metal sample was overly thick, he said, and not at all what he had handled. Jesse handled the foil next, and said that although it was too thin—the memory metal was thicker—it resembled the memory metal in its near weightless state. The memory metal, Marcel said, almost floated when you let it fall. And the near-weightless aspect of it astonished him almost as much as its malleability.

When it came to the acetate, however, Jesse, Jr., said it was the closest to the material he handled on the Marcel kitchen floor that night in July. He crumpled it and let it snap back into shape, remarking that this was so close it almost brought him back to that night. He and Earl Fulford identified the qualities of acetate, each in a blind test and each now knowing what the other had identified. Ted Acworth called it "amazing." "Both of them zeroed right in on the acetate making it clear to me that both of them found the weight, the thickness, and the malleability almost a one-to-one match with what they handled in 1947."

Ted pointed out that in 1947, acetate was a relatively new material that might have been unidentifiable back then. Brick Price suggested that using acetate for the test was the simplest solution because of its properties. Acetate had been around since 1910 as a component of glue, adhesive tape, and especially in the wings of early biplanes. And celluloid acetate was a component of film stock as early as the 1930s. But is there any evidence to suggest that acetate was used in weather balloons or in Project Mogul? If you look at the types of material that composed Project Mogul apparatus, you will not find acetate on the list. In fact, acetate in strip form was not used by the aircraft industry in the 1940s. Thus, acetate, although remarkably similar in its properties to the exotic metal strips handled by Earl Fulford and Jesse Marcel, Jr., would not have been material they handled in 1947. What we proved, however, regardless of what the material was, is that two witnesses, both of whom handled exotic material and who did not know each other, identified the exact same properties of the material they handled, which we re-created in the lab using acetate. It can be argued, therefore, based on eyewitness identification, that if two eyewitnesses pointed to an acetatelike substance as something they handled and acetate, according to the government's own records, was not a part of any Project Mogul component, then the eyewitnesses dispositively eliminated Project Mogul as the source of the Roswell debris.

Next stop, Seal Laboratories in Los Angeles for the testing of the Art Campbell artifact by metals expert Dr. Eric Kumar. The artifact to be tested was extremely smooth to the touch, but also very lightweight. It looked tantalizing, organic with its numerous folds that indicated the possibility of several layers. Dr. Kumar said he had never seen anything like this artifact before. After Ted had sectioned off a piece for a heat test, knowing the melting point might yield a clue about the artifact's composition, the object went off for observation into an electron microscope where small particles inside the folds could be examined for their chemical makeup. The object, preliminary analysis revealed, was primarily oxygen and carbon, elements of organic structure, but the object also had filler material, primarily sand from the desert. But, a further test revealed that the object was polyethylene, actually high-density polyethylene because its melting point was over 132 degrees Celsius. High-density polyethylene wasn't invented until the 1950s and wasn't used commercially in products like Tupperware until the early 1960s. This means that if the product was dropped on the Plains of San Agustin in 1947, it arrived before its invention. Or, it could mean that the artifact was dropped at the site after 1947, maybe as early as 1953.

High-density polyethylene or HDPE, as it's referred to, is also one of the primary components of aircraft and motor vehicles because of its high melting point. Ted reasoned that because the artifact's melting point was higher than the temperature in the desert, much higher, it indicated that something had melted the artifact because it couldn't have melted just from environmental factors. What did it say about Project Mogul? It meant that whatever the object's origin, it couldn't have come from Project Mogul because not only was HDPE not used in the device, there was no incendiary event that would have melted it. This means that whatever the artifact's origin, it was subjected to a fire or explosion. It doesn't indicate where the artifact came from even though it eliminates a Project Mogul apparatus.

The stunning testimony of Earl Fulford about the multiple craft Army personnel saw flying over the edge of the runway might suggest the multiple crash site theory, which might have included San Agustin, where witnesses reported the presence of an anomalous object before being forced out of the area by an Army detail. And Fulford's identification of an acetate material at the debris field as well as the confirming identification by Jesse Marcel, Jr., also seems to eliminate a Project Mogul apparatus. This means that unless Project Mogul contained material so far ahead of its time that it still hasn't been identified today, the material that both Fulford and Marcel described could not have come from Project Mogul. If reaching that conclusion was one of the goals of the episode, finding some truth that could be ascertained scientifically and objectively went a long way in eliminating Project Mogul as well as a standard weather balloon as the objects that crashed. Thus, the Army's cover story about the crash can be dismissed as false while the search continues for the real truth about the object that crashed outside of Roswell.

BILL'S BLOG

When we approach the subject of Roswell and its aftermath, the road we travel upon twists back on itself with tantalizing pretzel-like knots that not only beg to be unraveled but contain even more tantalizing clues to who might know what and where the red lines are concerning disclosure. For example, we have interviewed many witnesses from July 1947 whose stories revealed that the military seemed to be in a state of near panic as counterintelligence elements sought to cover up what some of the public safety personnel saw out there in the desert. Mortician Glenn Dennis told us that the Army had to dispose of the small ET bodies and pushed him hard to provide them with child-sized coffins. A local nurse also confirmed that there was deep concern over what to do about the bodies and how they should be examined.

Witness Frankie Rowe talked to us about handling the memory metal at the Roswell firehouse, wadding it up and then watching as it snapped back into shape. She described her father's reaction to the alien bodies he said he saw at the crash site. Alpha Boyd's father, a maintenance man at Walker Field in

Roswell, told his daughter after he had been diagnosed with cancer and was near death that he had seen an alien, or "extra-biological entity" firsthand, brought to Hangar 84 at the base on a stretcher. He stared right into the face of that entity and said it communicated with him, told him it was dying, and then passed out of his sight. These are multiple cited eyewitness reports.

Then there are the cryptic allusions to the relationship of Roswell to the UFO mystery and what can't be talked about in official circles. For example, Apollo astronaut Dr. Edgar Mitchell has repeatedly said that he had been briefed not only on Roswell, but also on the military's knowledge of a UFO presence, our government's dealing with an actual extraterrestrial presence, and the government's complicity in covering up its relationship with an extraterrestrial presence. Where did that information come from? Dr. Mitchell said he had been briefed, but by whom and why? Was it because he was going to the moon and was about to see something there that has not been officially acknowledged as being there? Did Dr. Mitchell have a need to know?

Then, as reported by UFO researcher and historian David Rudiak, retired NATO Supreme Commander General Wesley Clark made a cryptic reference to space travel and the human potential of developing ways to travel faster than the speed of light. Rudiak spoke to him in 2004 in Las Vegas during one of Clark's campaign appearances on behalf of then Democratic presidential candidate and current Secretary of State John Kerry. Rudiak asked the general whether he had ever been briefed on UFOs when he was active-duty military. Here is Clark's answer, as posted on Rudiak's Web site (www.roswellproof.com): "I heard a bit. In fact, I'm going to be in Roswell, New Mexico, to-night."

Notice the sudden reference to Roswell in General Clark's answer? Why the relationship of Roswell to what the general might have heard, as if the two were connected stories? Then, when pressed by Rudiak General Clark replied: "There are things going on. But we will have to work out our own mathematics."

Again, it's a two-part answer to a very straightforward question. Clark answered the question with a backdoor "yes"; he knew of things that were going on in relation to UFOs but did not explain or elaborate upon what they were, instead indicating that human beings would have to develop their own scientific and mathematical approaches to what was going on. And he related it to Roswell, which, he said, was where he was headed after Las Vegas. Were General Clark to have simply repeated the official government party line about Roswell—nothing happened there and it's all hype and, by the way, there are no UFOs—that he had never been briefed and he had no knowledge. But he didn't say that. In fact, he alluded to the opposite, indicating that he knew things were going on even if he couldn't talk about what things they were. According to UFO historian Grant Cameron, who writes about U.S. presidents and UFOs, General Clark would have to have been briefed on flying saucers because, given his status in the military command structure, any information about extraterrestrial anomalies would have been in his purview.

It's this background of semiofficial opinions about our government's involvement in the UFO question that was on our minds as we set up the Roswell episode. We'd attended the 2007 National Press Club conference on UFOs where distinguished pilots, military officers, and FAA investigator John Callahan all described their encounters with either UFOs and a UFO cover-up. But everywhere we turned, there were indicators that the UFO cover stories began after the stunning incident at Roswell where, in light of a public discovery of a UFO crash and the remains of actual anomalous life-forms, the government decided that this was a story that could not be revealed to the American people. Simultaneously, it was apparent an agreement was struck among military powers that there should be international cooperation about a cover-up, even though many retired military officers eventually came forward, such as Major Jesse Marcel, Lieutenant Walter Haut, and Air Force lieutenant colonel and deputy base commander of RAF Bentwaters, Charles Halt, to tell the truth about their experiences with UFOs. But it all seemed to have started at Roswell because it was there that the public and UFOs officially crossed paths.

In 1997, over ten years before the *UFO Hunters* set up its episode in Roswell, I had traveled there with my wife Nancy and the Corso family for the publication release of what would become the *New York Times* bestseller, *The Day After Roswell*. It was the fiftieth anniversary celebration of the Roswell incident marked not just by festivities, but also by lectures, exhibitions, and panel discussions by Roswell historians. You have to attend one of these yearly events to appreciate the depth of seriousness on the part of visitors to Roswell, most of whom are looking for new information, getting stories from witnesses, and searching for the scrap of truth that would become the dispositive confirmation that a UFO did crash in Roswell in 1947. Since the 1997 fiftieth anniversary, more information had come out about the crash, not the least of which was Art Campbell's research into the crash at San Agustin and Tom Carey's and Don Schmitt's research into new Roswell witnesses and what might be their most recent project—if it holds up—actual photographic evidence of an extraterrestrial biological entity, probably from the Roswell crash. We'll see.

And I was personally excited about returning to Roswell because, on the one hand, Roswell was almost an obligatory stop for us because we couldn't do a show about hunting for UFOs without hunting for some type of evidence at Roswell. On the other hand, even were we to have found nothing, the intensity of eyewitness stories and the background of Roswell itself was simply good television.

Excitement builds as you land at Albuquerque, and it's not

just anticipating the green chili peppers and salsa verde. It's the sense that you are getting close to a kind of UFO central, a place and a time when human history might have changed because of an encounter with another sentient and sapient species. The excitement builds as you drive from the Albuquerque airport down Route 295 south to Roswell through a desert of scrub brush, rolling tumbleweeds, and chaparral, a desert pockmarked here and there by a dairy farm, forlorn cattle staring out at you from behind fences, grain silos, and dirt paths heading from the road out over a ridge. Farm equipment here and there dot the edges of the roads, ancient-looking tractors, some of them scarred by rust, and often an old pickup truck with its bed stacked with hay. As SETI's Seth Shostak once said to me, why would any advanced alien race ever want to come to Roswell? Just to see a cow chewing its cud?

But then you come into the town itself, driving past the old Walker Field, now a maintenance airfield. And what do you see as you pull up to the airfield gate to get a glance at the Mecca of ufology? A stealth bat-winged Air Force fighter circling the runway, a giant stealth B-2 bomber, also sporting its black bat wings, making touch-and-goes off the runway. What's going on here? We thought this airfield had been closed decades ago, consigned to history, closed to the public: No UFOs here so move along. But that's not the case.

There were abandoned hangars, including Hangar 84, but there were also maintenance operations going on, real indicators that planes were being serviced and that, because of the presence of our nation's most classified aircraft, the base was still active. It made the return to Roswell and the set up of one of our episode segments at the base, all the more potentially exciting because if there was a UFO central, this was it.

We met old friends during this episode, met new witnesses, reconnected with stories we'd heard, and engaged in the same old arguments. Tom Carey and Don Schmitt took us to the actual crash site. We traveled back in time along that same road with Staff Sergeant Earl Fulford on a sentimental journey to one of the most chilling moments of his life when he saw something no human being had seen before. We walked the Plains of San Agustin with Art Campbell and if there was anything to test, we tested it. And we met up with Jesse Marcel, Jr., to examine materials that mimicked the strange metallic foil he'd held in his hand on the night his father brought it home in a box of other crash debris, laid it out on the kitchen floor, and told him and his mother they would probably never see its like again for as long as they lived.

This was Roswell, where, despite all the rumors, the cover stories, the hype, and the debunking, out there in a high desert so lonely you'd think it was another world, human beings from an Army airfield came into contact with entities from another place and time. And American history in that moment, likely changed forever.

"INVASION ILLINOIS"
THE TINLEY PARK LIGHTS

In our first episode of season two, we traveled to Tinley Park, Illinois, a suburb of Chicago, where, in 2004, local residents reported seeing huge formations of floating lights in the sky. Some said they had actually captured these lights on video. Were these real objects moving slowly across the sky? Or was this one large flying triangle something the military was testing? Were these actually airplanes mistaken by people on the ground, or were folks simply staring at constellations of particularly bright stars in the sky? There were so many witnesses whose sighting times corroborated with each other that the story of mass sightings of floating lights captured the attention of newspapers and local television. The case was less than four years old, relatively recent by UFO case standards, which meant that we could treat it as a current case. It was a good place to start our second season.

THE STORY

Remember some of the very compelling mass sighting scenes in *Close Encounters of the Third Kind* when folks stood by the side of the road and watched in awe as constellations of lights floated by? Somehow, hundreds of witnesses seeing the same thing at the same time and reacting en masse at an awesome spectacle of lights hovering overhead tugs at the strings of our imagination. So it was from August through October 2004, when hundreds of witnesses stopped to stare at large formations of lights as they moved across the night sky.

We were in contact with Illinois state MUFON (Mutual UFO Network) director Sam Maranto, who first began reporting the sightings and the videos witnesses were taking, calling attention to the fact that although the sightings were in areas in proximity to major airports, the constellation of lights did not bear any resemblance to the navigational lights on conventional commercial or military aircraft. The first series of lights on August 21, 2004, Maranto reported, was observed by multiple witnesses under ideal atmospheric conditions. The weather was warm, lots of folks were enjoying barbecues in their backyards, and because of the brightness of the stars, people were awed by the expanse of the night sky. Then a new set of lights appeared.

One witness, who would become a guest on *UFO Hunters*, was Bill Dooley, who told the press that there was a sense of excitement in the air even before the first sightings because his neighbors were all talking about the Chicago Bears preseason game they were watching. Folks were outside, Dooley said, when one of the neighbors said, "Look up." What they saw, Dooley reported, was amazing. They saw three moving bright lights, brighter than the stars in the background, which seemed to be moving very slowly across the sky and making no sound whatsoever. Then the lights stopped, hovered, and then moved from a single file into a stack, one on top of the other. Then, which seemed to belie any indication that they were simply stars that were misidentified by witnesses as moving lights, they moved from a stack into a triangular formation. Then the triangle moved and the lights seemed to change color to white. They were self-illuminating. Dooley said that after the triangular formation of lights left the area, again belying the fact that it was a constellation of stars, a single bright red light appeared in the sky forty-five minutes later. It followed the same path as the triangle, floated noiselessly overhead, stopped, and then floated away. Witnesses watching the light show were transfixed.

Just a block or so away from where Bill Dooley was standing, eight-year-old Justin Japcon noticed the lights overhead. Justin had seen his share of helicopters and conventional aircraft going to and from nearby airports and knew in a flash that whatever this light was, it was nothing conventional. He said that there were three lights moving across the sky and then, right over the heads of people in their backyards, the lights simply stopped and all was silent. Justin's father said it was eerie because even though the bright lights were hanging just over the rooftops, clearly not stars because they were too bright and had moved there from one corner of the sky on their way to the other. The silence was palpable. There was no sound of rotors or propellers, no sound of engines of any sort. All they could hear was a cacophony of frightened dogs barking in the distance, reacting to an eerie presence beneath a sky dazzled with an array of lights in a triangular pattern.

Then a police officer in a patrol car rolled by the neighbors, who stopped him and asked if he could see what they pointed to overhead. Not only could he see it, the officer said, he was keeping his ear tuned to his radio because the 911 switchboard was alive with calls from residents who were also looking at the pattern of lights. No, this was no ultrabright constellation of stars, residents said, because stars don't move from one corner of the sky to the other in less than fifteen minutes. This was something else.

Justin Japcon's father, T.J., ran inside his house to grab his camcorder. Whatever this was, he would eventually tell MUFON director Sam Maranto, to whom he would deliver the video, he had to capture these images because this was an event he wanted to memorialize. This footage would eventually wind up on our episode of *UFO Hunters,* one of the most compelling videos of real-time UFO manifestations we had ever seen to that point.

Witnesses to the August 21 sighting would not have to wait long for another strange event; the lights reappeared over Tinley Park neighborhoods on Halloween. This time there were even more witnesses because parents were out in force shepherding their trick-or-treating children from house to house under crisp skies. As T.J. Japcon told his friends, he never thought he would see the awesome spectacle again that he'd witnessed in August. But on Halloween, there it was, just as spectacular.

One of the immediate arguments raised by skeptics about the Tinley Park lights is that they were an elaborate hoax or a misidentification. Witnesses ruled out conventional aircraft right away because the proximity to local airports like O'Hare and Midway in Chicago would have meant that planes taking off or landing would have generated lots of noise from their jet engines. Residents were used to hearing the sound of engines from flights going in and out of the airports. But lights that close to the rooftops and hovering in place, then moving again, all without a sound, eliminated conventional aircraft. Could they have been balloons? Bill Dooley and others speculated that even if someone managed to launch balloons in a perfect formation, the air currents would have eventually separated them from a rigid alignment as they rose into the atmosphere. Also, Sam Maranto speculated, balloons simply don't hover motionlessly in the air. They rise and they move with the air current. Even if they appear to be in formation for a period of time, ultimately they separate from that formation. Another theory was that hoaxers had launched lighted model aircraft to fool witnesses on the ground. But that, too, was unlikely because model aircraft are still powered and there would have been the sound of engines everywhere. Maranto said that all the theories, some of which we would test during the *UFO Hunters* episode, simply didn't pan out. It left him, and the witnesses on those nights, with the feeling that the cause of the lights, albeit unknown, was most likely anomalous unless the military was testing a highly classified craft that did not behave according to the rules of conventional aeronautics.

The other aspect of this story is that although we informally referred to the episode as the Tinley Park Lights, the official name of the episode was "Invasion Illinois" because the lights appeared over many of the suburbs surrounding greater Chicago, dazzling residents and keeping local police agencies hopping from site to site as calls came in to 911 dispatchers.

OUR SEASON TWO INVESTIGATIVE APPROACH

This episode, the opener of season two, marked the first full use of what would become a standard feature on *UFO Hunters* for the remaining seasons. It was called the "white box," an interview format we introduced in the Stephenville episode in season one. We refined it in season two so that it became a mainstay of witness testimony in which each witness was photographed against a stark white background and stared directly into the camera while one of the producers asked questions that we developed from off-camera interviews. The effect was dramatic and very revealing because it looked like a confessional, an effect that no other show ever duplicated.

Another format change for season two, again, tried out at the end of season one, was the three-part story approach. Rather than Ted, Pat, or I pursuing the same on-location witness interviews, we decided that each member of the team would pursue his own investigation into the phenomena. Ted would pursue the scientific investigation and testing, gathering the evidence he would need to bring to one of our labs or photo analysts for expert opinion. Pat, probably the most people-oriented person on our team, would handle the person-on-the-street interviews, gathering and collating information for Ted to process, and I would be in charge of gathering the expert opinion, usually from MUFON investigators. So the breakdown was: Ted handles raw science data, Pat handles unbiased witness observation, and I was the UFO guy exploring the UFO explanation. The three of us would come together at various points in the episode to share information, beat a point of analysis back and forth, and agree on the steps we should take next. We would come together at the end of each episode to challenge the opinions of the others and see if we could come to any agreed-upon conclusion. There was a lot of joking about this approach in the critical media where folks said that the *UFO Hunters* never came to an agreed opinion except to say that the case needed more investigation. But that was not completely true because, essentially, we sought to eliminate, and often did eliminate, the theories of debunkers by knocking down the conventional explanations about phenomena. We debunked the debunkers.

THE EPISODE

We were attracted to the story of a mass sighting in the Chicago suburbs by MUFON director Sam Maranto's reports. Maranto emphasized that the sightings took place over a large area, by folks who did not know each other or share information, and were independently reported to police and emergency dispatchers. Some people said they saw lights from their backyards, from their front lawns, or through their windows on a very warm August night. Not only were the lights moving, but they were also sporting different colors, mostly red, and police were not disputing the veracity of the sightings. The lights, some of which stayed in a rigid triangular formation, floated across the area from west to east for about thirty minutes and could be seen from Lincoln Hills, Oak Forest, Orland Park, Madison, Mokena, and Frankfort. Witnesses speaking directly into the camera against the white background were specific in their recall, saying not only did the lights seem to form a rigid pattern at first, they moved as if parts of the rigid structure broke off and reformed from a triangle into a straight line. And the lights changed color.

We began our exposition of the story at the Tweeter Center (now the First Midwest Bank Amphitheatre) in Tinley Park. It was there, on August 21, 2004, that fans leaving the Ozzfest rock concert were caught in a traffic jam. They casually looked up at the sky and saw a dazzling light show. It wasn't a light show from the rock concert, but a light show of floating orbs moving across the sky. Pat Uskert commented, "Of course skeptics might challenge the credibility of witnesses leaving a wild Ozzy Osbourne concert." Given the types of light shows at rock concerts and the types of substances often imbibed therein one might

argue that folks leaving the concert were juiced and ready to see anything. But, Pat pointed out, that doesn't explain the identical nature
of the sightings by those in their cars and by those in their backyards.
They described the same thing. In his introduction to his investigation,
Ted said that he found this to be an interesting case because of the vast
number of witnesses observing the phenomena from different locations. Because one aspect of Ted's expertise was scientific measurement, the different witnesses who said they observed the same set of
lights from widely separate locations meant that Ted could evaluate the
metrics of the sightings to see if folks were seeing the same thing or
seeing entirely different phenomena.

We also discovered from our research that a similar pattern of lights
had been seen just two days before the Tinley Park sighting in British
Columbia, Canada. Then, the next day, a similar pattern of lights was
spotted in Minnesota. And the day after the Tinley Park sightings, the
lights appeared in Houston, Texas. On August 23, an array of lights captured on video and similar to the videos from Tinley Park was sighted
in Melbourne, Australia. We had to wonder, was this array of lights a
worldwide event?

Triangular UFOs, whatever their origin—ours or theirs—have been
around since before the 1980s, objects that seemed to defy the rules of
conventional flight. Unlike the flying saucer sightings of the 1950s and
'60s and the flying cylinder sightings of the 1960s, these giant triangles
fascinated witnesses because of their enormous size and because the
self-illuminated orbs at the corners sometimes broke away from their
positions and reformed themselves into a different shape. Other witnesses remarked that the triangles had an almost translucent body and
that they could see the stars in the sky through the formation of orbs.

The team broke into their separate investigations. Pat began by taking measurements along the lines of sight reported by witnesses to
pinpoint the precise locations of each observation. Ted planned to use
Pat's measurements and other data to calculate the size and speed of
the objects, compare them against star maps and routine commercial
air traffic in the area to see whether the lights were an anomaly or sim-

ply a misidentification. Ted worked with our photo analyst Terrence Masson in his analysis of the different videos we received from witnesses. Ted's primary question was whether the three lights at the corners were part of one object. And if so, how big was it? My path was to set up a balloon and flare test with some of the witnesses to see if on video, we could mimic the pattern of lights as they floated across the sky. Could the Tinley Park lights have been a hoax, a prank in which flares or candles were tied onto balloons and then tied on to a rigid structure such as PVC pipe so that it looked like a flying triangle? Maybe we would never know what these lights in the sky were. However, by the end of the investigation we would certainly try to figure out what these lights were not.

One of our first interviews was with Illinois MUFON's Sam Maranto, whom I described as the "squeal man" for the case, meaning that when the first reports about flying lights came in, Sam took the call and jumped on the case. Sam said that he had interviewed well in excess of a hundred people, collated all of their sighting descriptions, and collected their videos as well. He told us that the Tinley Park events were among the best documented sightings ever, in large part because of the number of witnesses, the precise locations of their sightings, and the number of videos that were taken. There were over twenty-five videos, almost all of them taken at the same time with date and time stamps imposed by the cameras; these time imprints Ted would use to analyze the direction and movement of the lights.

Pat Uskert remarked that this case not only made national news, it made international news as well. Therefore, for one of his first interviews he spoke to Jason Freeman, a reporter for the *SouthtownStar*, a local newspaper that first broke the news of the sightings. Jason was also a witness to the events and when he encountered reports that people were seeing floating balloons, he believed that there was more to the story. He told Pat that he was "two times a witness," both on August 21 and on Halloween and based on what he saw was not about to jump on the balloon story without considering other possibilities.

When he first saw the anomaly, he wrote in his column in the *Star*, he was driving. He stopped the car and got out to get a better view of the overhead lights. What exactly did he believe he was looking at? we asked him in his interview. He knew they were strange, although he didn't believe they were necessarily paranormal. But what kept bothering him was that nobody from official circles ever came forward to explain what the lights were. Did the Air Force not know? If they did know, were they keeping the truth close because the lights were from a classified aircraft? Or were the lights officially a taboo subject because they were simply an unidentified flying object? Freeman did not know, but he wanted to follow up on what other witnesses saw.

Sam Maranto said he had contacted the police department, who told him flat out that these lights were not balloons or flares. In fact, other agencies Maranto spoke to, including the FAA, did not know the origin of the lights. The FAA told him that because the lights did not register on air traffic control radar, they had no idea what the lights were and had no way of tracking them. We were perplexed, too. How could radar at two of the nation's busiest airports not pick up something overhead that was observed by thousands of witnesses as flying close to the ground. It made no sense to us unless the objects were below the level of radar contact. Nevertheless, the FAA's response caused us to rule out commercial or private aircraft because they would have turned up on radar.

Sam delivered the videos to us on a DVD, showing us the first video from Oak Forest in which the lights could plainly be seen moving and not stationary. While witnesses in Oak Forest were filming lights, T.J. Japcon in Tinley Park was filming the lights south and west of Oak Forest. Thus, as Sam pointed out, both videos being shot at the same time from different locations, but aiming at the same point in the sky, amounted to a triangulation of the object's position. As we reviewed other videos with Sam, shot from other locations, we could see that they seemed identical: lights that were rigidly in formation as they moved. It looked to us as if there was a solid structure holding them in place. Pat was the most skeptical member of the team, however, arguing that it was premature to call this a craft. "All we have," he said, "were three points of light seemingly moving in the sky and videotaped from different locations."

Skeptics argued that the lights were flares. Others argued that the confused witnesses were simply looking at an unusually bright constellation of stars, and they matched the light pattern with constellations. However the on-scene witnesses did not agree. Witnesses Bill Dooley and T.J. Japcon said that even though they did not know what the lights were, they were sure that because of the absence of sound from jets or propellers that these could not be commercial or private aircraft. But Ted Acworth was not convinced. He said that we had to eliminate dispositively the possibility that these lights were conventional aircraft.

Triangulating the air traffic routes in and out of Midway and O'Hare Airports, Ted demonstrated how the area around the Chicago suburbs was among the three busiest air corridors in the nation. It was heavy with commercial air traffic and nearby military bases also added to the crush of air traffic in the Chicago area. Tinley Park is between two military operations areas (MOAs) where there are on and off activities, which could also explain the presence of the lights or even strange noncommercial aircraft. But, Ted pointed out, even with two MOAs surrounding Tinley Park, you wouldn't get a presence of military aircraft in a commercial air traffic control area where the FAA's Chicago center would have to track military flights as well as regularly scheduled commercial flights. Therefore, Ted theorized, military flights would stay out of a commercial air traffic center absent some sort of emergency. But, as Ted urged, we had to check on military traffic on the nights in question even if only to eliminate that possibility. Thus, I telephoned the commander of nearby Scott Air Force Base to check on any military air traffic on August 21 and October 31, 2004. The base responded both over the phone and in writing that they had no information at all concerning any military activity in the air over Tinley Park and its environs on the dates in question. Their explanation was that because of the high turnover of personnel at Scott AFB, there was no one available to speak about the flight logs on August 21 and

October 31, 2004. Since we couldn't verify any military air traffic on those nights, it was time for Pat to get to the witness locations to collect the videos so that Ted and Terrence could review them.

First, Pat interviewed T.J. Japcon and Dave Wagner, who, at 10:45 P.M. on August 21, 2004, were at a block party with about seventy friends and neighbors. Suddenly T.J.'s son pointed to the tree line and told his father to look at the light that was moving over the trees. He said it was a UFO. Other partygoers turned to look and saw the formation of red lights heading their way. The lights were clearly on the move, not stationary in the sky like a pattern of stars. T.J. grabbed his video camera and captured the formation of lights on tape for an incredible eighteen minutes as they traversed the sky, stopped, and started moving again. The lights moved in ways that were too slow for conventional aircraft and moved without the thwap, thwap, thwap that helicopter rotors make. Over the course of the next twenty minutes, the lights crossed the entire sky. This is also not the type of movement that a formation of stars would make because stars don't move across the sky in minutes.

Pat also asked T.J. about the police unit he flagged down that night to report what they were seeing. Japcon confirmed that the officer told him that he couldn't stop to talk because of the intensity of dispatch switchboard activity from folks in the surrounding neighborhood reporting the same thing that Japcon and his friends were seeing. Pat followed up with the Tinley Park Police Department and found that, indeed, their incident report sheet noted a number of folks calling to report "bright red lights" moving across the sky, hovering, and then moving again. These reports confirmed that what Japcon and his neighbors had seen was more widely observed than just by a few people at an outdoor block party.

After twenty or so minutes, the lights disappeared from view as if someone had thrown the off switch. But at eleven thirty that same night, Japcon had another sighting. He and his neighbor grabbed a telescope for a closer look and what they saw was more than just a single red light. They told Pat that what was a single floating light to the naked eye through the telescope was actually an oval-shaped object with about ten or twelve red lights around it. Pat used his GPS locator to measure the precise location of the sighting and its direction across the sky, an inclinometer to measure how far above the horizon the lights appeared to be, and a chronometer to measure the time it took the lights to cross the sky. These measurements, along with the video he collected, comprised the kinds of data that Ted needed to calculate the flight characteristics of the lights and perhaps even speculate about their nature. But in order to be as precise as possible, Ted said that he needed one more location to complete the triangulation. He had video from Tinley Park and from Oak Forest. It was up to Pat and Sam Maranto to gather video from another witness, Bob Peterson.

Peterson told Pat that he was outside and just happened to look up, where he saw three red lights in the sky. "It was definitely an odd thing to see," he said to Pat, remarking that he could easily recognize conventional aircraft because his house was along the flight pattern in and out of Midway Airport. "I thought the lights were helicopters at first," he said. "But as they got closer, they were dead silent. With no noise coming out of them, at that point I knew it wasn't a helicopter."

Pat asked, "What about airplanes?"

"No," Peterson said. "Way too slow."

But was Bob convinced that the lights were not anything paranormal? If anything, he suggested, it was probably a prank or a hoax. His neighbor, Bill Dooley, also saw the lights. Dooley's neighbor, Don Wilkinson, had a high-powered telescope, and Bill and Don described the light they saw through the telescope as a magnified version of what they were seeing with the naked eye: a large, floating, circular red light in the sky. At first they thought it might have been a flare, Dooley said, and they thought if it were a flare they would definitely see smoke from the burning chemicals through the telescope. But they didn't see any smoke at all. Absent smoke, a flare as the cause of the floating light was very unlikely.

Pat logged all the locations and angle of inclination data from Bill Dooley and Bob Peterson to complete the triangulation requirement.

He brought it to Ted for his evaluation while I worked with the witnesses to build our own floating triangle complete with balloons to launch it and get it to fly and flares at the corners to mimic the red lights witnesses saw and videotaped. Our plan was to launch this device, videotape what it looked like as it rose, and compare our flare video with the videos shot by Japcon, Dooley, and Peterson. While Pat and I worked with some of the Tinley Park witnesses to assemble the balloon device, Ted and Terrence Masson analyzed the videos Pat and Sam Maranto had collected.

The first video Ted and Terrence evaluated was the one shot by T.J. Japcon on August 21, 2004, which Terrence believed needed to be stabilized in order to keep the lights in the video in frame. "The swimming motion of the video from a consumer handheld camera," Terrence explained, "distorted the image of the lights against the background of the sky." He began by stabilizing or "pinning" the location of one of the lights so that the motion of the other lights was around a fixed object. It helped him to analyze the nature of the three lights. Were the other two lights free-floating or locked in place, which would indicate whether the lights were rigidly attached to one another or simply three free-floating lights. And Terrence found that the other two lights were, indeed, locked to the stabilized light, meaning that they were either fixed to the same physical structure—such as a triangular craft—or, if a hoax, the object might have been an I beam or even a fabricated triangular structure such as the one Pat and I were building.

The witnesses, and this was recorded on video, said that the lights did move with respect to each other, changing their formation from a triangle to a straight line. What might that mean? Ted suggested that the lights actually never moved with respect to each other. On the contrary, what shifted were the viewers' perspectives as the object itself maneuvered in the sky. Ted concluded, therefore, that the three lights were fixed to each other by a rigid structure that was turning in the sky so as to give the impression that the lights were moving. But, if there was a structure holding the lights in place, what was the nature of that structure? A clue, Ted and Terrence believed, could be found in

the image of a helicopter captured on T.J.'s video that was flying close
to the lights. Perhaps, they reasoned, if the helicopter pilot could be
located, he or she might be able to provide a description of what either
one was flying close to. And, in fact, the team did find the helicopter
pilot, who said that he had observed a "weird" object flying close to him,
but he declined to go into any detail or file a formal report, claiming
he "feared for his job."

Next, Ted and Terrence tried to get a feel for the overall size of whatever the lights might have been fixed to. Was it ten feet across or a thousand feet across? They begin their measurements by taking the height
of the helicopter image in the frame and comparing it to the height of
the lights and then calculating the distance between the two images.
Terrence estimated just from eyeballing the screen that the ratio of the
helicopter to the lights was about 1:30, indicating that the lights were
about a thousand feet across. Next, using an estimate of a thousand
feet across, Ted and Terrence plugged in the location data that Pat
compiled from witness statements. The GPS locator pinpointed each
sighting on an area map. The inclinometer pinpointed the angle of el-
evation or the height of the phenomena above the horizon. And compass readings revealed the direction the array of lights was traveling.
Based upon the compass and inclinometer readings, the witnesses all
appeared to have seen the same object toward the west and low to the
horizon, between five and ten degrees. Using T.J.'s footage and laying
it across the map of the area, Ted estimated that the object was two
and a half miles away from T.J.'s location at an average of approximately
seven degrees above the horizon. With about a thousand feet between
the lights, Ted and Terrence could estimate the total size of the array.
They agreed that give or take a few hundred feet, the total size of the
array was about fifteen hundred feet. "Definitely not the size of a
conventional aircraft," Terrence argued. Ted agreed, saying that he
did not know of any object capable of carrying lights at about fifteen
hundred feet apart.

Ted and Terrence speculated that this array was an object flying
about several thousand feet in the air and fifteen hundred feet from end

to end, way larger than a 737, which had a wingspan of about two hundred feet. We would have to stack up about seven 737s from wingtip to wingtip to get the span of the array of lights over Tinley Park on August 21 and October 31, 2004. Terrence suggested that it was unlikely the array was a naturally occurring phenomena; certainly not a constellation of stars because it moved across the sky and was seven times larger than any conventional aircraft, and clearly a flying object. "I have no idea what it might be," Terrence said, underscoring the suggestion that this was, by definition, an unidentified flying object. But could that object have been an elaborate hoax, a structure suspended from balloons and carrying flares for lights? Many of the witnesses said yes while many others said no, it would have been impossible. Time for our experiment.

We first cleared our test with local police and fire authorities and let air traffic control officials know that we would be launching balloons and flares. We wanted to check on not only the ability of a rigid structure to handle balloons and flares as it ascended, but to analyze the intensity and color density of the flares to see if they matched up with the videos witnesses took. We also wanted the witnesses to be on hand to tell us if what we launched was similar to what they saw with their naked eyes. We began by laying out PVC pipe in the shape of triangles, making sure all the parts fit, and then gluing the pieces together. But before we could assemble it outside, the weather took an ominous turn for the worse as heavy thunderstorms moved into the area. As the bands of storms approached, we picked up tornado warnings on our radio. Pat and I quickly moved all the construction materials, the balloons, and the flares inside a garage to keep them dry.

With police and fire officials looking on, we tied and then secured the PVC pipe components together and inflated the helium balloons, balloons five feet in diameter, large enough, we hoped, to lift the PVC frame. It soon became apparent, however, that the larger we made the frame, the heavier it became and the more difficult it was to lift it with the balloons. We tested each corner as we tied on the balloons and found that the balloons simply didn't have the capacity to support the frame. Pat quickly realized that the idea of a hoaxed object made of any solid structure was impossible because it would have taken hundreds of balloons to lift it. Actually, if the object were fifteen hundred feet across, it would have taken thousands of helium balloons to do the job.

The witnesses, Bob Peterson, Bill Dooley, and their children and neighbors arrived just as the skies cleared and we had a window during which to launch our test object. The witnesses even brought the same cameras they used on the nights of the Tinley Park lights to make our video comparison as accurate as possible. But the frame we built was unusable because it was too heavy. Pat had another solution. Having served with the Army Corps of Engineers, he had learned to improvise. He laid out fine, lightweight rope, in the shape of a triangle and we affixed the balloons to it and then affixed the flares to the balloons so as to have the rough shape of a triangle, although not rigid, that would keep the balloons in formation while they ascended with burning flares.

"Gentlemen, light your flares," Pat barked, and our witnesses set the flares, now attached to the balloons, alight. It was time to launch. The eyewitnesses recorded their comments as soon as the balloons began to ascend. They remarked about the quality and density of the color, the brightness of the lights, and the difference between the rigid triangular formation of the 2004 lights against the sporadic triangular array of our 2008 lights and how both sets of lights moved across the night sky.

"What we saw in the summer of 2004," Bill Dooley said. "Was a much steadier formation of lights. There was no jerking around, the way these lights did." The 2004 lights were "bright red like you'd see on top of a cell tower," Dooley explained. The test flares we launched were "more orange, more pink, and not like the 2004 lights."

For witness Bob Peterson, who originally thought the Tinley Park lights were a hoax or prank, our demonstration gave him a change of perspective. "From what I saw tonight," he said. "I don't think [the 2004 lights] were a flare. There was just too much that was different about it." Moreover, the behavior of the lights, the way they stayed in a rigid formation in 2004, was different from the way our test flares separated from each other, tried to float at different speeds, and reacted individually to the air currents. For him, seeing the test, convinced him to change his mind about the possible nature of the lights from known to unknown.

Our next step was to meet again with Sam Maranto to talk about the Tinley Park lights as part of a worldwide phenomenon. First, Maranto pointed out, Tinley Park's history of strange lights in the sky didn't just begin in 2004. "This area has been a hotbed of activity," he said. "Project Blue Book, the official Air Force investigation into UFOs, actually had one of their cases right here in Tinley Park. Two young men reported having seen an unidentified flying object, and that case was investigated but is still an 'unknown.' It was a case from the early 1960s," Maranto said. He also told us that similar objects that witnesses saw in Tinley Park on August 21, 2004, were observed in Canada just days earlier. On August 19, the object was seen hovering over Minneapolis–Saint Paul for a period of almost nine hours. After that, the object appeared over Houston and then over Melbourne. Sam showed us video from Australia that appeared to show two of the types of objects folks saw in Tinley Park. And then, on October 1, 2005, the same configuration of lights returned to Tinley Park and was, again, witnessed by hundreds of local residents. The lights last appeared on Halloween 2005.

All that was left was for Ted to weigh in on the comparison between the test flares we launched and the videos he and Terrence Masson analyzed. First, Terrence pointed out, that even with completely calm air and no turbulence aloft, you would still expect to see some random motion from balloons loosely tied together in formation. Our test balloons, Terrence said, "were all over the place." They behaved erratically in the wind that night, pulling against the line as they tried to go in their separate directions. This was in stark contrast to the 2004 footage. On the night of our test, the winds were twelve miles an hour and our balloons moved in concert with the winds. In 2004, however, the winds aloft were over twenty-five miles an hour and the lights stayed in a rigid formation. In our test, the balloons were pulling against the tether. What this suggested to Ted and Terrence was that, indeed, the 2004 lights were held in place by a rigid structure.

"The longer the 2004 lights held their configuration in the wind as they traversed the sky indicates the greater the likelihood that the lights were held on a rigid structure," Ted said. "That's a pretty important conclusion."

"It definitely shows that the 2004 lights were not flares," Terrence said. But Ted and Terrence wanted to compare the colors between our test flares and the 2004 lights even though with consumer-grade cameras it was hard to match up color because of the way the colors would change according to the degree of optical or digital zoom in low light, nighttime settings. But in comparing the 2008 and 2004 videos Terrence noticed differences in the intensity of the light. "The flickering, for example, is very evident in the flares," Terrence said. Then there is the steady nature of the light. A flare will have greater scintillation, a shimmering, than a constant light source. This was another difference between our test flares and the 2004 lights.

"To me," Terrence argued, "the 2004 lights were an illuminated source rather than a burning source, which the flares were." And Terrence brought up another point of comparison, specifically that the flares were dropping residue as they burned off their fuel source. We could see the residue dropping off in the video and even with our naked eyes as the flares rose. But in the original video from 2004, there was no evidence of any burning or dropping residue.

Ted, whose job it was to evaluate all the conventional explanations, said, "I would love to say that our analysis showed that the Tinley Park lights were flares suspended in the air. But I can't say that. It's extremely unlikely that flares were the explanation for what we have here [in the 2004 videos]." And Terrence said that there was no way he could see any sort of tethered balloon or burning light source in the 2004 videos. Without calling it a flying saucer, Terrence said definitively that, "by the strictest definition, this was an unidentified flying object."

With all the data collected and the analysis thereof, Ted said, "I can't explain what it is. Yet it is a corroborative case with lots of witnesses. There was definitely something there."

And Pat said that he believed this was a real case of something that people saw, but there was no evidence that this was a hoax. Beyond that he could not go, except to say that this was real. "In my opinion," Pat said, "this case is still open."

Here's what we know: no evidence of a hoax; video evidence indicates the Tinley Park lights were not flares; photo analysis suggested a massive rigid object that held the lights together and turned as it floated overhead so that the lights looked as though they were moving when they weren't. As Terrence said, this fit the precise definition of a UFO because it was simply unidentifiable.

BILL'S BLOG

I nvasion Illinois" was the first episode of our second season that was an easy episode to produce because it fit all the requirements of our new format. The multiplicity of witnesses, men, women, and children, fit right into our new method of interviewing direct into the camera for personal testimony. We had a lot of faces we could get into the white box to tell their stories in sound bites. The many sighting locations offered Pat Uskert the opportunity to develop his style of witness interviews and measurement taking. And the successful teaming up of Ted Acworth and Terrence Masson from season one was also perfect for this episode because of the many videos we had at our disposal. Our guide into the intricacies of what was going on in Tinley Park and its neighboring towns was MUFON director Sam Maranto, an aggressive investigator whose ability to track down videos and the witnesses who took them proved invaluable in our investigation.

We had honed our new approach to investigation by the end of season one, primarily during the Stephenville episode, and the "Invasion Illinois" episode allowed us to refine that approach further with specific roles for each member of the *Hunters* team. "Invasion Illinois" also provided us with so much video that it fit into another sweet spot for us: display lots of videos and let television viewers, members of our audience, come to their own conclusions about what they were watching. And that's exactly what happened when some viewers came to their own conclusions and set out to duplicate the flares on balloons experiment to see if they could fool not only residents of some local communities, but *UFO Hunters* as well.

On January 5, 2009, two self-described skeptics from northern New Jersey decided to see if they could duplicate what they said they saw in the Tinley Park flare demonstration by launching their own lights attached to balloons at around eight fifteen in the evening. The appearance of the floating lights, which, according to local police, posed a possible hazard to flights in and out of the Morristown Municipal Airport, captured the attention of a number of local residents from the Morristown and Hanover Township area. The two young men who launched the balloons said they were demonstrating that a simple hoax could fool people into thinking that the lights were UFOs. However, by the definition set by UFO researchers, any flying object that's real and not an illusion and cannot be positively identified is a UFO. That's the approach we took in the "Invasion Illinois" episode at Tinley Park. Because Ted and Terrence could not positively identify the nature of the lights residents saw, they had to go down as "unidentified." The same was true for the residents who observed the Morristown lights and could not identify them as Chinese lanterns.

In late December 2008, we received notice from History that *UFO Hunters* was renewed for a third season. By early January 2009, we were set to assemble at our production facility in Santa Monica when I got a call from History about the Morristown lights. Were these lights a real UFO flap over New Jersey or were they, as the Hanover Township Police Department reported, simply a prank. Whatever they were, we thought that covering the lights story and especially the stories from eyewitnesses and looking at the video of the lights might be a good way to preview the third season. In the back of my mind, I thought that if we could include the Morristown story—whatever the nature of the lights was—with our first episode of the third season at Mount Shasta, California, "Giant Triangles," and have the Morristown video analyzed, it might be an interesting tie-in. Accordingly, a day before I was set to fly back to California from New Jersey, I went up to the Morristown area to meet a production crew from History for interviews with witnesses and a review of the video.

At first, the two hoaxers claimed to be witnesses to the lights themselves, telling a local news channel they were driving along a street in Morris Plains, New Jersey, when they saw the lights. Basically, it was a false claim, part of their hoax to report a fictitious sighting because, even though the police believed the lights to be a prank, the two hoaxers were trying to trick the media into reporting news of a UFO flap over the area. Simply stated, they hoaxed the hoax.

The two hoaxers weren't the only people to report seeing the lights. Hanover Township health officer Dr. George Van Orden, the first person I interviewed for this promo segment, told me that he saw the lights when he was out walking his dog at about eight thirty. He said he heard no sound of jet engines or propellers and did not believe he was looking at floating balloons. I specifically asked Dr. Van Orden if the lights seemed to be drifting or moving randomly with the wind, which would have been an indicator that they were balloons. But Dr. Van Orden, who was stressing his scientific credentials, said that he believed these were not moving in a random motion but seemed controlled. He was the eyewitness; I was the interviewer.

"These lights" Dr. Van Orden said, "were not lights on a jet, not lights on a helicopter."

My next stop was to the Hanover Township Police Department, where an officer told us definitively that the Morristown lights were flares attached to balloons and they were trying to find out who the pranksters were because the objects had interfered with air traffic at the Morristown airport and presented a hazard. The police were investigating. Accordingly, contrary to what was reported in the newspapers about how we investigated the lights, we knew at the outset that the Hanover Township police believed the lights to be suspended from balloons. But the witnesses to the lights told a different story.

My next stop was a visit with pilot Paul Hurley, whose daughter had witnessed the lights and been frightened by them. Hurley had videotaped the lights with his consumer-grade camera. He led me to his window where he had seen the lights.

"These were five red lights," he said. "They were moving over the trees. They were moving very slow. In my opinion, too slow for any aircraft to maintain altitude."

"You are a pilot, right?" I asked.

"I have my pilot's license," Hurley said. "I called the airport tower and asked the controller there if he was seeing the lights. He said he was, but was not in contact with them." He continued, "There were five lights in a pattern of three and two. One light simply took off in another direction."

I suggested that if the lights were an array attached to a rigid structure, then ultimately, that structure would have fallen down somewhere when the balloons exploded. But that did not happen. This was why I said that because of the absence of any rigid structure that would have come down, we knew that whatever this phenomenon was, it was not a series of balloons carrying a rigid structure to keep them together. And this was the case. In fact, what Paul Hurley and George Van Orden most likely saw were a pattern of Chinese lanterns launched separately without a rigid frame and carried by the wind, which is what the police said and which would have explained what Paul Hurley described as a single light taking off in a separate direction. But the premise of this preview segment was to build it into one of the first episodes of season three, which, for a variety of reasons, we could not do. Hence, this piece became a stand-alone, which was not our original intent.

Paul Hurley introduced us to his family, who also witnessed the Morristown lights. Paul's young daughter was one of the first to spot the lights. She explained that she was sitting at the kitchen table doing her homework while facing the window. Her dad, Paul, had his back to the window. She noticed the lights first and said that she was frightened because they looked so strange. She pointed them out to her father, who grabbed his video camera, ran out into his backyard, and videotaped the lights, which he played for us on his television monitor. Although the video was blurry and slightly pixelated, it seemed as though the three lights were moving in unison, as if they were attached to a rigid structure. However, the video only captured a few minutes of the lights so any independent movement, which the two other lights exhibited, might have not been caught on camera. My response, because this is what we were planning, was to take the video back to Ted and Terrence for their analysis so that any conclusions about the nature of the lights could come from them after subjecting the video to the kind of scrutiny they did for the Tinley Park lights.

But here's what happened: The production team from the network videotaped the Morristown segment with entirely different equipment than the VariCams we used for our regular episodes. The minicams used for the Morristown segment had different settings than the ones we used for our regular episodes, which presented a real problem in editing the different segments together. At the end, and because we were filming in Sonora, California, for our "Giant Triangles" episode, the schedules did not allow for a separate analysis of the Paul Hurley video by Terrence and Ted, which was what we had originally planned. As a result, the Morristown segment, incomplete as it was, was only a preview for the season and not a full segment in season three's opening episode. A full segment would have required the same kind of analysis that we did in Tinley Park.

On April 1, 2009, while we were filming on Andros island in the Bahamas for the Autec episode, the hoaxers came out with the story that they had launched the Morristown lights and posted videos of what they had done. The media, especially the Newark *Star-Ledger*, seized on this as an example of how *UFO Hunters* was hoaxed. But it wasn't true. It was only a claim by the hoaxers that resonated because we had never completed the full treatment—the analysis of the Hurley video—that we normally provided. The arc of the segment, as a part of "Giant Triangles," would have gone something like this:

I would have introduced the Morristown segment to Pat, Ted, and Terrence, all of whom would have pointed to the fact that the Hanover Township police had said that the lights were Chinese lanterns. Given that, Ted and Terrence would have analyzed the Hurley video along with the videos from Sonora, which actually revealed a triangular shape moving over Mount Shasta in daylight. And, I suspect, Ted and Terrence would have said that they identified, by color intensity and flicker, that the lights, which appeared to be self-illuminating, were actually burning objects: flares or candles. And we would have been able to contrast the Sonora giant triangle to the Morristown flares. But that's not how it turned out.

By the time *The Star-Ledger* story broke, we were well into our third season and off to Germany and Poland for our "Nazi UFOs" episode, a painful exploration of the ways the Nazis used their concentration camp prisoners as guinea pigs for radiation and space medicine experiments. It was chilling and blotted out any further response to the Morristown lights.

Next question: Could the Tinley Park lights have been simple constellations of stars, acutely bright on the nights in question, that witnesses misidentified as triangular anomalous craft? Some of our viewers heavily criticized the episode because we didn't challenge the witnesses on that explanation. One of our viewers argued that the triangle witnesses observed were really the stars Gamma, Schedar, and Caph in the constellation Cassiopeia, which formed a triangle and which was rising at eight thirty on the night of August 21 in the north to northeastern sky. Hence, it would have been in the line of sight for witnesses that night. At eleven thirty the star Capella rose from the same part of the sky, making for the second sighting, so the argument went. Because Capella was known for its display of various colors, it might have explained the reddish color of the Tinley Park lights.

However, as compelling as the argument might be for some for the misidentification of the Tinley Park lights, the witness testimony still stands because of the visual movement of the lights. More importantly, as Bill Dooley and T.J. Japcon described it, the lights, before their very eyes, transformed from a triangular formation to a straight line. And all of this took place within a thirty-minute sequence. Ted and Terrence suggested that the movement of the lights was really an effect made possible by the movement of what they believed to be the rigid structure itself, turning in the sky so that it looked as though the lights were moving. This type of visual activity during a thirty-minute period should eliminate a misidentification of a pattern of stars as a UFO.

A final word regarding the way we interacted with witnesses on *UFO Hunters*. As exasperated as some of our viewers, and our hoaxers, might be about what some called our "coddling" of witnesses, we recognized from the outset that many witnesses would be reluctant to tell their stories in public because of a fear of ridicule. Our job, whether we believed our witnesses or not, was never to ridicule anyone, even those whose stories were obviously based on delusion or simple mistake. Our approach was to take witnesses at their word and evaluate the evidence of what they said they saw in our final segment of each episode. Occasionally, we would push witnesses to reveal more, as we did in the second episode of season two of *Hunters,* "UFO Emergency," in which one of our witnesses finally came forward for the first time to reveal that she actually saw the flying triangle that police units in the field had reported seeing. She had previously denied ever having seen anything anomalous.

We treated our witnesses and our guests with respect and politeness and questioned them about alternate explanations of what they had reported seeing so as to give them a chance to qualify their stories. Where witnesses stuck to their stories, we went along with them during the interviews, using the analysis of evidence to come to our own conclusions. Therefore, even though the Hanover Township police in New Jersey said that the Morristown lights were Chinese lanterns, flares attached to balloons—which we acknowledged in the segment—we allowed the witnesses to tell their stories as they wanted. We never wanted to come off as bullies, and I was proud of that.

"GIANT TRIANGLES"

T his was the first episode of season three and the episode into which I had planned to insert the Morristown segment because one of our guests for this episode was Terrence Masson. The episode took us to Sonora, California.

Before *UFO Hunters* became a television series, Pat Uskert had gone on the road with his video camera to interview folks who were posting their UFO videos on the Internet. One of his interviewees was a gentleman named Mark Olson, who had spent a great deal of time videotaping odd phenomena over the mountains above Sonora from his rear balcony. Pat spent some time with Mark and was present when a huge bright triangular object floated overhead in the distance. Pat watched it with awe as Mark videotaped it. This videotape was what I had in mind when we set up the episode because it was where I was planning to get the okay to insert the Morristown segment for contrast. But the Sonora episode took a different direction by focusing on the "why" of anomalous activity rather than simply reporting on the anomalous activity. Were there UFOs after the gold from California's gold country?

This episode also introduced a new member of our *Hunters* team,

Kevin Cook, who had previously appeared on the reality show *Smash Lab* and who had been graduated from Penn State with an engineering degree. Ted Acworth, now a brand-new father as well as the owner of his own unique enterprise, was unable to travel with the team on what would be our accelerated schedule for 2009 as the network hoped to triple our viewer ratings.

THE STORY

For decades, residents in California's Sierra Nevada Mountains and the Gold Country have seen UFOs over the mountaintops, even from the small towns in the area. Residents had seen so many strange unidentified flying objects over the peak of Mount Shasta that some people wondered whether there was a secret facility inside the mountains where these objects were hangared. Was this a top-secret futuristic U.S. military base for a space command or, with our government's approval, had extraterrestrials set up a base high in the Sierra Nevadas? Speculation was rampant. But the videos coming out of areas like Sonora were very compelling.

Pat, lured by the stories and Internet videos of strange craft over Mount Shasta, decided to contact one of the most celebrated videographers in the area, Mark Olson, to ask if he could videotape UFOs with him. When Mark agreed, Pat traveled up to Sonora, California, to meet with Mark and spend quality time looking for UFOs to videotape. And Pat would not be disappointed by what he found; the discovery would become the basis for our trip to the Mother Lode Country to look for the UFOs and see if we could find any clues in an abandoned gold mine.

In this episode there was less of a backstory than a focus on what was an ongoing, current set of UFO sightings in the area. Instead, we were looking at a common thread of sightings, a theory that the flying disks of the 1950s and the cylinders or barbells of the 1960s and '70s were no longer populating our skies. Witnesses, from the 1980s forward, were reporting different types of flying objects: giant triangles whose presence filled the sky. What were these objects folks claimed to have seen? Were they our own secret aircraft, neutral buoyancy craft that acted more like balloons than heavier aircraft, but with the ability to project holograms, camouflage themselves against the night sky, and hover so silently that witnesses would be transfixed in awe? Our exploration of giant triangles would take us from a Mesoamerican artifact of a strange birdlike creature to a nighttime sky watch where Kevin and Pat hoped to see a UFO hovering just over their campsite.

Our main thrust in this episode was what would turn out to be one of the most fascinating photo analyses of the entire series, ranking up there with our UFO sighting over Area 51, the NASA analysis of Space Shuttle mission STS-48, and the chilling photo from Dulce, New Mexico, of the cow embryo with a human head, an embryo that was sectioned out of the womb of a mutilated cow.

THE EPISODE

Having seen video and heard from witnesses that flying giant triangles are in our skies prompted us to investigate stories that Pat had heard about in Sonora, California. This episode introduced our new team member Kevin Cook, a mechanical engineer whose express purpose in joining the team was to keep us honest and not to speculate about conclusions we had no evidence to support. It became part of my job to put forth evidence to challenge Kevin's skepticism. It was different from working with Ted because Ted's role was to test out evidence by analyzing it and seeing what the science revealed. Kevin's role was to challenge the logic of an assertion.

The evidence began with a review of some of the most celebrated giant triangle sightings. In addition to the video from Tinley Park, we looked at footage of the 1989 Belgian Air Force pursuit of giant triangles over Europe. Those triangles not only posed a challenge to NATO by intruding into protected air space but outmaneuvered and outran the Belgian Air Force's F-16s the fastest U.S.-manufactured jets they deployed. And, of course, we reviewed the 1997 giant triangles that floated over Phoenix, Arizona, encounters witnessed by then Arizona governor Fife Symington. But all the videos and sightings were at night. In California's "Triangle Alley," however, we discovered witnesses and video of triangular arrays of lights flying across the area during the day. That meant that these sightings couldn't have been mistaken for stars or other celestial phenomena. It meant that unless these arrays could be positively identified as conventional aircraft, including military aircraft and helicopters, they would have to go down into the "unknown" basket. Accordingly, we traveled to Sonora, California, to meet the witnesses and see their videos.

Our first major witness, with whom Pat had worked back in 2005, was the previously mentioned Mark Olson, who was fascinated by the many triangular arrangements of lights that looked like orbs, but were traveling in unison as if they were fixed to a rigid structure that proliferated in the California Gold Country area. Olson told us that one of the primary reasons he didn't believe these lights were airplanes is that they were traveling so slowly that if they were planes, "they would have fallen right out of the sky."

Pat, the lead interviewer in our Mark Olson segment, reminded everyone that on June 15, 2004, Pat had visited Mark in Sonora, where the two had an amazing sighting of a daytime flying triangle. Mark said he was blown away by the sight, saying on the video, "Oh, my God, I have three lights in a triangular formation." It was indeed an eerie sight. "I was right there next to him," Pat said, pointing to the balcony from where the two were filming. "I was fumbling with my camera, but by the time I got everything up and running, this thing was gone."

"You missed it?" Kevin Cook asked.

"I missed it, but luckily Mark captured it."

Good thing for us that Mark was already videotaping the sight because it gave us some of the most striking footage we had ever seen.

Pat conceded that he understood Kevin was skeptical about the nature of the object on the video. But Pat also admitted that, "I'm personally invested in this and I'd be very embarrassed if this turns out to be nothing but a small airplane."

Kevin, who reviewed the video, said that he noticed that the lights were equidistant, stayed equidistant as the object traversed the sky, and seemed to be rigidly held in place by a structure. "They didn't vary as they flew across the sky," Olson said. "They stayed fixed. All I could think of was this was not of this world."

But Kevin sought to explore every possible conventional explanation. He asked about military bases, particularly Air Force installations, and commercial or private airports. Olson said that a small airport, Columbia Airport, was right over the mountain ridge. But that airport didn't have radar in 2004, Olson said, and the nearest military airport was in Merced, not very far away from Sonora. Kevin also asked Mark how he captured the video he showed us and what he did to surveil the skies to get that video at exactly the right moment.

"I have watched the skies for thousands of hours just to get a few minutes of video," Olson explained. This was more than just a hobby, Kevin suggested. And Mark admitted that, "For a while it became more of an obsession. Just wanted to know what they are." But, he admitted, he still doesn't know what they are even though he captured them on video. The daytime footage, Kevin explained, was "exceedingly rare" and believed that it would be very revealing when analyzed. That was also Olson's expectation, who said that any independent analysis of the footage would reveal more than he was able to figure out from just watching the lights in the sky.

Kevin, because he was basically a skeptic, although impressed by the quality of the video, still claimed that because Olson's testimony was essentially an eyewitness observation, it offered no real proof that something was there. Pat, however, said that because he was present when the video was taken and was an eyewitness himself to other lights that Olson had seen, fully believed that what was on the video was real.

For my part, I was struck by the similarities between the Olson video and the video shot in Belgium in 1989. The Belgium video in at least one respect was even more compelling than the Olson video because it actually showed the triangular structure holding the three lights at the corners in place. My hope was that when we took the

Olson video to Terrence Masson's lab, he would be able to subject the video to the kind of analysis that just might reveal a structure holding the lights in place. As an image analyst, Terrence would have the tools to be able to stabilize the video, enhance it, and see what it is that was holding the three lights in place. Terrence and Kevin planned to analyze the Olson video frame by frame for answers to what looked like a mystery. If the lights in the triangle were lights from a conventional aircraft, the analysis would reveal it.

Terrence Masson began by stabilizing the frame, as Kevin suggested, so as to enable him to analyze it frame by frame. Then he cropped out the background to focus on the image itself, the three lights. As he moved through the frames, Terrence remarked that it was clear that the lights were "locked solid" in formation. If they were separate lights without being affixed to any structure, he pointed out, you would see some fluctuation and independent motion of the lights. But the images revealed that they stayed together as the array itself moved across the sky. Next question from Pat: "Was this anything like a helicopter?" Terrence said that he was almost certain that the array displayed none of the obvious features of a conventional aircraft such as a helicopter. Of course, one of the major features was that the Olson footage picked up no sound from the lights even though you could hear Mark commenting with Pat on the audio track. Then, working from the still frames and altering the background, Terrence was able to show that there was a dark triangular structure quite visible in the frame. This was strong evidence that there was a craft in the frame and that it had a triangular shape holding the lights in a fixed position. It was a black triangle, clearly apparent in the video stills.

Kevin wasn't convinced, however, and asked whether there was some other explanation for the image of a black triangle in the frame. There was one video phenomenon, Terrence explained, in which a very bright light against a light background might generate a dark halo around it. It was an anomaly of color in a still frame. But, he went on, because the dark triangle around the three rigid lights was consistent from frame to frame throughout the sequence, it was unlikely that the triangle was a feature of the video and more likely that it was an object that was captured on video. Therefore, Terrence said to an excited Pat and a skeptical Kevin Cook, "What I believe we're looking at is a dark triangular craft capable of self-propulsion and holding three bright lights at its corners that is not consistent with any man-made craft."

Encouraged by Terrence Masson's analysis of Mark Olson's video, Pat and Kevin headed up to what the locals call "Triangle Alley," a three-hundred-square-mile area where giant triangles are routinely spotted by UFO sky watchers to see if they could videotape their own giant triangle. They trudged up the side of a steep hill, making their way across snow-covered loose rocks to reach a vantage point from where they could get a clear 360-degree view of the area and set up a camera to videotape anything interesting in the sky. It was to be a nighttime sky watch above the snow line, but Pat, whom Kevin called "the wilderness guy," was used to the climb and the outdoor camping out, especially after his experience at Tikaboo Peak during the Area 51 episode.

While Pat set up the camera on its tripod, Kevin pounded a marker into the ground on a spot where he would take a GPS reading so that they would have a record of the exact location of any sighting, just in case a triangular craft popped into frame. They focused their attention on the ridgeline in the distance of their stakeout location because, as Kevin explained, most of the witnesses we interviewed said that they saw flying triangles rise and then descend right at the ridgeline.

As the night wore on and the temperature continued to drop, Kevin finally noticed a light changing color from red to white and moving very slowly just above the ridge. Was it a star? It was off in the distance and looked like a star, which prompted Pat to use the star map on his smart phone to see if he could identify it. He did. It was the star Pollux in the Gemini constellation in the northern sky, which has an orange hue. It is brighter than its twin star Castor, and on a clear night can be confusing to anyone who might mistake it for a flying object. But Pat knew what he was looking at. Kevin admitted that at night, from their vantage point, many objects, mostly conventional aircraft, came into view and the stars were particularly bright. He said he could see how anyone at night could "get easily excited by things they see in the sky, but which can be easily explained." However, that did not in any way mitigate the effect of the Olson video that he and Terrence had analyzed.

Witness Mark Taylor, whom we interviewed as part of the Sonora segment, told us that multiple witnesses had viewed strange objects over the mountains, objects that could perform maneuvers that were impossible for conventional aircraft. "What these things could do," he said, "were amazing. Just amazing." He confirmed what Mark Olson told us about the array of strange sightings that fascinated residents of the Sonora area, who often stood in awe as they watched giant objects float over the city.

While Pat and Kevin made their way back down the mountain after their sky watch, I went off to interview Northern California's MUFON director and a guest on our first season, Rubin Uriarte, about his take on why there was so much anomalous activity in California's Triangle Alley, where, since 2000, there have been over sixty reported giant triangle sightings. Rubin began by pointing out that Triangle Alley runs from central Southern California all the way to the Oregon border. It's also adjacent, he said, to Area 51. The Nevada test sites were only 250 miles away from the Sonora area; literally, Rubin said, a blink of an eye from where we were standing. Rubin showed me sketches made by witnesses of a giant triangle from 1986, before the government released any news about the B-2 bomber. Witnesses who saw the craft depicted in the sketch Rubin showed said that the craft was huge and was flying over Corning, California, which was north of the Sonora area.

"What's interesting," Rubin said, referring to the sketch of the triangle that witnesses made, "was that this thing was just hovering and witnesses observed it for over a half an hour."

The object that was observed in Corning was similar to craft that had been seen over the years throughout northern California. It was three lights that may have looked separate at first, but were in a rigid configuration with respect to each other. These craft hovered silently in the sky and then shot off at tremendous speed. It boggles the mind and makes you ask, What is the link among all these craft?

The first thing that came to mind, I told Rubin, was that it reminded me of the Phoenix lights. What did he think about that? "These craft have all the same characteristics," he said. "There are lights around the perimeter, sometimes a light in the center of the triangular formation, and there is no sound as the lights hover overhead." Planes, he agreed, and helicopters behave entirely differently.

Rubin said he believed that the sightings over Northern California go all the way back to the great airship sightings of the late 1890s, not that everything in the sky was unexplainable even though it might have been called a UFO back then in the very earliest days of powered flight. From San Francisco north, as well as parts of the American Southwest, was home to many hobbyists piloting metal-clad balloons propelled by small gasoline engines. Miners in the area also reported seeing strange airships, some of which were brighter than stars. What might have been truly anomalous advanced aircraft—flying saucers—and what might have been conventional metal-clad balloons, we truly can't say even over a hundred years later.

If flying triangles, anomalous craft, were present in the Northern California area going back into the early twentieth century, what might they have been looking for? "There are plenty of minerals in this area," Rubin said. "And there is also an entire system of caves running through this mountainous area. And, remember, this is Gold Country." Could the presence of gold in the mountains of Northern California be what was attracting the flying triangles? Strange as it seems, the relationship between gold and extraterrestrial craft has been a theme in ufology dating back to the work of Erich von Däniken, who wrote about ancient astronauts. Because gold has very high conductivity, ancient alien theorists have suggested, the presence of large deposits of gold on planet Earth might have been attracting astronauts from other planetary systems for thousands of years. "Sonora might be an intersection," Rubin said. "Think of this area as a beacon drawing alien craft to it because of the gold and its use in electronic circuitry."

Here's what we believe we know: It wasn't just Sonora that was home to many UFO sightings. It was the entire Sierra Nevada range. It's not just flying triangles; it's all sorts of objects. And it's not just now, it is a phenomena dating back to the beginning of the last century. And if gold is attracting craft, maybe there's evidence of activity inside spent or abandoned gold mines. Pat and Kevin decided to go caving to see what evidence they could find. This excited Kevin, who said he could easily fantasize about discovering a mother lode and retiring early, very early. Pat, however, wanted to test for what he called "invisible energy," levels of radiation and magnetism, which could be clues of some former technological presence inside the mineshaft. There also might be evidence of energy levels that could be a signpost or a beacon attracting UFOs to the region.

With their miners' helmets and lights in place, Pat and Kevin adjusted their instruments. Kevin was not expecting to find any significant radiation levels, but he believed he would get some magnetometer readings if there were ferrous material inside the shaft. Kevin said, however, that he was nervous about entering the mine because "for all my life I've been trying to stay out of small cramped places." And here he was, on camera, going deeper into a mine that was dark and looked ominously uninviting. "It was even smaller than I expected," he said as the two entered the shaft. "But as long as I keep my mind on my instruments, I can stay focused. But why am I thinking about bats?" Pat, however, was thinking about finding significant radiation readings that might indicate that the presence of gold in the mine might have been used to power alien spacecraft. Or even, he hoped, they would find levels of magnetic energy, trace energy that had been found at the scenes of other UFO encounters.

Pat and Kevin traveled down to the end of the mine, where they set up their measuring equipment. They started with Geiger counter measurements. Because standard background or atmospheric radiation levels were about fifteen counts per minute, the number of radioactive rays moving through the Geiger counter, Kevin was looking for a higher number to confirm an anomalous presence. As Pat explained,

"Ufologists claim that high levels of radiation are a residual effect of UFO contact." If they measured high levels of radiation, they did not plan to spend any more time in the mine than they had to. The radiation would have spoken for itself. But Kevin found that there was nothing significant about the radiation level along the mineshaft walls. "Not different from background atmospheric radiation," he said.

Next up was the magnetometer test. Higher than normal levels of magnetic energy might also indicate that there was an abnormal presence in the mine. A magnetometer measures the changes in the magnetic energy levels in the mine. "It has been reported," Kevin said, "that UFOs are attracted to high levels of magnetic energy." But Pat's measurements showed that the magnetic field was jumping around, hovering at zero and then showing tiny spikes. In other words, Kevin said, just like the radiation readings, the magnetometer readings were essentially normal. "Just because there's gold in the mine, and gold is one of the best conductors of electricity, doesn't mean that aliens were here to get it." And the idea of aliens visiting the area was also a stretch. But Pat reiterated that there was a theory that heavy mineral deposits, especially gold, might indicate an alien presence. "You're smiling at me as if I'm crazy," he said to Kevin. Kevin said that if Pat were suggesting to him that aliens were hovering over the mine to extract minerals from it, "It sounds like *Star Trek*." He would much rather focus on the magnetometer and Geiger counter readings.

"If there are beings from another planet who wanted our minerals, they could just come here and take it," Kevin said. "They wouldn't even have to fight us for it." Even though it was only Kevin and Pat's theory, it was what made the UFO investigations fun and interesting, Kevin said. "We get a lot of leads. Some take you straight to a dead end. Some take you right into a gold mine."

By the time Pat and Kevin were exploring the mine, I had traveled back to Southern California to meet with my friend and fellow publisher Giorgio Tsoukalos of *Legendary Times* magazine.

"I might have something that might make your triangle mystery a bit less mysterious," Giorgio told me, holding a tiny reproduction of a birdlike artifact in his hand. "This artifact was found in Colombia, but it's pre-Colombian in origin. Dozens of these have been found. But to the untrained eye, they look like modern fighter jets." The object certainly looked more modern than ancient. Giorgio continued, "For mainstream science, experts have said that this looks like a stylized insect or a bird." However, just by looking at it, you could tell that the wings were in the wrong place. "Birds' wings are actually connected to birds' bodies just like our arms are connected into our shoulders, right below the neck," Giorgio said. Holding out the representation of the artifact, he explained that the wings on the artifact were not connected to a shoulder girdle. Rather they were set back closer to the tail. "This is not a bird," he asserted. "The question is, what is it?" One clue, he pointed out on the object, was the upright tail fin. "Birds do not have upright tail fins," he said. "Their tail fins are horizontal."

This presentation was certainly intriguing. It demonstrated that ancient Mesoamericans had been witnessing and then depicting in their art, triangular shapes they used as talismans. What did these talismans represent? What were the ancients depicting? Were we looking at an artistic representation of the Space Shuttle, a modern jet fighter, a spacecraft capable of navigating in Earth's atmosphere? How would a Colombian cult from fifteen hundred years ago understand, aerodynamically, the function of a tail fin?

"They saw something," Giorgio said. "But not only did they commit what they saw to writing and art, they also re-created stuff, saying that their heirs should be able to look at these things, what they depicted, and not forget what happened during their time."

Could the artifact representation be the missing link between what the ancients saw and flying triangles in our skies today? Either some culture came here from another world in triangular craft, which the artifact that Giorgio presented depicted, or, even more stunning a possibility, was some culture time traveling?

After Pat and Kevin returned from the mine and I returned from meeting with Giorgio, the team shared its findings. I presented the ar-

tifact and what Giorgio Tsoukalos theorized about it. "This representation of a real artifact," I explained, showing them the object Giorgio
had given me, "depicts a real object of art almost fifteen hundred years
old that has been found in caves all over South and Central America.
Legend has it that these were craft flown by ancient astronauts now
memorialized and idolized as a birdlike device. We don't know if
these came from another planet or if they came from the future or if
they really depict an aircraft. We just don't know."

"You're telling me," Kevin said, "that fifteen hundred years ago there
were aircraft in the sky, flying around, and people were making mod-
els of them and drawing them and making little trinkets just like this?"

I explained my theory. "Indigenous peoples on planet Earth were
visited by ancient astronauts, perhaps extraterrestrials who left their
mark on the cultures they encountered by seeding them with advanced
technology. Hence the explanation for the existence of a fifteen-
hundred-year-old artifact that looks more like the Space Shuttle than
a bird. Maybe they weren't extraterrestrials at all and the artifact that
Giorgio showed me was really a depiction of a time ship. That got
Kevin's attention.

"Time ships from the future?" Kevin said in his white-box interview.
"Time travel? It just doesn't exist, at least not today. It's just science
fiction."

"Just consider the possibility," I said. "Flying triangles from our own
future seeding the past for purposes we don't yet understand. The native cultures see the ships and memorialize them in their art."

Kevin was still incredulous at the whole concept. "All you're saying
is that some flying craft from our future time traveled into the past.
That's it? Is there any kind of proof of this or is this all theory?"

I pulled out some heavy artillery. "I'm telling you that some twenty
years ago a United States Army officer went into the future. We have
that totally documented." Kevin and Pat simply stared, not knowing
whether to believe I was completely delusional or that I had been led
down the rabbit hole following the Mad Hatter. "But," I cautioned, "does

this constitute any evidence that time ships are coming back from the future? Not at all." While Kevin stared with a mixture of shock and disgust as if he were tweezing a large spider crawling up his sleeve. Pat simply said that what I had said was one of the reasons he enjoyed the interplay among us. At the very least, it made for interesting conversation. "You know a hundred years ago when people said it was impossible for heavier-than-air powered flight and they laughed at Darwin's theory of evolution, they were proven to be wrong. That's why I'm not dismissing the possibility of time travel," Pat said.

"Regardless of what inspired the creation of this artifact," Kevin admitted, "it does look like a triangle more than it does a bird. And it does look aerodynamic. I propose we build a model identical to this right here made out of Styrofoam or something like that and throw it in the air. Let's see if it performs like a glider. Let's see if it flies."

"You got it," I said. And we planned to visit our modeling and special effects expert, Brick Price.

But before that, we made a stopover in Houston, Texas, to interview a retired Air Force pilot, Mike Daciek, who, though a self-described skeptic, said he saw a flying triangle over his own house. From what he saw from the performance maneuvers of the triangle he watched, he said he believed that no government on this planet had the technology to do what that triangle did. Mike had over forty years experience in the cockpit and either flew or saw every type of plane in the U.S. arsenal and he said he still couldn't explain the nature of what he saw. Kevin was impressed with Mike's credentials, explaining that because pilots are trained observers, what they report having seen usually has a high credibility. "When a pilot says he sees something flying through the sky and he can't explain what it is, we have to give it special consideration," he said.

Mike began his story. "It was the eighteenth of May 1996, at about 1:20 A.M. when I looked out of the corner of my eye and something caught my attention off to the left. I saw three red lights forming a triangle. It was coming toward me pretty fast and the triangle was getting bigger. It was almost like it was climbing a little bit because it didn't follow the curvature of the earth. It just disappeared into infinity."

I asked Mike how he would estimate the speed.

"I've seen the Sputnik," he said. "I've seen the SR-71 and even the 71 couldn't go that fast."

"The SR-71 is the fastest airplane ever built," Kevin said. "It can fly at Mach three plus, that's over twenty-four-hundred miles an hour. And what Mike Daciek saw in the sky was even faster than that."

Pat joined in. "It would be impossible for me to believe that an experienced pilot with over thirty years in the cockpit would not be able to identify an SR-71." He asked Mike a very pertinent question about his expertise in identifying foreign aircraft. Mike said that it was part of his training as an Air Force pilot. "You had these black silhouettes that would flash up on a screen and you would say, 'P-51, F-15.' You wouldn't want to be shooting down your own airplanes."

"And you would say," Kevin asked, "what you saw was not one of those silhouettes that you could identify." Mike said that this was not like anything he had ever seen. If Pat had any doubts about Mike's sighting and description, Mike's assertion that this was nothing he could identify, he was now convinced that Mike had witnessed an overflight of a flying triangle.

"For the first time in my life, I would say that I saw something very unusual," Mike said in answer to my question about what he thought he saw. "Before, I might not have said that there were aliens visiting us, but now I believe there are."

The usually skeptical Kevin had to admit that he doesn't know what's going on anymore. Before meeting Mike and hearing his testimony, Kevin admitted, he believed that the flying triangles were top-secret military aircraft. "But now I don't know what to think," he said. But if Kevin thought that what Mike Daciek revealed was astonishing, he would be even more surprised when we met another aeronautical expert, Gordon Scott, also in Houston, Texas.

Scott told us about a giant triangle flying at a low altitude along a creek bed behind his home. Reluctant to speak on camera at first, Gordon Scott ultimately felt that his story had to be told in public and agreed to appear in the episode as a witness describing an event that took place on August 15, 2001, at about eight thirty in the evening.

"When we first saw this thing going down the creek, we were scared to death," Scott said. "We were getting ready to call 911. We run out into our backyard and watched this big black thing approaching. The bright red light on the bottom lit up the whole creek probably a hundred feet across. And I assumed it was an aircraft ditching. I could have hit it with a softball underhanded." That's how close he was to the object. He heard no noise and felt no heat, felt no breeze and smelled nothing. Kevin was running Scott through the routine questions we asked all of our witnesses to eliminate any aspects of a conventional aircraft. But Kevin said that he still found the story suspect because Scott was close yet he heard, felt, and smelled nothing.

The object, Scott said, followed the creek bed as low as possible. Then as it approached a bridge over the creek, the object rose straight up vertically about fifteen to twenty feet so that it cleared the bridge, then it dropped down vertically, hugging the creek bed, and continued on its way. It moved vertically and horizontally, but not like a helicopter. As the object moved along the creek, an F-16 fighter suddenly appeared, flying slowly and sporting two Sidewinder missiles under its wings with two more under its fuselage.

"It wasn't chasing the flying triangle," Scott said. "I believed it to be an escort. It was flying with it."

Scott explained that NASA's Johnson Space Center was only thirty miles south of his property, the direction the flying triangle was heading. And this prompted him to think that the craft and the fully armed F-16 escorting it were somehow connected to the Space Center. Kevin believed that this indicated that the flying triangle was actually one of our own aircraft, experimental, but not extraterrestrial. I speculated that one could explain the craft's presence with the F-16 as a hybrid design, perhaps developed with alien technology or reverse engineered from downed alien spacecraft. And that might explain the prevalence of flying triangles over California, Phoenix, and other locations. But Pat was very skeptical about that theory and said that without evidence he couldn't get on board. We had to leave that idea on the table while we flew back to Los Angeles to meet with Brick Price to test out Kevin's challenge of Giorgio's representation of an ancient flying object. In order for it to be something more than an idolized bird, we would have to test its ability to glide like a plane.

Brick, turning the artifact representation over in his hand after we joined him at his facility, said that given the architecture of the object and the ratio of its delta-shaped wings to its body and the vertical tail fin, he believed it was capable of real flight. But the acid test was, will it actually fly? Ever skeptical, Kevin challenged Brick's theory, suggesting that it looked like Brick had altered some of the object's aerodynamic features, particularly the attack angle of the wing, when making a scale model of the artifact. But Brick Price adamantly said that nothing was changed. The model was scaled up from the artifact, but the ratio of wing to body, the angle of the wing, and the height of the tail fin were exactly the same as Giorgio's artifact. What Brick also discovered was that the fuselage itself served as a lifting body, making it, at least in theory, capable of flight. But, put to the test, would it fly?

We set up a catapult launcher and a ramp to get the model airborne. And once launched, the model actually demonstrated lift, rose into the air, and settled softly on a landing pad. It was a stunning demonstration as the model hovered in the air before its descent. Even Kevin was impressed, saying that he'd hoped the test would have been less spectacular. But, according to Pat, if the model was true to scale and the ratios were all the same as the artifact, the simple fact that the model flew, meant that whatever its ultimate origin, the culture that created this artifact, understood flight. I was impressed not only with the object's ability to glide, but with its actual aerodynamic performance. The model gained altitude, stalled in midflight, righted itself so its angle of attack gave it the ability to land, and then landed nose up as if it were an actual Space Shuttle touching down on a runway. This, to me, served as proof of an ancient flying triangle. How could the indigenous peoples living in Colombia fifteen hundred years ago conceive of a design that mimicked the flight characteristics of the Space Shuttle? I still held to a theory more plausible than simply design by accident: time travel.

But, true to the organic nature of argument in season three, Kevin asserted that the flight characteristics of the model proved nothing more than that those ancients who designed it watched the flight of birds and designed a "trinket" as a toy for private enjoyment. Giorgio disagreed, as did I. The aeronautical technology was too advanced for ancient peoples to have designed simply by watching birds because the model didn't resemble a bird at all.

At the end of the investigation into flying triangles, here's what we found out: Witnesses all over the world had seen flying triangles that hovered noiselessly and shot off at tremendous speeds. Pilots who had seen these objects also reported that they attained speeds greater than any conventional aircraft. And we even analyzed a video in which we could actually see the triangular shape of a craft. The Giorgio Tsoukalos artifact also indicated, at least to me, that the ancients had seen something, perhaps a flying triangle or even a Space Shuttle that made its way back thousands of years in time. Whatever the inspiration for the design of the model, we learned that fifteen hundred years ago, the ancient designers of this model had seen something in the sky of very advanced technology. Who flew it, we may never know.

BILL'S BLOG

Giant Triangles" was our first episode of season three, and it marked a change in our format from seasons one and two. In our first season, Pat, Ted, and I pursued our stories together, with Ted and special-effects producer John Tindall putting together scientific experiments in the final segment of each episode. Toward the end of the first season, in addition to adding what came to be called "white-box interviews" for witnesses, we also separated the three team members, with science assistant Jeff Tomlinson joining Ted to pursue independent story lines. We refined this in the Stephenville and "NASA Files" episodes. When season two started with the "Invasion Illinois" episode, we had solidified our format so that Pat, Ted, and I conducted separate investigations into the same case and came together in the final segment, after the science segment, to compare notes and challenge each other's findings. The heavy reliance on science in season two, especially in the Roswell, Phoenix lights, Aurora, James McDonald, and Area 51 episodes were the high points of the series. However, after the final episode of season two, "Area 51 Revealed," Ted Acworth, whose own business startup had begun to get some traction and whose new baby and the demands of parenthood precluded him from traveling along with the team, exited the series because of conflicts in his schedule. The network, therefore, came up with a new idea that would eventually find its niche in shows like *Ice Road Truckers* and *American Pickers* where the focus was on character interaction. In fact, organic character interaction shows were becoming a staple on reality television.

The network and production company, now absent a Ph.D.-level scientist, developed a new type of story approach for season three, which was reflected in this "Giant Triangles" episode. The network hired Kevin Cook as a type of "everyman," the guy on the street who, although open-minded, was not about to be swayed by theories of an ET presence on Earth or any sort of conspiracy theories. Kevin was not a true believer. He was more of a gearhead who needed to see how things worked, how mechanical devices operated, and always looked for a conventional explanation for the physics of an event even in the face of high implausibility for the conventional explanation. Therefore, when confronted with the near-paradox of an ancient artifact that, when scaled up to a model, flew like a glider, Kevin was unhappy with a clear challenge to his conventional belief system and would not look at our experiment as an example of something that was clearly out of its own time. The same was true when analyzing the Mark Olson flying triangle video with Terrence Masson, which revealed in stark contrast that the image Olson captured on camera was a solid triangle and not at all conventional. Kevin looked at it, accepted the unconventional nature of the image, but refused to go beyond what he was seeing to draw any conclusions as to its nature.

The change in format for *UFO Hunters* in its third season also highlighted the watershed in reality television. The idea for *UFO Hunters* was born out of the old *UFO Files* series on History that ran for over a decade. In *Files,* a small film crew used on-camera interviews with experts looking off camera, stock footage, and some special effects to highlight a particular aspect of ufology or a UFO case such as alien implants, alien abductions, pilot UFO sightings, or the Bermuda Triangle. In our first season, we modified the *UFO Files* format to account for the different personalities and respective expertise of the cast. By the time we developed the independent story line approach toward the end of the first season and then refined it in season two, the series was consistently hitting a million-plus viewers for each episode and became one of the highest rated series on History. But times were changing with series like *Ice Road Truckers*, a more character-based format.

Kevin Cook's arrival on *Hunters* gave us the opportunity to incorporate the organic character interaction of *Truckers* into a paranormal investigative format. In so doing, while our series itself was transformational in its approach to evaluating all types of evidence of paranormal activity, it also marked the transformation of the reality television genre itself into something more character-driven within an unscripted but quasidramatic format. From a purely media perspective, it was fascinating to watch even as Pat and I adapted ourselves to the new format. Almost like the fan takeaway in the dramatic morality play of, dare I say it, professional wrestling, viewers in our season three found themselves siding with or against the three different characters on *UFO Hunters*: Pat's exploratory approach, Kevin's skeptical everyman, and my theories about alternate realities and the paranormal.

The Morristown lights incident and the discrepancy among the witness reports, the video shot by Paul Hurley, and the Hanover Township Police Department's assertion that the lights were actually Chinese lanterns had given me the idea to insert the video and witness reports into the Terrence Masson analysis of the Mark Olson video for the "Giant Triangles" episode. I had seen the Olson video years before we began our series because Pat Uskert had brought it back to Venice Beach, where we were neighbors. It would have been a great contrast between a nighttime video of unexplained lights over north Jersey and daytime video of unexplained lights over Northern California. However, because of the dramatic witness testimony from Mike Daciek and Gordon Scott as well as the appearance by Giorgio Tsoukalos and our experiment with his artifact, there was simply no time for inserting any additional material. Nor was their time to squeeze in the image analysis of the Hurley video because of how crowded the episode had become. Moreover, even if there were the possibility of fitting in the Morristown story as a contrast to Sonora in this first episode, I was told by the folks in editing that the camera settings from Morristown, as well as the nature of the camera itself, meant that cutting in the Morristown footage would have been impossible. As a result, my plan to compare the Hurley video with the Olson video had to be abandoned and the Morristown segment was dropped. Thus, when the hoaxers told their story to the media about their prank, it was already too late for our show to respond or cover the story in a subsequent episode.

The Giorgio Tsoukalos segment was popular with our audience because of the flight test of the artifact. Our audience loved scientific visual effects, especially when they proved or disproved a point in contention. The footage and analysis of the strange light over Area 51; the modeling of the farmer's field adjacent to Rendlesham Forest in the Bentwaters episode; the materials analysis of the metallic implant in the alien abduction episode; the fire started by overloading the circuit breaker panel in the Maury Island episode; and the memory metal test in the Roswell episode all delighted viewers who loved to see scientific demonstrations played out on television. It was no surprise, therefore, that the flying model test of the pre-Colombian artifact was the visual that was responsible for what became History's popular *Ancient Aliens* series. Pat Uskert and I had been pushing for an ancient aliens episode since the beginning of season one. We were excited, therefore, to host Giorgio Tsoukalos in the third season and to see the *Ancient Aliens* series become a popular show in its own right on History.

"ARIZONA LIGHTS"

You can imagine the guffaws when, after worldwide coverage of a startling triangular array of lights that floated on March 13, 1997, at approximately 8:30 P.M. and then, again, two hours later, a startling triangular array of lights floated across Arizona from Henderson, Nevada, to Sonora, California. You can imagine the guffaws when, after worldwide coverage of the event, Fife Symington, then governor of Arizona, announced at a press conference that he had, in fact, solved the mystery, and thereupon introduced a tall, glittering EBE with long fingernails and an oversized head. Oh boy, did the press in the room fall on its collective journalistic face, laughing out loud at the witnesses and the rest of the press for even reporting the story. Now, imagine over a decade later when that same governor publicly apologized to those witnesses he had offended and to the world at large when he appeared on *UFO Hunters*. He revealed, in startling detail, what he actually saw that night when the triangular array of lights floated barely a hundred feet over his head while he was standing in his backyard after having dismissed his security detail for the night. Having Governor Fife Symington tell the story of what he actually saw and apologize for his joke on the Phoenix lights witnesses was one of the highlights of our second season and a moment that made our Phoenix lights episode more than a story about UFOs. It turned it into a personal story of contrition, a plea for forgiveness, and compelling multiple eyewitness testimony.

The story of the Phoenix, Arizona, lights became one of the hottest, most covered stories in 1997, witnessed via media coverage by the entire world. It involved then president Bill Clinton in a strange disappearance, as if he had to be sequestered while the government decided what to do about the thousands of witnesses to the lights, and brought debunkers out of the woodwork like termites hoping for a feast.

It pitted photo analyst against photo analyst, theory against theory, and witnesses against the U.S. military as the Air Force and Air National Guard tried desperately to explain the nature of the lights— flares versus UFOs—even conducting an exercise to convince a skeptical public that what they really saw were flares and nothing more. And how much did that flares exercise cost taxpayers, which at the end of the day only wound up serving as evidence for the UFO theory?

The Phoenix lights story contained all the elements of a great UFO explanation from multiple witnesses, folks looking out into the night sky to catch the appearance of the Hale-Bopp comet, but seeing an array of lights instead. The lights also inspired a mass suicide in San Diego when a cult leader promised that after the deaths of its followers, they would be beamed up to a spaceship, then the appearance of a possible spaceship. There were also close-up witnesses, credible military witnesses, photo evidence, and a government explanation that only reinforced what the witnesses said they saw. All of this, and the promise of an exclusive interview with Fife Symington and the participation of *Out of the Blue* filmmaker James Fox promised to make this one of the best episodes of all three seasons. For an episode of *UFO Hunters*, this was just about as good as it gets.

THE STORY

The stage was set for thousands of witnesses across the Southwest scanning the sky for the appearance of the Hale-Bopp comet. But the story began when witnesses in Henderson, Nevada, at the Arizona border, reported a strange sight: six orange lights in a triangular pattern slowly moving toward the southeast and making no sound except for what they said was the wind. About fifteen minutes later another witness, this time behind the wheel of his car, saw a formation of lights heading his way as he drove north. He headed home, retrieved binoculars, and kept watching the lights as they headed south and west toward Phoenix.

Minutes later, the lights appeared over Prescott, Arizona, but this time witnesses said that as the triangular formation of lights passed overhead, the starry nighttime sky was blotted out between the lights as if there were a solid object holding the lights together. These reddish lights with a white light in the middle of the formation were low in the sky and moved over Prescott Valley in what looked to observers to be a controlled flight. Just after they passed silently overhead, the lights seemed to turn in unison as if they were attached to a solid structure and continued to head in a more southerly direction. At this point, phone calls to local 911 dispatchers began coming in. Witnesses also began to call media outlets and even local airports to report something in the sky that did not appear to be an airplane. Even Peter Davenport at the National UFO Reporting Center (NUFORC) in the state of Washington, began receiving reports of what witnesses said was a V-shaped formation of what looked to be self-illuminating orbs. But in one report, the rearmost light moved within the formation toward the point of the V just before the lights turned toward the south. Again, it seemed to those reporting that the lights were not flying independently even though one of the lights moved to a new position while the others stayed stationary with respect to each other.

Within minutes, folks just north of Phoenix began seeing the array of lights off in the distance toward the north–northwest, heading their way. It passed very low right over private streets, possibly as low as one hundred feet, and traveling slowly toward the south. Then it seemed to stop dead in the air. Then it picked up motion and continued through the narrow valleys toward the outskirts of the city suburbs where more people, some on the roads, spotted the object that many people described as "unearthly." In fact, one of the witnesses was Arizona governor Fife Symington, who said in 2007 and on *UFO Hunters* that despite what he'd said at his faux news conference when he had his chief of staff dress up in an alien garb and show up as the explanation for the lights, Symington himself saw the eight thirty lights. He said they were not a conventional craft because they flew too slowly for an airplane, did not have the thwapping sound of rotor blades like a helicopter, and were completely noiseless. A plane would have stalled at the speed it was moving, a helicopter would have shown distinct navigational lights and made noise, especially at the low altitude at which it was flying, and the lights, if they were attached to a flying structure, made the craft larger than a football field. Also, Symington said, as commander in chief of the Arizona National Guard and Air National Guard, he called Luke Air Force Base and was told no military craft were in the sky at eight thirty over Phoenix. Thus the Air National Guard's official acknowledgment of the lights was not confirmed as military.

About two hours after the first sighting of the lights, a second set of lights flew over the same area, causing even more confusion and frenzy than the first set. Were the ten thirty lights over Phoenix a different object, the same object returning, or flares from Air Force or National Guard planes to establish a conventional explanation for the eight thirty lights? At first, when the ten thirty lights appeared, residents called Sky Harbor air traffic control again and were told that no planes were picked up on radar. Residents also called Luke Air Force Base again and were told none of their planes were in the air. However, after the initial responses from Luke AFB, the Air Force said that the lights were ground illumination flares from a flight of A-10 Warthogs over the Goldwater bombing range. Months later, the Maryland Air National Guard announced that there were planes in the air on the night of March 13, 1997, from the 104th fighter squadron flying out of Davis-Monthan Air Force Base in Arizona as the unit that dropped LUU-2B/B ground illumination flares in an exercise over the Goldwater test range. Our frequent guest on *UFO Hunters* and naval photo analyst as well as CIA UFO consultant Dr. Bruce Maccabee conducted a triangulation analysis and said that it was indeed likely that the ten thirty lights were flares that could be seen over the Phoenix area at ten thirty. However, our guest photo analyst for the Phoenix lights episode, Jim Dilettoso of Arizona's Village Labs, said that after he had performed a spectral analysis of the lights, he determined that the colors of the lights were inconsistent with flares.

Witness and award-winning filmmaker Dr. Lynne Kitei has said that the ten thirty lights were not flares and that a subsequent flare-dropping demonstration by the Air Force to prove that flares were what people in Phoenix saw on the night of March 13, 1997, showed, again through an analysis of the aerial performance, the colors, and the residue actually proved that what witnesses saw were not flares. The controversy over the nature of the lights still remains today.

THE EPISODE

Our guest researcher for this episode, who led us through interviews with firsthand eyewitnesses, folks who reported that they were less than a hundred feet away from the object floating over Paradise Valley, and in one instance below the balcony of one of the valley rim's houses, was *Out of the Blue* and *I Know What I Saw* filmmaker James Fox. James aired on History and Dr. Lynne Kitei were among the first researchers to compile all the witness testimonial evidence and video from the Phoenix lights incidents, and Fox's relationship with Governor Fife Symington provided the forum for the retired governor to reveal what he really experienced on the night of March 13, 1997, a narrative that was as eerie as it was riveting. The vast number of witnesses, the video, the attempts by the military to prove that all the witnesses were confused by flares, and the science behind the event deconstruction itself combined to make this a must-do episode for the *UFO Hunters*, especially with the added benefit of association with James Fox and Dr. Lynne Kitei.

It was the night of the comet, an event that thousands of sky watchers were set to enjoy even as members of the Heaven's Gate cult in San Diego, led by Marshall Applewhite, prepared to take a lethal overdose of sedatives to commit a mass suicide. But what sky watchers saw that night along a corridor running from Nevada to the Mexican border across Arizona was something far more than they bargained for. As Ted Acworth explained it, they saw a triangular or arrowhead formation of orange/red circular orbs, self-illuminating lights moving slowly and silently overhead, low to the ground, which seemed, at times, to be hovering, not dropping, even though there were air currents aloft. Witnesses to the eight thirty lights say they actually saw a rigid object holding the lights in place, describing it as a V-shaped craft or a boomerang almost a mile wide and stretching across the entire sky.

The people who watched the spectacle were actually in shock, commenting on video that it was nothing like anyone had seen before. The first sighting was at 7:55 P.M. over Henderson, Nevada, then farther south at 8:15, and over the Phoenix area at 8:30. Then another set of lights made their way across the Phoenix area two hours later. The *UFO Hunters* were looking for clues to determine whether there was one actual craft and whether the eight thirty and ten thirty lights were part of the same event or whether these were two entirely different incidents with two different explanations. As we did with the Tinley Park lights and Northern California giant triangles, we broke our investigation up into three different avenues of pursuit. Pat Uskert began with looking at the history of reported UFO sightings in the area. Pat said that he thought we were looking at a top-secret black budget aircraft that was being tested over a populated area or a real extraterrestrial craft. Ted Acworth obtained as much video as he could of the ten thirty lights as he set up an experiment to compare videos of the lights to flares that he launched so he could compare the aeronautics performance, the color and intensity of the lights, and whether there were any distinctions between the residue from the flare and any residue visible in the lights videos. He explained he was most interested in the dynamics of the flares he launched and how the image looked on video against the night sky. And I pursued an analysis of the nature of the craft itself, if, indeed, it was a craft. If not, what was it and why was it appearing all across the state of Arizona?

We enlisted the help of James Fox, whose film *Out of the Blue* was one of the first in-depth investigations of the Phoenix lights via extensive interviews with witnesses. He would be our guide through the maze of witness reports and speculation concerning the lights. Fox had been investigating the Phoenix lights since 1997 and said he believed it was a craft even though its nature was officially undetermined. We also met up with our friend Bill Scott, a retired NSA officer, Rocky Mountain bureau chief of *Aviation Week & Space Technology,* and a test pilot, to describe to us the nature of the U.S. military's black-budget program and how it might explain the Phoenix lights.

As Pat had discovered on an earlier trip to Phoenix, unexplained lights in the sky were nothing new, dating back over a thousand years. They had not only been witnessed by area Native American tribes, particularly the Hohokam, but also depicted as images drawn on rocks, shapes that are otherwise unexplained by traditional culture and history. Native Americans said that their ancestors had seen these images flying through the skies and handed stories about them down through the generations. Pat was learning that the history of the Phoenix area was replete with descriptions of sightings of unidentified objects in the sky that, he believed, led straight to the 1997 Phoenix lights.

In his interview with James Fox, Pat asked the basic question: If the lights episode occurred over eleven years earlier, why are people still talking about it today? "Because most people aren't buying the government explanation," Fox explained. What the Air Force said both on the night of the lights and even years later simply didn't wash, according to Fox. We received the official Air Force explanation ourselves directly from the Pentagon concerning the ten thirty lights. They said in a letter that the lights were actually a formation of LUU-2B/B ground illumination flares deployed by A-10 Thunderbolts in a test, called Operation Snowbird by the Maryland Air National Guard over the Barry Goldwater testing range. This was, I suggested to Fox, the only official explanation for the ten thirty lights. "But a lot of the videotaped images and the testimony from eyewitnesses would suggest otherwise," Fox said.

Pat's exploration of the history of unexplained sightings in the Phoenix area took him to *The Arizona Republic*'s Richard Ruelas, who had been covering the Phoenix lights story from its beginning. "A lot of times UFOs are seen in isolated and rural areas, usually by a single witness or a small group. However, this was the first mass sighting in a heavily populated area," Ruelas said. Even more important, the witnesses were not just folks out for a stroll at night. These were, in many cases, professional individuals, doctors and former military, who lived in the vicinity of Sky Harbor Airport and knew what conventional aircraft, including helicopters, looked like in the night sky and how they performed.

"One of the big confusions," Ruelas explained, "was that there were two separate events. At around eight to eight thirty folks see a V formation. At around ten thirty there are hovering orbs over the western part of Phoenix." He continued, "Most people on the ground who saw the first lights saw the flying V." This seemed to them to be a real anomaly.

The mystery of the flying V prompted Phoenix Councilwoman Francis Emma Barwood on May 6, 1997, to ask the Air Force what these lights were and why they'd caused so much confusion, a question she raised with the mayor and city council when she asked for an Air Force explanation. She wanted an explanation for the phenomenon and to express her query as a public safety concern because of reports of an unidentified object over a populated area. She had asked, "What's hovering over the city?" Ruelas said that when Barwood raised her concerns, it indicated that a public official requesting an expenditure of public resources because of a possible UFO, "gets her laughed at." *The Arizona Republic* reported that Barwood didn't want to be known as the "UFO candidate," but that description follows her everywhere still today. Pat asked, albeit rhetorically, why it would be that people in official positions would stick their necks out and get burned if there was nothing going on. "It wasn't a case of much ado about nothing,"

Pat said. "It was much ado about something." Folks just didn't know what something was.

In my interview with Barwood and with James Fox, she reiterated that she never said the word "UFO"; it was not mentioned at all. All she asked about was whether any official investigation revealed anything about the nature of whatever was in the sky over Phoenix because it was close enough to the airport, as well as over a densely populated residential area, that in her mind it touched on the area of public safety. "I never said, 'UFO,' 'flying saucer,' 'extraterrestrial craft.'" She reiterated over and over again never having said anything like that. Barwood told us, "I couldn't understand why no one wanted to find the truth. Why didn't anyone want to know what it was that night?" But she was ridiculed in *The Arizona Republic,* which, she said, "ran a cartoon of me with flying saucers over my head and another with a switch embedded in my head." Newspapers and even some of her colleagues on the city council became very derisive toward her, some referring to her as "Beam-me-up Barwood" even though she never suggested any extraterrestrial explanation for the lights over Phoenix. She continued that she started getting phone calls at seven in the morning, calls that didn't stop until after eleven at night. "Over the summer, I tried to call back everybody, over seven hundred people," she said. Asked if she pursued any independent investigation on her own, Barwood said she referred all the phone calls she received to Governor Symington.

Barwood also talked to us about Governor Symington's news conference early on June 19, 1997, when, pressured to find an answer to the sightings, he promised to "look into the issue." "We're going to find out if it was a UFO," he announced. That afternoon, the governor called for another unscheduled press conference, at which he said he had found the culprit behind the whole incident. "I will now ask Officer Stein to escort the accused into the room so we may all look upon the guilty party," the governor assured the assembled media representatives. Barwood said that at first there was excitement in the room because he said, "he was going to look into this." But when the governor's chief of staff walked into the room dressed in an ET costume, large head, long fingers, and a long shining nightgown, "we realized," Barwood said, "that this was a big joke. Given the thousands of witnesses who wanted answers, the governor was laughing at the entire incident." But, Barwood said, "this was not at all like Fife. He doesn't have a sense of humor." As the costumed alien began to take off his false head, Symington told reporters that, "This goes to show that you are all entirely too serious." The laughter resounded through the room. But there was no laughter from the witnesses.

"Was it your perception," we asked Barwood, given all the media and derision surrounding the lights incident that, "there was something organized against you because you brought up your questions at a city council meeting?"

"It seems that way," she said. "Many people wanted to know answers, but never did I have any negative comments from my constituents or anybody in the city or anybody in the state. The negativity came from government officials."

Eyewitness Mike Kristin, whom Fox and I interviewed, gave us his firsthand account. Mike was out on his balcony, he said, enjoying the cool night air, when he saw spots of bright orange light in the distance. "You tell me what you think that is," he said to himself right before he went back inside his house to get his video camera. "As I was doing that," he said, "one of the lights went out and another one appeared right to the left of it just a little bit lower. Then that light went out then another one appeared and next the entire array of lights appeared, eight or nine lights and they formed this arc. I videotaped it for about two and a half minutes and then and the lights started to go off one at a time, but not in the same order as they went on." But the Air Force explanation that these lights Mike saw were ground illumination flares dropped over the Barry Goldwater gunnery range behind the Estrella Mountains would also comport with Mike's sighting because the sky over that range would be visible from Mike's balcony. We asked Mike whether he had ever seen lights similar to what he videotaped before. "I never have," he said, reporting that he had in the past seen one or two lights in the distance, but never this close and that far to the east of his house. "They were extremely bright compared to the lights I had seen before," he said. "And I thought it was unusual the way they held their pattern." We asked whether this was the pattern that flares had appeared to him in the past. "No," Mike said, "because flares tend to drop fast, are responsive to the wind, and do not hold their position with respect to each other." Thus, from what we gleaned from the interview, the lights that Mike saw looked nothing like the flares Mike had seen before, and their appearance was preceded by a glowing orange orb that Mike couldn't identify. Therefore, we had to figure out if these lights Mike saw were different types of flares or something else entirely.

James Fox asked Mike what he thought he captured on videotape that night. "Could have been one of three things," Mike said. "Number one, it could have been a hoax, which I don't think it could have been because it was pretty elaborate. Could have been an alien spacecraft, but I have no proof of that. The only other thing I can think about is that it could have been a military experiment."

Ted commented that, as described by the witnesses, some of the behavior of the lights struck him as strange. The nature of their appearance and aeronautical performance required further investigation, so Ted set up a flare test over Santa Monica Bay in Long Beach Harbor. His maritime test involved actual ground illumination flares suspended by parachutes to give them more glide time in the air. He was looking for as close a match as possible with the videos of the ten thirty Phoenix lights. As Ted in California set up his experiment, James and I interviewed another witness and subsequent UFO researcher and documentary filmmaker Dr. Lynne Kitei, who chose to remain anonymous about what she learned about the Phoenix lights until seven years after the event because in 1997 she feared for a negative impact upon her reputation.

In 2004, she went public with the revelation that the 1997 lights had appeared before. "I was experiencing this phenomena for two years before the mass sighting," she told James and me. "They were orbs about three to six feet in diameter and a uniform amber color throughout and it didn't glare at all." And then on January 23, 1997, another set of lights appeared to Dr. Kitei. She said she saw a massive triangular formation, which she was able to capture on film. "There were six points of light that seemed to be attached to something," she said, "moving slowly behind South Mountain." Thus, she was not surprised, she said, when she saw the lights formation two months later in March. "I saw the six lights pop on and fumbled with my camera and by the time I got in focus, I captured them." The lights were near South Mountain in the direction of Sky Harbor Airport.

"What would you say to someone who said you saw a military flare?" Fox asked, conceding that he was deliberately playing devil's advocate.

"There's no way it could have been military," Dr. Kitei answered. "Military flares flicker and they can't keep a formation and they drift with the wind. These were orbs."

Another witness was Steven Blonder, author of *Oracle of the Phoenix*, who captured his own video of the ten thirty lights and who said that he, like Dr. Lynne Kitei, had also seen lights before the March 13 sighting, this time on March 10, 1997. He said that when he saw the lights he got out his video camera and managed to get an extreme close-up of an orange, orblike pulsating light, "unlike anything I had ever seen before in my life." Steve's neighbor became involved because she said that Steve's wife came over to her house on March 11, telling her that she had seen the most amazing thing, something she had ever seen before in her life. And for the next three nights, Blonder's balcony became the scene of nightly viewing parties because the lights had appeared on three successive occasions. Each night, sky watchers were not disappointed at what they saw. And just like most of the other witnesses, neither Steve Blonder nor his neighbors accepted the official Air Force explanation that what they were really seeing were flares. "I was very upset when I saw the flare story come out because I knew it wasn't flares," Steve told me. But Ted told us that even though witnesses dismissed flares because they couldn't see any glow around the illumination, nor could they see smoky residue, it was possible that the environmental conditions on the night of March 13, 1997, wouldn't have allowed for any reflection of light around the flare.

Steve's neighbors, Jaylene and her husband Jason, also a witness, volunteered to join Ted in Long Beach for his flare experiment to compare what they saw with the incendiaries that Ted was set to launch over the bay. Would the eyewitnesses say that Ted's flares looked like anything they saw in the skies over Phoenix? The only difference between Ted's experiment and the Phoenix lights was that Ted was using a maritime flare instead of the LUU-2B/B the Air Force said the Maryland Air National Guard used. But Ted said the difference in illumination and the aeronautical performance would be minimal. Maritime flares are used by ships in distress to signal rescuers visually while ground illumination flares are meant to light up targets. Maritime flares are launched hundreds of feet in the air and, like ground illumination flares, are suspended after launch on parachutes so they stay aloft longer and descend gradually. Ted was specifically interested in the way the maritime flares' flight characteristics would be perceived by the witnesses: Jaylene and her husband Jason. Ted launched the flares in sequence from the deck of a small craft out in Santa Monica Bay and then called Pat and me who were on land with Jason and Jaylene. Jaylene reacted first to Ted's flares, saying that the difference she noticed was that after the maritime flares were launched, they each seemed to descend at different rates and fell to different altitudes quickly. The Phoenix lights seemed to stay in line and moved in a straight path without any deviation. Jason said that the Phoenix lights never dropped at all, maintaining a steady altitude as they traversed the sky. "The lights we saw in Phoenix were totally different than what we're seeing now," Jason said.

"Even though we only spoke to two witnesses in this test," Ted said, "lots of other witnesses gave descriptions of what they saw that night as totally inconsistent with flares. The hang times, the blinking on and off, the velocities and the spread over the distance are all inconsistent with any flares that I know. So it leaves me wondering at all whether there could have been flares that night back in 1997."

Ted then turned to another analysis of what the Phoenix lights videos might suggest. He and photo expert Terrence Masson reviewed the Steve Blonder and Mike Kristin videos of the ten thirty Phoenix lights. We knew the exact locations of each witness, who were about fifteen miles apart on the northern and southern ends of the basin where the lights were observed. The curious thing to both Ted and Terrence was the way the lights went out. "If they were flares," Terrence said, "they would be going out in a certain order. Yet these lights didn't." Also, Ted and Terrence agreed, if they were dropped from a plane, they would go out in the order they were dropped. These lights didn't behave that way either. But the general appearance of the lights themselves, compared to the maritime flares, and the way they burned bright orange, still may back up the Air Force claim that the Phoenix lights at ten thirty were flares. The videos, however, don't indicate that the colors of the lights are truly flares because on the consumer camera, the colors of the lights are distorted because the cameras are overcompensating for reduced light entering the lens. The orange color that witnesses saw with their naked eyes turned up white in most of the videos. Flares, therefore, while not a conclusive answer, could not be ruled out as a possibility, Ted and Terrence concluded from their analysis of the videos, even though Ted conceded he was on the fence. While the performance of the lights, he said, did not look like flares descending on parachutes, he did not have quantitative data to make a positive determination.

Pat and I went back to Arizona to talk to witnesses who saw the eight thirty lights. However, because there were no videos or photos of the eight thirty lights, Pat and I worked with a forensic sketch artist John Barbaresco to take down witness descriptions and translate them into a police composite sketch of a craft folks said they saw.

Our first description came from Dana Valentine, who, at 8:13 P.M., was sitting on his father's back porch when he saw five lights in a line in the sky approach. Intrigued by the weird nature of the lights, he brought his father outside to observe them as well. "At first we couldn't tell whether we were seeing five individual objects or one huge one,"

Dana said. "But as it got closer, we could tell it was one object because of the spread of lights across the sky that moved together."

"It looked like it had a body shape to it," Dana's father said.

Both men said they estimated the object to be over a mile in wingspan. Police artist John Barbaresco took down all of Dana's information and keyed it into his graphic program generating an animation of what Dana said he saw. It was a huge V-shaped object spanning over a mile with five lights along the legs of the V. Dana confirmed that the animation was accurate, depicting almost exactly what he saw.

Next witness was Terry Mansfield, who said that she saw a boomerang-shaped craft, an actual craft she could have almost touched because it was so close to her house. She was hosting a meeting in her home when one of the volunteers in a project she was working on pointed out the window and said, "Oh, my God, look what's outside." Terry said the group all looked straight from her porch and realized that the sky seemed to have gone black because there were no stars. They had been blacked out by something. They realized also that they were looking at a black, shimmering, piece of satinlike material that comprised a rigid shape. "The craft was so big," Terry said, "that I couldn't see the back or front." The craft, she said, spanned the entire horizon, completely blocking out the sky overhead. She described the underside of the craft as undulating and fluid and that it was so close as it floated overhead without a sound it was something she could reach out and touch. Terry, who had been in an Air Force family for over twenty-five years said that she had seen every type of military aircraft in service. The craft she described to John, James, and me resembled nothing she had ever seen before. If anything, it was the size and the undulating nature of the craft's skin, as well as its noiselessness, that impressed her most, as it did her friends who witnessed it with her. Yet, Terry revealed, there was another aspect to this craft's appearance and its effect on her group. After being struck by the proximity and awesomeness of the spectacle, the women went back inside to their meeting without saying a word to each other about their shared experience. It was as if the women had come to a collective agreement not to talk about what they had seen. Maybe it was the nature of the spectacle, Terry wondered, but it also seemed as if they had silently agreed among themselves that they were not supposed to talk about it, an instruction somehow inserted into their minds by the object itself or by those navigating it. Or maybe it was just the shock and awe of the nature of the experience. For his part, Pat was struck by the number of identical witness descriptions, each corroborating the other about the characteristics of what they saw.

If it wasn't flares or mass confusion among witnesses over the nature of the lights, we reasoned, could there be another conventional explanation, perhaps a top-secret, stealth, giant aircraft that the military was deliberately testing over Phoenix to gauge witness reactions? Our aeronautics expert, Bill Scott, said that the military has classified weapons systems far in advance of what laypeople believe exist, a technology beyond what we think modern technology is. He suggested that experimental aircraft in our nation's arsenal could well have performance features that fit the descriptions witnesses gave of the Phoenix lights. Bill had done research on similar types of aircraft for a series of articles in *Aviation Week & Space Technology*. For example, neutral buoyancy craft, essentially very advanced blimps with stealthy camouflage and the ability to generate holographic projections in the sky, can trick enemy antiaircraft radar as well as eyewitnesses that the craft, while still silently hovering, is shooting away at high speed. Moreover, by capturing light from the topside of the craft and projecting it toward the ground, the craft can trick observers into believing the craft is not really there. It is a form of invisibility. Just imagine the potential of such a craft, especially if a neutral buoyancy craft is extraordinarily large and can float to very high altitudes allowing it to traverse great distances in a fraction of the time it now takes large conventional transport planes. You could move equipment and personnel from home base to a battlefield front in a matter of a few hours. And in the private sector, Bill Scott speculated, imagine such a craft in the employ of the United States Postal Service, UPS, or Federal Express. It would revolutionize parcel delivery and pay for itself in the commercial marketplace. Could something like that have been what witnesses saw over Phoenix in 1997?

Bill Scott said that his team at the magazine came across a number of black-budget programs that suggested the existence of a rigid-hull, helium-filled neutral buoyancy craft, much like a blimp, but very large with the wingspan of a football field. They typically were triangular shaped—some were boomerang shaped—but were so secret that no diagrams or blueprints were ever released by the government, and the craft still remain secret. The craft might have been developed for Special Forces operations, stealthy large-payload capacity craft that could get teams directly into a battlefield position along with their equipment. I asked Bill whether the existence of these black-budget craft would ever be revealed. Bill said that, pragmatically, why would the military reveal anything officially about these craft as long as the secrecy surrounding them gave the military a battlefield advantage? Besides, everyone believes that it's a UFO so why disabuse them? "It's the way the black world thinks," he said.

Bill Scott admitted that some of the rigid-hull airships that he had seen did not display all of the characteristics of the craft reported over Phoenix. "The idea of blinking out and disappearing immediately," which was a feature of some of the witness descriptions, Bill said, "I don't know how to explain that."

Next stop for Pat's investigation was his interview with Arizona native Jeff Woolwine, who had spent years exploring the Native American petroglyphs in the hills near Phoenix. These are rock art carved into large stones by the Hohokam, an indigenous people who lived in the area from 200 B.C.E. to 1400 C.E. before they mysteriously disappeared. Woolwine suggested that the petroglyphs represented depictions of strange lights and objects that the Hohokam actually saw in the sky and wanted to memorialize with their art much like early cave dwellers memorialized the animals they saw and hunted on the walls of caves. In one of the most telling images, Woolwine showed a drawing of a barbell-shaped object. Then, he showed Pat a video he personally shot in January 2005 of a barbell-cylindrical object flying over the Phoenix hills. His video, he believed, and the object sketched into the rock were probably the same. He said that local tribes were inspired to create their own art by the objects they actually saw.

Pat, still skeptical of this extraordinary interpretation of an ancient alien theory, suggested that we really do not know what the glyphs in the rocks depicted. Perhaps Woolwine was right and they depicted UFOs. However, they could have been depicting celestial objects, events in the heavens such as eclipses or the appearances of comets that were entirely natural and had nothing to do with UFOs. He acknowledged that the petroglyphs had been studied by experts for years and still posed a problem in interpretation.

Subsequently Pat interviewed Doc Tallboys, a park ranger at White Tank Mountain Regional Park in Maricopa County and one of the local experts on Native American petroglyphs who works with the Arizona Historical Society on cataloging and mapping all the art in the White Tank Mountain Regional Park. Tallboys told Pat that the Hohokam were great observers of events taking place around them, especially celestial events, and left a pictorial history of what they saw from their point of view. Some of their depictions actually looked like alien beings, including one figure that looks like it is wearing a space helmet and one object that looks like a saucer with fire coming out of the bottom. Was this reminiscent of Ezekiel's vision of a wheel turning like a fire in the sky? Of course, Ranger Tallboys said, this is only our modern interpretation of what we think the Hohokam saw. Absent a Rosetta Stone to translate these petroglyphic images into modern objects, our own perception allows for a wide range of speculation.

We next interviewed former governor Fife Symington about his first Phoenix lights news conference. If Governor Symington's news conference was aimed to put the kibosh on any further investigations, it did just the opposite, arousing anger and more conspiracy speculation among the witnesses. Then, years later, Governor Symington made a stunning public reversal of what he said at his news conference mocking the sightings. James Fox and I interviewed the governor at his home in California. What did he see with his own eyes?

"I saw a large, velvety, illuminated triangular-shaped object," he said. "I believed and described it as otherworldly." But why, we asked, did the governor mock the entire event the first time he promised to investigate it? "First of all," Symington told us, "the world was descending on us. Media from everywhere appeared in Phoenix wanting to know what's happening. I made the decision at that point to spoof and to lighten the atmosphere. But I didn't realize that I was offending so many people. I was simply trying to lend a little levity to an atmosphere that I thought was getting too hyped up, too over the top, too much hysteria."

We asked the governor that, in light of his initial promise to pursue all avenues of investigation into determining the cause of the Phoenix lights, what he'd learned. He said that he had ordered his staff to contact the Air Force at Luke Air Force Base and to call the Department of Public Safety and the commanding general of the Arizona Guard to find out what it was. "But the Air Force totally blanked us. They just said, 'We have no comment.' That was it."

Wasn't that a nonanswer, a refusal to confirm or deny anything, an admission that it's something you can't talk about?

Symington answered, "As a governor, I can say that the worse comment you can make is 'no comment.'" But "no comment" means that there is actually something an official can't comment about. It's a way to suggest that something that can't be confirmed or even talked about does exist. The Air Force knew there was something there, Symington suggested, but would not talk about it. Thus, for the first time on television, we got an admission from a high government official that his inquiry into the Phoenix lights indicated there was something the military was keeping secret even from the civilian official in command of the military in Arizona. Again, we debunked all the self-proclaimed "science guys" and debunkers who said that there was nothing anomalous in the skies over Phoenix and that the Phoenix lights had either a conventional explanation or simply didn't exist.

In 2006, Governor Symington had agreed to be interviewed by

James Fox for his documentary *Out of the Blue,* where he first made the startling admission that he, too, had been a Phoenix lights witness even though he had spoofed the entire incident. Symington, a retired pilot and Air Force officer, admitted that he, with his own eyes, saw the boomerang-shaped craft. Asked by Fox to describe exactly what he saw, Symington said, "It was a large dark object, which I had described as a delta-shaped object. It was enormous. It was so big it was hard to determine just how fast it was going. It was very odd, the whole thing. It had a kind of an iridescent quality to it, and it was just astounding, much bigger than anything I had ever seen in the air. I realized that I was seeing something that was truly extraordinary."

"Why did you decide to come forward?" Fox asked.

"I figured that enough time had passed," Symington said. "I knew there were a lot of people angry at me, and I decided to set the record straight. I'm no longer the governor, just a 'Joe Citizen' and I don't want people who were my constituents to be upset with me for something about which I'm really on the same page."

In our interview with Symington for the "Arizona Lights" episode we asked, "As a former Air Force officer and pilot, do you think this craft you saw was military, extraterrestrial? What do you think?"

"I've used the word before, which I described the craft as being 'otherworldly,'" he said. "I just don't believe it came from anything we know on Earth. So you call it extraterrestrial, otherworldly, the most incredible thing to see. I just don't know of any earthly explanation for what we saw."

Governor Symington's revelation impressed Pat, who said that he couldn't imagine that all the credible eyewitnesses, including the governor, a former Air Force pilot, could mistake a real craft for a formation of flares. Pat trusted the witnesses and believed it was an otherworldly event. Ted also said that he was skeptical about the flares explanation because nothing he heard from witnesses, especially during the demonstration, could be written off as flares even though that was the official explanation. This was something different and much bigger, Ted suggested. And I agreed with both Ted and Pat that we were looking at a real craft that had amazing aerodynamic qualities, a solid craft, but I still think it was our craft, a neutral buoyancy craft rather than an extraterrestrial spacecraft. But if it was our own top-secret craft, why would the military test it over a residential area where thousands of witnesses would see it, where the media would report on it, and where it would cause a worldwide stir? And if it were extraterrestrial, why would whoever was directing it or flying it choose Phoenix again and again for years prior and years subsequent as a location to observe? Was something of importance in Phoenix that had gotten an extraterrestrial species interested in what was going on? It was certainly something for speculation.

BILL'S BLOG

When I think of the Phoenix lights story and the controversy among opposing camps of witnesses, debunkers, official spokespeople, and researchers into the incident, I think of all the related events surrounding the March 13 lights appearance. There were:

The night of the Hale-Bopp comet.

The Heavens Gate mass suicide.

The immediate Air Force and Sky Harbor denials of any unidentified objects flying over Phoenix.

The subsequent Air National Guard confirmation of a flare drop by the Maryland Air National Guard in an operation called Snowbird.

The Air Force's "no comment" response to Governor Fife Symington's request for information about Air Force activity or Air Force knowledge of craft in the air on March 13, 1997, at eight thirty and ten thirty.

The subsequent flare drop tests to address the concerns of Phoenix lights witnesses, tests that only reinforced the beliefs of many that the lights they saw were not flares.

Fife Symington's fake news conference, unscheduled and completely unresponsive to his earlier statement that he was investigating the incident.

The official smear campaign launched against city council member Barwood after she asked questions about the nature of the lights and the potential threat to air traffic over the Phoenix area. Why was she targeted and by whom?

Among the conspiracy theories that included Symington's press conference and the attacks on Barwood, was Bill Clinton's disappearance. President Bill Clinton's mysterious disappearance on the night of March 13, 1997, when, staying at a friend's house, he fell, injured his ankle, and was out of communication. Was there a connection between Clinton's disappearance and the Phoenix lights incident?

Just looking at the list of concurrent and subsequent events, it strikes me that there is much more to the Phoenix lights story than a bunch of people standing on their balconies in anticipation of a once-in-a-lifetime comet sighting. Even if there were only conflicting statements from the Air Force, it would be intriguing enough to suggest that someone was hiding something. But when you put all of these disparate pieces together, they point to a story much larger than what has since been reported. Indeed, the strenuous denials of anything strange by debunkers and so-called science guys are belied by the Air Force's "no comment" comment to the governor. And just the vehemence of the debunking was enough to get the *UFO Hunters* team out to Phoenix, especially since investigations into the case were alive and well and new evidence was turning up all the time.

In fact, there was so much evidence about this case that there wasn't enough time in the episode to cover it all. For me, there were the deliberate obfuscations between how debunkers handled the eight thirty lights—as if they didn't exist—and the ten thirty lights—definitely flares even though witnesses said they weren't flares and video analysis of the lights leaned against ground illumination flares. If experts were so convinced of the flare explanation, what explained the eight thirty sightings of a floating object directly over people's homes, including the governor's?

The eyewitness descriptions of the eight thirty lights were some of the most compelling testimonies I had ever heard about UFO encounters. First there was Governor Fife Symington's description: an object so large it filled the sky but through its "undulating" surface he could still see translucent stars as the object noiselessly floated overhead. Then there was Terry Mansfield's description of a floating satinlike velvet surface, again, showing a translucent starlight through its skin, that was floating so low she could have touched it from her balcony. And if that weren't enough, the sense of awe and shock she and her friends experienced was so intense that they never even spoke about it after the object had passed over. Was there a psychological component to the entire event, compelling the governor to make fun of it in the immediate aftermath and only coming out publicly seven years later? Then there was the Dr. Lynne Kitei story of seeing similar lights earlier in January and even two years earlier. But it gets more compelling when Dr. Kitei describes herself shooting rolls of film of the lights that she doesn't remember ever taking. Dr. Bruce Maccabee, who analyzed the photos she took, discovered that Dr. Kitei's loss of memory and photos she took are the first documented extrinsic physical evidence of episodes occurring during the phenomenon of missing time.

And then there are the backstories. Governor Symington, for

example, said that his observation of the object over his house came after he told his security detail he was going to bed for the night and dismissed them. Then he stepped out into his backyard, even though he said he would not leave the house, where he saw the object. Did the navigators of the object, assuming it was not an Air Force classified craft, somehow send him a message to go out into the night to watch the object? The governor also said that he had had an earlier experience with a UFO encounter while he was an Air Force lieutenant. He said that he caught an object on radar that should not have been there and that it did not behave as a conventional aircraft. However, when he reported his radar hit to his commanding officer, he was told to forget about what he saw and if there was any tape of that radar hit, to erase it. To me, that sounded just like a story Philip Corso told about the time he was commanding an antiaircraft missile battery at the Army's Red Canyon test range in White Sands, New Mexico. He said he caught an anomalous object on radar, reported it to his commanding officer, and was told to erase the tape and forget it ever happened. Then Lieutenant Symington said that after he was told to forget about what he saw and keep silent about it; he did just what he was told and tucked the entire incident away, never to be discussed. But that was all before he saw the triangular object over Phoenix and before our interview on *UFO Hunters*.

Symington mocked the sightings and Barwood was smeared, literally driven out of office, just because she asked the city council to investigate the lights. Her description of the way the smear campaign operated was also very compelling. If she had walked into the council meeting holding up a copy of *UFO Magazine* and demanding full disclosure of a UFO incident, even I could see that there would be a media reaction to her jumping to conclusions. But that never happened. She never even uttered the dreaded three letters: "U-F-O." Why were the attacks on her so completely well orchestrated, as if she had to be squelched lest an official request for an airspace alert gain any traction? The mayor and a cabal of his council members went after Barwood with gusto, according to Barwood. Why do that if there was nothing to hide because nothing had happened? Just that activity, even absent Governor Symington's sighting and derisive mocking of the event he witnessed firsthand, is enough to raise suspicions.

Then, consider the lengths the Air Force and National Guard went to in trying to prove that the ten thirty lights were nothing more than flares. First came the pro forma denial of any air activity. Then the "oops" moment when they reported the flare drop, almost as an afterthought. Then, when that report didn't immediately squash suspicions and opinions from photo analysts, there was the public demonstration of a flare drop years later. Again, why try to prove a point if there was no point? As Dr. Lynne Kitei said, even the photo analysis of the flare drop demonstration showed that the color and intensity of the subsequent test lights didn't comport with the photo analysis of the 1997 ten thirty lights.

Let's say, for the sake of argument, that the ten thirty lights were truly flares. Why drop flares so obviously in public after public safety switchboards and the media had been alerted to the eight thirty lights? And, again, the eight thirty lights weren't just floating over Phoenix. They were floating all across Arizona from Nevada to the Mexican border. Why drop flares after all this? Perhaps because the eight thirty event was so widely reported that the Air Force had to come up with an ad hoc explanation as quickly as possible and dropped flares two hours later to give themselves an excuse to explain the nature of the lights people had seen earlier that evening. The Air Force's actions point to a cover-up, a way to deflect public inquiry into a cul-de-sac of misinformation.

And this brings us to elements of evidence pointing to a real UFO—either ours or theirs—encounter, which are:

- A mass sighting over a wide area by professional witnesses in different locations, including pilots and the state's governor.
- Photo and video evidence of the objects in the sky, whether flares or not.
- An official denial, which is then reversed and hammered home as if to squelch all inquiry.
- An official smear campaign, first of a city councilperson and then an oblique denial by the governor, one of the official witnesses.
- Actual trace evidence in a sequence of photos, just like the "tale of the tape," indicating that one of the witnesses was experiencing a form of missing time as she was photographing the strange lights.
- Clear psychological reactions from some of the up-close witnesses to the eight thirty lights in which they were uncomfortable talking about what they saw and felt until years later. And isn't it interesting that both the governor and some of the other firsthand witnesses seem to have had the same reaction: Don't embrace the lights, but deny the reality until a safe number of years had passed.

All of this as a result of a routine flare exercise and nothing more? The implausibility index, at least for me, indicates that a UFO, again, ours or theirs, is a more plausible explanation than a flare exercise confused with a UFO.

And even though the *UFO Hunters* didn't produce the actual UFO, we did come up with one striking piece of evidence buried amid the denials, obfuscations, smears, and disinformation. In Governor Symington's later revelation of events, we learned that rather than a flat denial from the Air Force about the existence of an object over Phoenix at eight thirty, what we got was a big, juicy, tempting "no comment." About flares? Because the obvious response to a "no comment" is why refuse to comment on something that didn't even exist, the mere refusal to comment means that something did exist, something you can't comment about. That, to me, says it all.

"ALIEN CRASHES"

In 2008, residents of Needles, California, including a former chief of operations at Los Angeles International Airport, a riverboat pilot, and a local radio commentator, all reported the military retrieval of a strange object that fell from the sky into a ditch along the bank of the Colorado River. In 1965, the year of the great northeast power black-out, residents in Kecksburg, Pennsylvania, a rural suburb of Pittsburgh, reported the controlled crash landing of a strange object that swooped out of the sky in a long S-curve and landed in a ditch outside of town and was retrieved by a U.S. military and NASA team. And in 1945, a bell-shaped object that German scientists had been developing as a "wonder weapon," a device so powerful it could change the outcome of the war even as Soviet troops were marching through Poland on their way into Germany, disappeared without a trace from the Owl Mountains cave where it was being tested. Where did it go?

These seemingly unrelated events across over sixty years inspired us to investigate them over the course of two episodes in seasons two and three, where we found that they indeed might all be related. We found that it would be a secret that stretched across a century and in-volved the possibility—at least that was my speculation—of time travel experiments by the Nazis and by former Nazi scientists working inside NASA. Our travels for these episodes took us from Needles, California, to Kecksburg, Pennsylvania, to Berlin, and to the Owl Mountains in Poland, where, guarded by machine-gun emplacements built into the tunnels overlooking huge caves, the place where the Nazi Bell, Die Glocke, was built and tested. We began in Needles.

One of the less publicized cases, but one that was recent and, in fact, was taking place right while we were filming the show, was the crash and recovery of a strange object along the banks of the Colorado River near a town called Needles, California, in the Mojave Desert, on the Arizona border. We were so impressed with eyewitness accounts of the crash and retrieval of the object and the credibility of the former LAPD witness that we wanted to get on this case while it was happening. But when we arrived and found that our friend George Knapp had been there and been confronted by armed government personnel in unmarked vehicles who said they were dispatched from Area 51, things got even more exciting. Then, when we matched the story of Needles up with the story of Kecksburg in 1965, we thought there night be enough of a similarity we could mesh the cases into a single episode. But when we researched the story of the Nazi Bell, we realized there might be an opportunity to relate the three stories even though our season two episodes were locked in. We hoped for a third season to research the Nazi UFO story and, fortunately, we got it. So here, over the next two chapters, are the stories of the 2008 Needles incident, the 1965 Kecksburg incident, and the 1945 disappearance of the Nazi Bell, the Wunderwaffe or "wonder weapon."

THE STORIES

Needles, 2008

He called himself "Riverboat Bob," and he traveled along the Colorado River, a river whose bends and banks he knew very well. Therefore, when, one night on May 14, 2008, he looked up and saw a large, turquoise, cylindrical device that soared overhead and seemed to crash-land along one of the riverbanks, he tried to locate exactly where it had fallen. But almost immediately, as he was watching from behind the wheel of his boat, a large military Skycrane helicopter flew over the area and, surrounded by other helicopters, the Skycrane lifted the glowing crashed object off the bank and flew away.

At the same time that Riverboat Bob saw the object, a retired LAPD security chief and operations head at Los Angeles International Airport and current Needles resident, Frank Costigan walked out into his backyard to find his cat. He looked up and saw a turquoise object fly overhead and pass into the distance, where he saw it descend toward the river. He thought he would soon hear the crash as the object fell, but he heard nothing. The very next day, residents in Needles saw black unmarked utility vehicles and a large truck with a dome on top. It looked like a government convoy, but where was it from, what was it doing in Needles, what was under the dome, and did where they were going have any relationship to the object that Costigan and Riverboat Bob saw? And then *Coast to Coast AM* radio host and KLAS-TV news correspondent George Knapp came to town to find out more about what had happened.

Knapp reported that he was confronted by the, for want of a better term, "Men in Black," whom he confronted in return, asking who they were and where they were from. Eventually he found out they were from Area 51, the location of one of Knapp's most important stories that he'd reported on concerning Bob Lazar.

What we would learn about the object, the individuals who saw it, and the sudden military presence, even interacting with us a year later, was astounding.

Kecksburg, 1965

Folks on the East Coast of the U.S. were already jittery by the beginning of December because of a blackout along the eastern power grid just weeks earlier. Then on December 9, folks in Canada and the northern U.S. were in for a shock when some people noticed what looked like a fireball sweeping down from the sky across Michigan, Ohio, and into western Pennsylvania, where residents heard a sonic boom as it descended.

As it came down across the Midwest, some observers thought they were seeing a meteor crash, others thought it was a plane crash, and still others thought they saw a satellite falling out of the sky. Pilots in the area reported seeing the fireball, too. But as it passed over the Kecksburg area just prior to its landing in the woods, a young boy told his mother that he had actually seen the object land in a ditch in a small clearing. The boy's mother also saw the falling object and noted that it had a purplish color and had smoke coming off the surface as it seemed to slow down in the sky before disappearing behind trees. Still others near the crash landing site felt the earth vibrate when the object hit. A member of the fire department said he saw the artillery shell–shaped object lying on its side in the ditch, glowing a light purple. A local radio reporter interviewed some of the witnesses who had gathered at the crash site where they saw the object and a military unit with transport apparatus retrieving it and hauling it away. That unit, according to some witnesses, also included personnel from NASA. As for the radio reporter, according to one of the production team at the station who'd witnessed it, unidentified men showed up at the station's broadcast booth and confronted the local radio announcer, who backed off the story. He was later killed in a car accident.

Over the years the cover story that the object was either a meteor or space debris from a satellite or space probe has come to be the standard explanation for the event, but political insiders like John Podesta, one of the managers of President Obama's transition team and now a member of his advisory staff, and author and UFO researcher Leslie Kean, have said there are gaping holes in the government cover-up and have demanded a better response from the government. Leslie Kean had filed a Freedom of Information request from NASA, and received a response, which did not hint at a UFO. If the incident at Kecksburg was a UFO, the cover-up would make perfect sense, especially if the

UFO, we speculated, was an object that had traveled through time from its origins in a Nazi engineering and testing facility toward the end of World War II.

Poland, 1945

Deep in the Owl Mountains in Poland lies a strange hollowed-out mountain, a huge cave dug into the side of a mountain so camouflaged that World War II Allied bombers would never know what was inside that mountain without firsthand human intelligence. It was inside this mountain that Nazi scientists, utilizing prisoners from a nearby concentration camp, prisoners whose lives were sacrificed for the top-secret weapon the Germans were developing, were experimenting with a high-radiation bell-shaped device that, reportedly, was so powerful that it had the ability to change the outcome of the war even in its final months.

This object was referred to by the SS officers overseeing its development as a wonder weapon. They called it the Bell or, in German, Die Glocke. There is a lot of speculation about this device. But the story that many have come to believe is that the weapon was composed of two counterrotating cylinders containing a dense liquid metallic substance referred to in the Hindu Vedic texts as "red mercury" a substance that when spun at high speeds was highly radioactive. The counterrotation generated a radioactive energy field, the story goes, that could propel the Bell great distances not only through space, but also through time. Now imagine a device that could transport itself back to Washington, D.C., circa 1940, where it would detonate, wiping out the United States government and rendering the U.S. helpless in joining the war. Imagine such a device detonating in London in early 1939 or in Moscow in 1940. Hitler would have been in control of all of Europe.

The radioactive energy field from the experiments with this device was so powerful that hundreds of workers in the cave were irradiated and killed, even some of the Nazi scientists. Now imagine that this project, managed by an SS officer named Kurt Debus, simply disappeared from inside the cave as the Soviet army smashed through Poland, overwhelming the German Wehrmacht. Where did it go? Now imagine that that very same SS officer Kurt Debus turns up at Cape Kennedy in 1965 as a launch director for NASA. Now imagine even further that a bell-shaped object glowing a purplish blue crash-lands in a ditch in Kecksburg, Pennsylvania, and is retrieved by an Army unit waiting for it, protected not only by the military but possibly by security personnel from NASA and even from a U.S. intelligence agency. Why was NASA at this crash site? Was the NASA official Kurt Debus waiting for his precious wonder weapon to return to its developer? Could that device, after landing in Pennsylvania in 1965, have made its way farther to the waiting arms of a unit from Area 51 after it crash-landed again over forty years later in Needles? And why would the Nazis, in their attempts to develop such sophisticated technologies as ballistic missiles, rocket planes, and jet engines, have focused so much of their attention upon the Vedic texts to find, among other things, the concept of Die Glocke? The answer, you may be surprised to learn, lies in a phenomenon called the Age of Spiritualism that spread across Europe and the United States in the late nineteenth century and informed part of the Nazi philoso-phy of the origins of Aryanism.

The seemingly outrageous theory of a World War II weapon that could travel through time, as far-fetched as it may seem, is what drove the *UFO Hunters,* to investigate the alien crashes in Needles and Ke-cksburg and the possible origin of the bell-shaped object that dis-appeared from its facility in the closing months of World War II.

THE EPISODE

It was a current story. Like Stephenville, Texas, in season one, the events in Needles, California, were popping even as we set up our epi-sodes for season two. And Needles had all the elements of a great case. It was current, it was witnessed by one of the most credible witnesses we could have hoped for, an operations director from a major interna-tional airport and a former high-ranking LAPD officer. There was also an eyewitness at the site of the crash; a radio station manager who was reporting the story and was threatened by a strange group of armed quasimilitary operatives; and folks in the town worried about the presence of armed personnel vehicles. And the events surrounding this incident in the desert town of Needles were very much like the events in Kecksburg. Thus, to compare and contrast, we revisited the Kecksburg story as well. We wanted to find out what had crashed, what the object was, and why the government wanted it back while keeping it secret.

The episode began with the basic report from Riverboat Bob, a reclusive fisherman who motored along the Colorado River and who said that at 3:00 A.M. he saw a flaming turquoise object streaking out of the sky and hitting the ground along the banks of the river. As Bob pulled his boat up toward the bank to get a closer look, thinking it was possibly a meteor, albeit one with a very strange color, the sky above within minutes was filled with double-rotor helicopters—which looked military to him—and a large helicopter that had a Skycrane attached. The Skycrane lifted up the object, which was about thirty feet long and bulky and looked like a tanker truck. With the object still burning with a bright turquoise glow, the Skycrane hauled it away. But Riverboat Bob wasn't the only witness to the object's crash. As Ted pointed out, this was a multiple-witness sighting, which, for him, lent more credibility than if the only witness was a guy who lived on the river. He said that there was even greater credibility to witness reports of the event because they described military units coming into the area and the sight of helicopters removing the object that likely crashed. And for Pat, the immediate question was, where exactly did the object crash, and what physical trace evidence might still remain? We split into three units to pursue our separate trails of evidence gathering.

Ted pursued the investigation of the crash site, searching for its location and looking for physical traces on the ground. "If a vehicle crashed into the desert along the river," he said. "You should be able to find hard physical evidence of that crash." He remarked that the number of witnesses who saw the large helicopter lifting something off the ground and escorted by a number of other twin-rotor helicopters indicated that this was more than a simple exercise. They were removing something they had expected to find there because of the speed at which they arrived on scene.

Pat Uskert was set to take the river route to find the crash site while Ted looked for it along the riverbank. It was a pincer movement, with Pat saying that if he could identify the site and excavate in the area, he might be able to find the answers solving the mystery of what had crashed. And I was dispatched to interview the eyewitnesses who said they saw the entire event unfold. I wanted to find out, by comparing eyewitness statements with statements from the military, why, in the face of what people saw, the military denied that anything concerning the crash had ever happened. To the military, this seemed to be a nonevent even though the actions of the military, including aerial surveillance, continued to take place and belie what they were saying. After all, why surveil an area in which you deny anything was out of the ordinary?

Before we went down our separate investigative paths, Pat and I met with David Hayes, the owner-manager and host of Needles KTOX radio station. "We're still trying to figure out what happened on May fourteenth," Hayes said. "With Bill Birnes and Pat Uskert of *UFO Hunters* in studio, we're looking for any information from anyone who saw the event," Hayes announced, joining us in our investigation. He told us that on the morning of May 14, right after folks saw the strange object descend, they began calling in reports to 911 and to the radio station. One caller reported, while Pat and I were on the air, that, "it was coming down fast, but it angled."

"Did you notice the shape?" I asked the caller.

"It almost looked like a huge meteorite from where I was," the caller answered. "I expected to hear an explosion when it hit."

David Hayes explained that folks at first thought it was a meteorite, but when it came down from the sky, a team of helicopters retrieved it. That was strange. "I have no idea what it was," Hayes said. "But they were here to recover it so quickly." In fact, Hayes reiterated, because the aerial recovery team got to the site so fast, in a matter of minutes, he believed they were tracking the object as it fell. "You couldn't have gotten there so quickly unless you were staged and ready to go," he argued. He also suggested that some folks saw the actual impact, as Riverboat Bob did, albeit from a distance alongside the bank. But what struck him personally was the intense presence of military units in the town. "I saw some unmarked official-looking vehicles coming off the freeway. But one was really strange because it was sporting multiple antennas and a dome atop its cabin. And its front license plate read 'U.S. government' and it had blacked-out windows and a guy inside who was staring at me." Later, Hayes saw the same vehicles outside the radio station, watching. He described the scene: "It was actually parked about a hundred yards from the station. And the kinds of equipment and the vehicles they were in was like high-tech possible surveillance." But surveillance on the ground from unmarked vehicles was only one of the strange events after the crash. Folks also remarked about unfamiliar conventional aircraft flying over the city.

The craft folks saw arriving at a local airport in nearby Billhead, Arizona, right across the border with Nevada and California, were white passenger aircraft with red stripes along the fuselage. Although otherwise unidentified, to some residents in the area these planes were very familiar. These planes, David Hayes told us, were Janet flights. "We had these reports of Janet air traffic coming in and out of the airport." But we knew that Janet was not a commercial airline even though it had been seen a lot over the skies of Nevada and Arizona. Janet planes were usually seen at the far end of the Las Vegas McCarren International Airport and were used to ferry high-level defense workers to top classified locations, including Area 51. It was the call sign of an airline run by the CIA. Why were these planes being seen at the airport serving Needles the day after the crash of the object along the Colorado River? I headed to Laughlin-Bullhead International Airport in Arizona to find the answer by interviewing airport manager David Gaines, a former Marine, to see what he could tell us.

We asked whether he had seen military aircraft landing at Bullhead before, and if yes, could he recognize them. But when we asked him whether he had seen any planes with a white body and a red stripe along its side and blacked out windows ever landing at his airport, he said definitely not. In fact, if such a plane existed, he said, he wouldn't be able to identify it or recognize it. And then I asked, "If you were told, ordered, not to divulge any landings by the planes I described at this airport and I asked you what you know about those planes landing here, what would you tell me?"

"I would tell you," he said, "that no aircraft of that nature had ever been here. We've never seen it."

Witnesses had told us that on the evening of May 14, they saw a Janet plane land at the Bullhead City airport under the cover of darkness. We, therefore, had an issue to resolve.

While both Ted and Pat set out on their respective paths to meet at what they believe should be the crash site, I set out from Arizona to join them. Our plan was to bring in archeologist Garth Baldwin, who had joined us at our very first episode in Kelso, Washington. Garth was a soils and landscape specialist who would be able to differentiate the physical scars left on the landscape from an impact and the normal wind and water erosion in the area. But a crash site would not be easy to locate because, as Garth pointed out, the vegetation was so dense you would have to walk carefully to find a path into the brush, where, Garth hoped to find some indications of a burn or an impact. Those would be big clues that something happened there. But help came in the form of a witness who had heard our broadcast on David Hayes's radio show. He told us he had a general idea of the location of the crash site.

Our witness was Frank Costigan, friends with David Hayes, and a retired LAPD captain and chief of police and superintendent of operations at LAX, who had longtime professional experience with observing and identifying controlled flights. He knew what to look for and what was anomalous. I joined him at his house. He said that at a little after three in the morning, he went into his backyard to hunt for his cat when, "all of a sudden the ground seemed to light right up, not like the sun or the moon, but enough to make me look up." The object he said he saw was round in front with flames coming off it. It was blue and turquoise and "five or six times longer than it was wide." He said that he thought he was about to hear a sonic boom when the object came closer or the sound of a crash as it descended over a ridgeline near the river. But, he said, he "didn't hear a thing."

From what he could see of the object and its trajectory, he said that it couldn't be anything but out of the ordinary. He said that the object was nothing close to what he had seen before. This was in no way like a commercial or private aircraft or similar to anything he had seen in the military. "It had to be something like a controlled flight of some sort." Frank said. "That maybe went haywire." That was his professional opinion.

Frank's description of a craft that had been a controlled flight immediately raised three questions: Whose was it, who's controlling it, and where did it come from? We knew that the desert around Needles was ringed by military bases and facilities. Just to the northwest was the China Lake naval range, the Marines' Twentynine Palms, the Army's Fort Irwin was to the southeast, farther to the east was the Yuma Proving Ground where the Army tested long-range artillery, and to the north was Area 51. In basic terms, Needles sat in a military hotspot where, for decades, strange craft of all kinds were tested. This opened up a question of origin: theirs or ours? An alien vehicle or one of our pieces of controlled flight ordnance, such as a small cruise missile? Frank also said that entire Mojave Desert area was surrounded by military test facilities and that he wouldn't be surprised if the object was meant to land in nearby Lake Mojave but missed its mark and came down along the Colorado River instead, which would also explain why so many military helicopters seemed ready to retrieve the object within fifteen minutes of its impact.

Ted and I met up and then visited with Riverboat Bob on his boat along the Colorado River to assess his story and see whether he could pick out the spot in daylight where he was when he saw the object go down. Maybe by working in from the edge of the river, we could make our way through the brush to the crash site. Riverboat Bob was a key witness who had seen the entire crash and retrieval. He told us: "As I was sitting on the boat fishing at three in the morning, when the whole front of the boat lit up. I looked up and saw a bright, turquoise, blue something falling out of the sky. It came straight across from one side to the other. And it hit. It just kind of made a thump." He said that it made an impact just west of where his boat was sitting when it hit the riverbank about two hundred yards away near the railroad tracks that ran alongside the bank.

Bob claimed that within fifteen minutes helicopters appeared. "Almost immediately after the first helicopter appeared, there was a second and then a third. And that's when the big one came overhead. That thing circled over my boat, went to the site, dropped out of sight for a moment, and the next thing I knew it was up and flying." Bob not only saw a crash, he saw a helicopter fleet over the crash site, and then the helicopter team leave the area with the crashed object in tow. "I saw the object being lifted by the helicopter. That's when I saw the shape. It was well lit by the other helicopters; they were shining their lights on it." Bob could see clearly that the object was still very hot.

Both Riverboat Bob and Frank Costigan said they believed the object hit at the edge of the desert close to the riverbank, deep in dense clumps of shrubs. Before we set off down the river and Pat set off along the riverbank near the railroad tracks, Garth Baldwin told us what we needed to look for that would indicate we were approaching the crash site. He said, "Given the size of the object that Bob described, there should be a large and significant displacement of the soil and a clear change in the texture of the sand and soil. Because the grass and sagebrush grow very slowly, if the area looks disturbed in any way, it would be obvious and that should be an indication." Ted believed that if an object crashed along the riverbank, the military retrieval team would have a difficult time covering it up because of all the old growth. But the area was so dense, the site could be well concealed by sagebrush on the ground. That was why we developed another search technique: an ultralight aircraft equipped with a high-definition camera that the pilot flew along the riverbank. We hoped that if we couldn't find the crash site while hiking along the ground, perhaps the camera could spot it from the sky. The plane took off, in radio communication with Pat and Garth traveling by land along the railroad track, while Bob, Ted, and I started motoring down the river to find the place where Bob had stopped for the night and saw the object crash in the distance. If Bob recognized the spot, Ted suggested, he should notify us immediately so that Ted could call in the ultralight to fly over the riverbank to see if there was any physical damage to the shrubbery, which might indicate a crash site.

We traveled along the river for about an hour with the ultralight crisscrossing both sides of the river, looking to position its camera at the best possible angle to pick up any disturbance in the sagebrush along the bank. Then Bob recognized the spot where he stopped for the night: a very thick clump of brush adjacent to a flat, sandy, mini-beach, a perfect spot to bring the boat ashore. We beached the boat as Bob pointed out a bend in the trail that he thought would lead us to the impact site. It was right next to a train trestle, which suggested to Bob that we were in the right spot. Ted called in air support, directing the ultralight to circle the area on either side of the trestle—just to make sure—as Ted, Bob, and I headed into the thicket. After a few passes, the ultralight hit what we believed to be pay dirt. Pat and Garth pulled up in his SUV and Pat told us, "The pilot in the ultralight told us there was a burned spot just south of here. That corresponds with what you saw, right Bob?" Pat asked. Bob pointed to a spot on our map of the area and said that the site should be due south of our position.

Garth set us up into two-person teams—Pat and himself and Ted and me—walking in a lazy S pattern, but crisscrossing so that the teams could survey the entire area between our position and what the pilot picked out as a burned area. With daylight fading away, we started out. But before we got to the burned site, Ted and I spotted another likely indicator of a crash, a scorched area with a huge mound of dirt pushed up as if someone had tried to cover up a scar in the ground. Ted thought that the berm of dirt might be covering up a crater, which would indicate a prior impact. In fact the shape of the berm and gouged earth leading up to it looked as if—assuming an object had crashed here—the object came in from the south over the river, just as Bob had described it to us. Ted called Garth on the walkie-talkie to bring him in for his opinion. But Garth said that he didn't see an actual impact. Moreover, he said, there would have to be a well-defined scorched area differentiated from the surrounding area of living vegetation. This was all old growth. So we made our way farther inland to the burned site that our pilot had spotted. It would take us another hour to find it.

When we arrived at the spot, we were impressed with the area of damage. There was burned foliage all over the place. I suggested that the amount of burning indicated that the object had been here. However, Ted pointed out that because Bob had said the object had landed with a thud instead of an explosion, the lack of a crater and the wide area of burned brush suggested just the opposite: that the object had not crashed here. Garth agreed with Ted, asserting that the burned material was uniform across the area, interspersed with live vegetation and old growth that would have been incinerated in the heat from the object. This led him to believe that the fire that had obviously been here was natural and not the result of a foreign object burning on the ground.

We pushed on, Pat scanning the ground with his metal detector, but our light was fading fast and we had over an hour's trek back to our SUV. We had to admit that although our pilot had spotted a number of burned areas from the air, we had not found any clear impact site, which still might be farther into the brush. But as darkness set in, we had to head back. And it was time for me to head back to Las Vegas to meet up with George Knapp, who had not only spoken to witnesses, but confronted the strange contingent of men in armed vehicles and dressed in black cammies. Were these members of an investigative and retrieval unit or were these the real Men in Black, charged with intimidating witnesses to UFOs? George Knapp was an eyewitness to these people, who they were, where they came from, and where they were going.

While I flew back to Las Vegas, Pat and Ted flew first to Pittsburgh and then drove to Kecksburg in rural Pennsylvania to meet up with

Stan Gordon, one of the key investigators of the Kecksburg UFO incident, dubbed "Pennsylvania's Roswell."

KECKSBURG

In ways similar to the Phoenix lights, albeit more than three decades earlier, the Kecksburg incident was a very public event, covered by many media outlets, local as well as national. Ted brought along a number of measuring instruments, including plans for a ground-penetrating radar search that might reveal any anomalies in the immediate area where witnesses said they saw the glowing object on the ground. Its similarity to Phoenix, as well as to Needles, lay in the media coverage of an event witnessed by many people and the presence of military units and explanations, but, ultimately, the cause of which the government refused to divulge. If something was still under the soil, Ted said, he believed they could find it, or at least an electronic trace of it.

The event began on December 9, 1965, at about 4:45 P.M. when a glowing fireball swept over the Midwestern United States, crossed the Ohio border, and appeared over western Pennsylvania. But observers looking at the spectacle across three states said that it didn't act like a descending, out-of-control fireball because it was moving too slowly. But then, according to witnesses, the object seemed to lose control of its landing momentarily and then fell to earth. What happened then had a strange similarity to what would happen in Needles over forty years later.

My first job in this episode, after I had returned from interviewing George Knapp, was to talk to Stan Gordon, the primary investigator on this case, who became involved in the 1970s. Stan set up the background for this case, the basic facts, the key witnesses, and what has happened in the aftermath of the incident. Stan began with the collective witnesses' observations that the object appeared overhead as if it were navigating and coming down in a controlled landing. And as it fell into a thicket of woods, there was a bluish smoke rising out of it that dissipated into the clouds very quickly. Stan said, as did John Ventre from Pennsylvania MUFON, that this object was likely reported in the skies over Ontario, Michigan, and Ohio, before it crossed into western Pennsylvania. As it was falling, smoking, and brightly illuminated, Stan said, "The police department, the fire department, and radio station were all being bombarded with calls. And as it proceeded into Westmoreland County, local county first responders were over-whelmed with calls coming in."

The entire town of Kecksburg was consumed by the incident, be-fore and after the landing and in the weeks, months, and even years after it. The images of the event have stayed with witnesses for de-cades, as Pat found out from Billy Buelbush, who was one of the first witnesses to the object, watching it fly over and crash. "Heard this sizzle noise," he said. "Then I seen this red fireball coming. I watched it come over and heads for the mountain. Then I saw it turn, a perfect turn, and come back. It came just like it was looking for someplace to land." Pat asked whether the object seemed to be under intelligent control, and Buelbush said that, "it had to be."

Buelbush said he drove to where he believed the object, which he at first thought was a downed aircraft, had come to rest. He said that he pulled his flashlight from his car and walked over to the impact spot in the woods. "I could see it down there," he said. He wondered how he could extract the occupants because, "there were no windows, no doors, no rivets." Standing approximately eight feet away from the object, Buelbush said it smelled like sulfur, smelled like it was made of rotten eggs. Pat said later that he was most impressed by the descrip-tion of the object's turning, looking for a place to come down, which meant that it was under intelligent control and not just tumbling out of the sky. At the site, immediately after he discovered the impact site, Buelbush was joined by units from the Kecksburg Fire Depart-ment, responding to reports of a burning crashed object in the woods.

Volunteer firefighter Jim Romansky reached the object first, survey-ing the damage he believed he would find. "I was shocked," he said, "because I was prepared for a smashed-up airplane, and here was this humungous piece of metal buried into this drainage ditch. Buried into brush because it came flying down from the trees." It was acorn-shaped, Romansky said, and had a ring of strange markings that circled the entire object. This object, however, displayed none of the traditional features of UFOs. It looked like an artillery shell or a large bell, not a flying triangle, disk, or cylinder. If anything, it resembled the shape of the object that would fly into Rendlesham Forest outside of RAF Bentwaters fifteen years later. The strange graphics on the side of both the Rendlesham and Kecksburg objects made for a chilling similarity, which became even stranger when one considers the strange graphics the late Jesse Marcel, Jr., saw on the materials that his father brought back from the Roswell debris field in 1947.

"I'd never seen anything like this in my life," Romansky said. "My impression after I looked at this thing, after I walked around it, after I thought about it some more as I stared at it was that this thing wasn't from here."

Just as would happen in Needles over forty years later, within hours after the crash a contingent of military personnel arrived, including both Army and Air Force, fully equipped with retrieval and transportation apparatus. They cordoned off the area around the drainage ditch where the object lay, still smoking, still glowing. They prevented the public from viewing what was in the ditch, pushing away those already assembled at the site and keeping others outside the area. Inside the newly restricted zone, the military began searching.

Bob Gatty, a reporter from the *Greensburg Tribune*, a local paper from the next town over, was dispatched to the scene by his editor to cover the event. He told Pat that he remembered very clearly the heavy and intimidating military presence. "There were at least a dozen military personnel in addition to Pennsylvania State Police. I said, 'I need to go down there.' And they said, 'There's nothing down there.' I said, 'If there's nothing down there then why can't I go in there?'" He told Pat his impression was that the military and not the state police were in charge of the scene. "I had never experienced a situation in which the military had come into a civilian situation and taken away control of an accident site. Why would the Army be there?"

Witness P. David Newhouse told us in a white-box interview that they were stopped by the military as they walked up to the site. "I heard the bolt snap on the rifle. We stopped and talked to the soldier for a second, and he told us to get out and get back to where we came from." Witness Robert Bittner said that a soldier looked at him as he approached the site, pointed his finger at him and said, "Nobody goes down here." And Bittner turned around and left the immediate area. Witness Billy Buelbush also claimed to have seen officials from NASA wearing Hazmat white disposal uniforms at the retrieval site. Later that evening, however, according to Stan Gordon, witnesses reported seeing a large flatbed truck enter the area. In an hour, the truck left from the site in an obvious hurry carrying something under a tarp.

Stan Gordon told us that years after the incident itself, he conducted interviews independently and separately with Billy Buelbush and Jim Romansky, both of whom led him to the site where they remembered seeing the object. It was the exact same location. Ted suggested that if Stan could lead him to the precise spot, Ted could search for any physical traces of impact or damage to the scene by bringing in equipment such as ground-penetrating radar and metal detectors. If the location had been undisturbed since the crash, Ted suggested Locard's Theory of transference might have resulted in traces from the object itself to still be in the area.

Ted, Pat, Stan Gordon, geologist Steve Kite, and ground-penetrating radar operator and electromagnetic surveyor Pete Hutchinson, who confirmed, from photos Stan Gordon took twenty years earlier, that the team was precisely at the right spot where the impact happened. Ted believed that a search for any physical evidence might also resolve an issue that debunkers had been proposing for years, that the Kecksburg object was really part of a Soviet space probe, the Cosmos 96 Venus probe, that had fallen back to earth. If the object was Cosmos 96, its tiny nuclear reactor might have left traces of radiation whose signature could identify it. However other evidence had already eliminated the Cosmos 96 as the crashed object. The National Space Science Data Center, for example, said that according to Air Force tracking data, Cosmos 96 entered the atmosphere and was destroyed earlier than the first sighting of the Kecksburg object.

Ted laid out the course of the search and Pete Hutchinson calibrated the equipment that would be able to identify metal under the ground and any spike in the electrical conductivity of the ground in the area against the conductivity in an adjacent area. And the search was positive for an area of high conductivity that showed up as a two-dimensional bright red spot on the chart. Even more promising was that the metal return on the ground-penetrating radar was anomalous to the area, different than the earth surrounding it. The electronic signature, Hutchinson told Ted, was consistent with the signature of a crashed vehicle. Time to dig, turn over the surface soil. Time to see if, when the lower level of soil is uncovered, the ground-penetrating radar could see the image of whatever might be buried there. And it worked. The GPR picked up an object just a few feet below the surface that, according to Pete Hutchinson, did not belong there. It was completely anomalous and was located at the exact spot where witnesses Billy Buelbush and Jim Romansky said they'd seen the object.

By this time, I had rejoined the team, returning to Pennsylvania from Las Vegas after interviewing George Knapp. And I joined in the archeological dig to find out what the source of the electrical conductivity might be, to see if we could uncover it. But we could not. We quickly hit bedrock and Hutchinson said that it was the bedrock itself, which was very high in iron, that was the source of the conductivity. Nothing had penetrated beneath the bedrock. The military and NASA, if the witness accounts of their presence are accurate, had certainly cleaned the site well and left no traces of any residual evidence from a crash. Despite the absence of any physical trace evidence, though, Pat accurately summed up what we learned from the folks at Kecksburg. Folks had seen something crash, witnesses saw military and NASA personnel, the object was not the Cosmos 96, and the government had still not released its full documentation on what it had retrieved.

Eventually, John Podesta, a member of President Clinton's administration, an adviser to President Obama, and now a member of Hillary Clinton's presidential campaign came forward to demand the government, and particularly NASA and the military, reveal their findings concerning the nature, origin, and purpose of the Kecksburg object. Journalist and author Leslie Kean (*UFOs: Generals, Pilots, and Government Officials Go on the Record*, 2011), whose 2007 National Press Club press conference featuring commercial and military pilots who had experienced UFO encounters and even aerial dogfights with UFOs, filed under FOIA for information about the Kecksburg crash and what NASA had discovered. But her organization, the Coalition for Freedom of Information (CFI), said that NASA was still hiding important facts about the crash. NASA had first stonewalled the CFI's FOIA request, but, after the CFI filed a lawsuit to compel the government to release whatever Kecksburg information it had, NASA released some information. However, as Kean said, the information raised more questions than it answered, specifically relating to the filing of Kecksburg discoveries in a file called "Moondust." Moondust was a government program, referenced in State Department documents, under whose auspice unidentifiable objects from space that fell to Earth were cataloged. In fact, not to digress but to make a point, when actress Marilyn Monroe placed a call to then attorney general Robert Kennedy demanding that his brother, President Kennedy, with whom she was having an affair, call her back, she threatened to expose information JFK had told her about Area 51 and the artifacts stored there from the crash at Roswell. Her phone had been wiretapped by the CIA, whose transcription of the call she placed to Bobby Kennedy was filed under Moondust. This indicated that Moondust was a live file back in 1962 and continued to be a live file in 1965 after the Kecksburg crash. What Kean believes she found out dispositively eliminated the Soviet Cosmos 96 based on the U.S. Space Command and Soviet Space Agency records. Therefore, if not Cosmos 96 or a meteor, what was it? The NASA documents offer no affirmative clue and, Kean said, the trail might have gone cold. But, according to some UFO historians, the object that crashed in Kecksburg, and possibly in Needles in 2008, might have had its origins in Germany and then in Poland in the 1940s as a Nazi military experiment that succeeded all too well.

MEN IN BLACK

Among the commonalities between the Kecksburg and Needles incidents was the almost immediate military presence, fifteen minutes in Needles and under an hour in Kecksburg, as if the military were prepared for the retrieval of whatever fell. Witnesses in both areas said that the government presence was intimidating, consisting of surveillance by unidentified vehicles, interrogation by men who seemed to be government agents aiming to suppress the sharing or disclosure of any information about what witnesses saw, and out-and-out threats to anyone going public with information the government wanted to keep secret.

In Kecksburg, the most chilling story about information suppression involved local radio newscaster and reporter John Murphy from WHJB, who interviewed one of the first witnesses to the glowing blue object, Francis Kailp. Based on his first phone call with Kailp, Murphy called the state police, who arrived at the crash site to investigate. After arriving at the site, however, the state police unit informed Murphy that they were contacting the military, an explanation for the sudden appearance of a military security and transport team. Then the state police told Murphy that they could find nothing and there was nothing to report. Another question: If there was nothing at the site—a statement that eyewitness testimony belied—why call in the military? It was a question that Murphy wanted to answer, especially after he heard a trooper on the phone talking to someone official about the police discovery of a pulsating blue object in the ditch. Murphy made a trip to the site, tagging along with a police unit. At the site, he discovered it was cordoned off and he was stopped from going any farther. Convinced that something was being hidden by the authorities, Murphy continued his interviews with witnesses, recording them on audiotape

and taking photographs, until he was confronted in his radio broadcast booth by two men who had identified themselves to radio station
personnel as government agents. One witness who saw them talking
to Murphy in the broadcast studio said she believed Murphy was being intimidated because she could see him shrink and withdraw from
the two men standing over him. Murphy's plans for his documentary
were quickly abandoned after that confrontation, replaced with a version that made no mention of the object that had fallen. People also
noticed that Murphy was a changed man after the confrontation and the
broadcast of his documentary, seemingly withdrawn and prickly to
the point of being incommunicative. Four years later, in 1969, Murphy
was killed in a hit-and-run accident. That crime was never solved.
Was Murphy a victim of government Men in Black who had frightened him into altering his documentary and then, because he knew
too much, eliminated him and the threat of disclosure of secrets
they were assigned to protect?

In Needles, folks also talked about the intimidating presence of Men
in Black. My interview with George Knapp about possible unidentified
military units in Needles turned up some surprising information about
the retrieval team that Riverboat Bob might have seen. "We were working on a story about black helicopters before we started working on
this Needles story," George Knapp said. "We figured out who the personnel in this unit were. They worked out of a very interesting outfit
in Fort Campbell, Kentucky, the 'Night Stalkers.'" The Night Stalkers,
or Project 160, was a very interesting special operations unit with a
history dating back to 1980, when Jimmy Carter was planning his second attempt to rescue the hostages held by the Iranians in Tehran.
When his first operation, Operation Eagle Claw, failed, in part due to a
lack of coordination among the different military units involved and
miscommunication among the personnel on the mission, the military
formed an elite special operations airborne command called Project
160. This top-secret unit might have also been responsible for the Cash-
Landrum incident, which UFO Hunters also covered in our season two.
In that incident this same unit was transporting a flaming radioactive

object across a lonely Texas road outside of Houston and irradiated Betty Cash, Vicki Landrum, and young Colby Landrum.

In 1980, the military was planning the second Iranian hostage rescue attempt, so it made perfect sense to keep the Night Stalker unit top secret. However, when the unit was dispatched on an emergency basis to dispose of a flaming nuclear reactor and, as they flew it in convoy, they had no warning they would fly over a car, which would stop and get an unhealthy dose of radiation. When Cash and Landrum filed suit against the Army for physical damages resulting from the object the Night Stalkers was transporting, the Army refused to acknowledge responsibility because they would have had to disclose the existence of the unit and the case against the Army was dismissed.

George Knapp said that this team was driving back to Las Vegas from Needles, when he ran into the black-suited personnel in the armed convoy. The KLAS-TV team was also in Needles and were confronted by the military team. "They flashed a badge," Knapp said about his meeting with the military unit. "Sure enough they were federal agents, they worked for an agency I had never heard of before, and they transported nuclear weapons." Nuclear weapons? In Needles? "They are highly trained," Knapp said. "They're a dangerous group of people. These guys are commandos. They carry all kinds of weapons. They're very tough customers. I'm not sure they're going to be happy getting this much attention." Even though George Knapp doesn't believe the unit he met up with was necessarily a Men in Black team or that they were in Needles specifically because of the crash, their presence does comport with the military presence in Kecksburg over forty years earlier.

What we do know is that there have been countless witness reports of strange quasimilitary units in black SUVs or trucks shortly after UFO incidents who asked lots of questions, cautioned witnesses to be quiet, and threatened those who they believed would give them trouble or talk too much. And the Needles incident was precisely the kind of incident that would have been a likely target of Men in Black because of all the witnesses and the presence of media. Adding to this suspicion of a government cover-up was the presence of Area 51 Janet planes landing at the Bullhead City airport just days after the crash and retrieval of the object, a crash that might have involved a radioactive device or a nuclear weapon. This led me to the speculation, based on what we knew was true, that this craft, perhaps similar to the device that the Night Stalkers were transporting in the Houston area twenty-eight years earlier, was so radioactive that, like Kecksburg, it had to be retrieved so that it didn't fall into the wrong hands and did not become a public safety hazard. The government responses were too similar to be a coincidence, especially the presence of the Night Stalkers and Area 51 personnel.

However, as Ted said, "What's missing is hard physical evidence and an actual crash site." Both in Kecksburg and Needles, the areas, if there had been a crash, had been completely cleaned up. Pat was struck by the immediate presence of military units in the aftermath of both incidents, units composed of agents who intimidated witnesses. And I believe that the similarities go even deeper, especially the government responses to inquiry. At first they cordon off an area while they retrieve whatever crashed. Then they warn people not to talk about what they've seen. Then they deny anything ever happened, belying the reasons for their own presence in the area. Whatever fell out of the sky, the military seemed intent to keep it secret.

BILL'S BLOG

Subsequent to our episode, George Knapp made contact with a source who told him the unit he'd encountered in 2008, was a unit working out of the Office of Secure Transportation (OST). The source explained that the mission of the unit was nuclear transportation, a high-risk job. The unit was armed and if threatened because they might be transporting nuclear material, they were authorized to protect what they were transporting with all necessary force, even lethal force. Eventually George Knapp was able to meet with the director of the OST who gave him his first ever interview about the unit and the OST. Although their job is transporting nuclear material and anything related to it, Knapp said to me that he has come across other strange rumors about the group, "legendary" among truck drivers, because of their mysterious appearance as quasi Men in Black. Rumors also have circulated that this unit transports downed UFOs, or parts thereof, and even alien bodies. But these are only rumors, Knapp reiterated. But, he conceded, if the government needed to transport aliens or UFOs, this would be the unit that would do it. In

Knapp's words, when he encountered them on the road, his first impression was these guys were "tough customers." And after he learned from the OST director that if the unit Knapp encountered believed he was carrying any nuclear material, they would have taken him out.

My opinion? What a great way to move a UFO, what a great cover for Men in Black, especially if the OST can pick personnel for temporary duty from any federal agency, in which the individual picked has the necessary security clearance, on an as-needed basis for a one-time job. Once picked and assigned, they go black because of the high-risk nature of the assignment and because the government doesn't announce when it's moving highly secure material.

As for the updates pertaining to the Kecksburg episode, the request for information under the Freedom of Information Act and subsequent lawsuit filed by the Coalition for Freedom of Information, the government's response was that it was simply the Russian Cosmos 96 probe even though the government's own tracking information revealed that the Cosmos 96 had a different trajectory and was tracked all the way down. Even so, it would have made perfect sense, had the probe come down in Kecksburg on December 5, 1965, for the OST, had it been in existence, to be the unit to retrieve the Cosmos because it would have had a nuclear reactor, thus requiring the highest security even to the point of threatening uncooperative onlookers with violence. And simply the threat of dangerous radiation would have been enough to scare off anyone. Author and witness Clifford Stone (*Eyes Only: The Story of Clifford Stone and UFO Crash Retrievals,* 2011) once told me, as a specialist in an Army Nuclear Biological Chemical (NBC) retrieval and cleanup unit, that unit was actually used to retrieve downed UFOs and debris and use its NBC designation as a means of keeping witnesses, onlookers, and interlopers away. In fact, Jim Romansky told me that from his first encounter with the Kecksburg object, glowing and pulsating blue in the ditch, that he has had medical problems and illnesses consistent with radiation exposure.

The Kecksburg case is still heavily researched, still importuned, and still tantalizes not only residents of western Pennsylvania, but UFO researchers in general because of the weirdness of the event. But the strangest aspect of the case may not be where the object landed, but where the object began its journey, possibly in Poland in 1945. But this is only speculation.

"NAZI UFOS"

Most people have heard the story of the German experimental superweapons in World War II, such as the rocket-propelled ballistic missile, the jet plane, the rocket plane, and night vision. These were tremendous advances in weaponry and at least one of their scientists, Hermann Oberth, as told to me by Phil Corso (*The Day After Roswell*, 1997), said, when asked about the German rocket program and technological weapons superiority the Germans enjoyed, "We were helped by people from other worlds." That cryptic statement, upon which Oberth did not elaborate, is what motivated *UFO Hunters* to investigate whether there was a weapon so unconventional that there might be a plausible ET connection. What we believed we found, was far more than we expected.

This episode, out of our third season, was, for me, one of the most intriguing and yet disturbing stories we ever covered. The episode took us to Germany, of course, where, in Berlin we met with a ninety-year-old physicist and former member of the SS and later a member of the East German government, who told us the story of the Nazi Bell. We traveled to the Owl Mountains in Poland to see where the alleged Bell was constructed and tested. And we traveled to the shores of the

Baltic Sea to meet with German technology historians at Peenemünde, the location of the first German test range. It was later moved to thickly forested Tuchola and underground to the Owl Mountains in Poland to protect the program from English and American bombing.

THE STORY

Although the story of the Bell dominated our thinking, the larger questions were how did the Nazis acquire the technology they used to develop rockets as modern weapons and propulsion systems for ordnance such as flying bombs, cruise missiles, and rocket planes? Hermann Oberth's statement that the Germans had been helped by people from other worlds, tantalizing enough as it is because it means just what it says, that the Germans were working with extraterrestrials, also brings up the question of how did the Germans come to encounter people from other worlds and what was their relationship?

The Nazi march to explore their extraterrestrial relationships began, believe it or not, in 1871 when Kaiser Wilhelm of the Second Reich sought to expand a version of national socialism, which he called the "pan-German nationalist movement." With that as a planted seed in the German nationalistic psyche, the fertilization came from the Theosophical movement started by Helena Petrovna Blavatsky, the Russian immigrant and controversial medium who settled in New York City and founded the Theosophical Society in 1875. Blavatsky had roamed through Europe and the East, especially India and Tibet, learning new philosophies, "ancient wisdoms," and taught herself to speak a number of languages. It was during her travels that Blavatsky learned of the Great White Brotherhood, "superhuman adepts or masters," believed by many Theosophists and occultists to have directed the development of humankind and prophesied by Blavatsky to become the leaders of all mankind in a new, spiritually adept and advanced society. German nationalists embraced her racial ideas and distorted them into a combination of the occult drawn from Theosophy, virulent anti-Semitism, and the principle of Aryan racial superiority.

Although she could not have known it in her lifetime, Theosophy was destined to exert a strong influence on the German nationalist movement that became the National Socialist, or Nazi, Party some thirty years after Blavatsky's death in 1891.

What would attract some in the Nazi leadership to Theosophy? German nationalists eagerly embraced Blavatsky's racial prediction, which they transformed into the infamous Nazi belief of Aryan racial superiority or the rise of the Übermenschen or "supermen." They also welcomed Darwin's theory of evolution that, when combined with Madame Blavatsky's racial beliefs, concluded that certain races would survive and evolve, while for other races, such as the Jews, their days were numbered. For the virulently anti-Semitic, racist theories couched in pseudo-mystical wrappings that supported their twisted thinking were well received and also gave rise, in the early twentieth century to the idea of eugenics, the creation of a genetically engineered superrace.

Eugenics experiments, the attempts to create a superior race, were carried out by the butcher of Auschwitz, Dr. Josef Mengele, in his experiments on twins, which fascinated him. Even when he was on the run in South America, remaining just steps ahead of the Nazi hunters on his trail, he continued his experiments on fertilization in his attempts to create a master Aryan race. He once bragged to residents of a small Brazilian town where he conducted some of his experiments that he could use a cow to host a human fetus. As we discovered in our trip to Dulce, those Mengele statements seemed to have come to fruition in a series of interspecies hybrid programs after World War II.

Besides stories in the Vedic texts about strange creatures from a distant planet flying around in saucer-type craft, Blavatsky was also inspired by popular occult mysteries by nineteenth-century British author and occultist Lord Edward Bulwer-Lytton. His book *Vril, the Power of the Coming Race*, first published in 1871, talks about a mysterious force called Vril that imbues those who can wield it, the supermen, with incredible powers. Not only did the Bulwer-Lytton novels influence Theosophists, they also had an effect on the whole occult or spiritual underpinnings of German Aryanism. The book's plot concerns an underground utopian society controlled by these supermen, essentially superior beings, who had mastered the Vril. If you're thinking that the Vril sounds like the Force in *Star Wars,* you're right. The Vril can also stand for the chi, as in tai chi, the idea of the life-energy force from Chinese culture. In Bulwer-Lytton's *The Power of the Coming Race,* the force was a psychic power that could be used for good but could also be a destructive force, such as a death ray.

The novel inspired a young Viennese woman, Maria Orsic, who also believed in the psychic power of the German superman and became part of the movement in Germany, in the early twentieth century, to annex Austria to create a union of all Germanic peoples. It was the Vril Society, ultimately linked up with the Thule Society or Thule-Gesellschaft that is credited with being among the early German nationalist organizations to employ the swastika as a symbol or emblem. Orsic was a trance medium who, when she demonstrated her abilities to Rudolf Hess, inspired him to look for a cultural history that would form the philosophical underpinnings for the supremacy of the Aryan race. This, when combined with the Vril theory of the superior masters of society and the virulent hatred of Jews after the World War I armistice, led the early Nazi leaders to fashion their horrific vision of the eradication of all European Jews. Ironically, Maria Orsic was Jewish.

Other early pronational occultist socialist philosophers also weighed in on the supposed coming to power of the Aryan race before the collapse of the Weimar Republic. One of the better-known occult groups was the Armanenschaft originated by Guido von List (1848–1919) who fancied himself a descendent of a long heritage of Teutonic warriors reminiscent of the characters J.R.R. Tolkien described in his *Lord of the Rings* trilogy. Von List had concocted his own premise of a Nordic race imbued with supernatural psychic powers, whom he called the Armanen who used as its emblem, the swastika and were virulently anti-Semitic. A branch of the Armanenschaft, Guido von List's cult, was known as the German Order and began right before the First World War. Like other similar groups, the German

Order embraced virulent ultraright, nationalist and occult societies, and racist beliefs. The German Order was the model for the Thule Society that became a source of influence for the Nazi Party in its early days. There was also serious interest in what was believed to be the continent of Thule, in Greenland, which the occultists described as the earthly origin of the Teutonic race or the Nordic Atlantis. Not surprisingly, the Nazis coalesced around the occultist tradition of racial purity, neopaganism, and occultism, and targeted their evil at the people of Germany, focusing specifically on the Jewish population, the Roma people, those they considered mentally unfit, gays and lesbians, and then throughout nearly all of Europe as their iron-fisted grasp increased.

The defeat of Germany in 1918 by the British, French, and Americans ended World War I, but left Germany thoroughly demoralized and in financial ruin. The armistice, signed in 1919, called for Germany to disarm, eliminate nearly its entire military, agree to new border limits, acknowledge a new, independent Poland, and relinquish all of its colonies. In his unpublished memoir, Dr. Max Jacobson—codenamed "Dr. Feelgood" by JFK's Secret Service detail, according to retired agent Paul Landis (*Dr. Feelgood*, Lertzman and Birnes, New York: Arcade, 2013)—described firsthand the conditions in Berlin, where he grew up, after World War I. He talked about the rationing, the inflation of the German currency, the unemployment, and the desperate nature of veterans of the Kaiser's army once they returned to civilian society. And he described the ominous threats made by proponents of the Third Reich, especially threats against the Jews and other minorities. It was against this background that Adolf Hitler, a World War I veteran, a lance corporal who was awarded the Iron Cross, rose to power as his nationalist rhetoric caught the imagination of a group of former high-ranking army officers, now out of power, who saw in Hitler the ability of a skilled and impassioned orator to galvanize the masses with his vision of Aryan supremacy.

Before he came to power, Hitler was a penniless sketch artist trying to sell his artwork anywhere he could, especially in taverns. He was already virulently anti-Semitic, and when he had money, he would visit inexpensive coffee shops and cafés where he'd expound his warped political beliefs to anyone willing to listen. He blamed Jews and Marxists for Germany's problems and argued that the elimination of international socialism and the resurrection of a nationalist German state, National Socialism, under the hand of a strong leader, would restore Germany. That brought him to the attention of disaffected former army officers.

Hitler's many biographers wrote about his psychic abilities and his strong belief in the occult (Joel Martin and William Birnes, *The Haunting of the Twenty-first Century,* 2013). Hence, he was tantalized by the teachings of the Thule Society and the Vril Society concerning the power of the life force and the belief in the destiny of the Aryan race. He surrounded himself with those who sought historical proof of the origin of the Aryan race, looking to the mystical planet of Aldebaran as the celestial home planet of the Aryans who migrated to Thule. Aldebaran is actually a giant orange star. However, the mythos of an extraterrestrial origin for the supposed super-Aryan race drove the early Nazi thinkers to search for any evidence in all cultures of an extraterrestrial presence in human civilization. Thus, as depicted in the *Indiana Jones* feature films by George Lucas, the Nazis traveled the world, especially to India and the Middle East to find their proof of Aryan supremacy. This search for extraterrestrial origins also dovetailed with early German rocketry pioneers, such as Hermann Oberth and Wernher von Braun.

Oberth is a particularly important figure in the German rocketry program because not only did he experiment with early rocket designs, theorized about multistage rockets, and was a space travel consultant during the 1920s, he believed that flying saucers were real objects navigated by real beings visiting Earth from outer space for centuries. Former NASA manager and MUFON founder and national director John Schuessler, also a guest on *UFO Hunters* in our first season's NASA files episode, has written extensively on Hermann Oberth, his rocketry experiments, and his belief in the existence of flying saucers and extra-terrestrial life, citing Oberth's article in the *American Weekly*, a Sunday supplement published by Hearst and reprinted in *The Milwaukee Sentinel* (October 24, 1954), wrote that it was his opinion that an extraterrestrial presence does exist and that, "It is my thesis that flying saucers are real and that they are spaceships from another solar system. I think they possibly are manned by intelligent observers who are members of a race that may have been investigating our earth for centuries."

Lieutenant Colonel Philip J. Corso wrote in *The Day After Roswell* that Oberth, who'd belonged to an ad hoc "brain trust" in Army research and development in the early 1960s, said the Germans had been helped by people from other worlds after Corso related to him an experience in the Army's New Mexico desert missile testing range at Red Canyon in which he said that he saw a strange craft on the ground disappear before his very eyes. Oberth told Corso that it was probably a "time ship." Simply stated, the pioneer of the German rocketry program believed that not only did ETs and their flying saucers exist, but they had been visiting Earth for centuries and were capable of traveling in time. This is an important underpinning to speculation that there was an ET theory circulating among German rocket scientists, a theory that dovetailed with the philosophers of national socialism who believed that Aryans were descended from extraterrestrials and were destined to rule over civilization on Earth. Hence, scientific, spiritual, occultist, and historical theory all pointed to a belief held by some of the Nazi leaders, including Hitler, that there was an ET connection that bestowed upon the Third Reich a stewardship over the earth.

The Nazi historical researchers also believed that the Indian Vedic texts, which described ancient flying machines called the vimana upon which the ancient deities traveled and wielded powerful explosive weapons, depicted real events not myths, and they sought to discover the power that these deities wielded. The propulsion systems of these flying machines, it was believed, counterrotating cylinders of heavy liquid metal called red mercury, generated an enormous energy field that could power these craft enormous distances and charge their beam weapons. This technology fascinated German scientists, who experimented with a device called Die Glocke, "the Bell," and hypothesized that this could be an antigravity device, a war machine, and, most importantly, a time machine. Hence the Oberth statement to Corso that what he saw in the New Mexico desert was a time ship. Of course, much of the story regarding the hypothetical Bell came from an unnamed former SS officer, who told his story to Polish writer and research Igor Witkowski, our guest on this episode of *UFO Hunters*.

The Germans also had many other "wonder weapons," including the V-1, V-2, and V-3 guided missiles, the rocket plane, and the jet-powered fighter-interceptor, which, because Hitler wanted it to be retasked as a bomber, was never as effective as it could have been in engaging Allied heavy bomber squadrons and the escort fighters who protected them. There was also a theory that the Germans saw in the Horten brothers flying wing the possibility of the development of an intercontinental bomber that could reach North America. The Nazi Wehrmacht believed that if Germany could bomb Washington or New York, they could knock the United States out of the war, strike a separate peace with them, and then focus on the Soviet Army that was pushing toward Germany after the collapse of the eastern front. During the final months of 1944, there was a German plan to fit U-boats with launch ramps on their foredecks for mounting and then launching guided missiles—the first guided missile subs—and maneuver them close enough to New York and Washington to hit them with missiles. *The New York Times* reported in November 1944, that Mayor Fiorello La Guardia was urging the Navy to intercept the German submarines and protect New York, which the Navy did, decimating the U-boat fleet. As recently as thirty years ago, divers off Port Jefferson on Long Island's North Shore described a U-boat, its numbers and insignia removed along with its weapons, lying on its side on the bottom of Long Island Sound, empty, now, of those who navigated her across the Atlantic and a testament to what might have been had Admiral Dönitz's plan to launch missiles toward New York been successful.

We'll never know what happened to the crew, whose bodies simply disappeared from the shipwreck. Was the boat scuttled? Did the crew slip ashore and integrate themselves into American cities? And were the missiles, torpedoes, and other weapons covertly removed by the U.S. Coast Guard? This, like the mystery of the German attempts to package a nuclear warhead; to send airmen into space aboard a rocket plane; to deploy radio-controlled bombs over London, New York, and Moscow; and to reverse engineer a functional flying saucer from the Haunebu flying disk that crashed in the Black Forest are still mysteries of World War II.

THE EPISODE

Was there a connection between the Nazi war machine and something out of this world? We know that one of the greatest evils of the twentieth century was the rise of the Nazi Party in Germany under Adolf Hitler. But what if that evil was connected to one of the greatest secrets of the twentieth century, the appearance of UFOs and encounters with the beings that piloted them? We traveled to Germany and Poland to determine if there was any evidence of the connection between the two. Pat commented that it was right after World War II that the U.S. experienced one of its greatest UFO waves. Did that mean there was a connection? Kevin conceded that the Nazis did have technology that was at least a decade ahead of the U.S. and Britain at the outset of the war, but it was conventional technology at best. We might have been researching the technology, but the Germans actually put much of it into wartime development. It wasn't UFO technology, that was true, but as soon as we brought the Nazi rocket scientists to the United States after the war ended, we suddenly were able to launch V-2s into the upper atmosphere. I reminded Kevin of Hermann Oberth's statement about the Nazis having been helped by people from other worlds. It was too important a statement by one of the fathers of modern rocketry to dismiss or ignore.

Our first guest was U.S. Air Force veteran Bill Lime in Albuquerque, who wanted to show us a mysterious German World War II compass and explain his theory of why it had to be related to UFO technology. The serial on this particular compass was traced all the way back to Nazi Germany where it had been fabricated in 1943. Bill Lime told us that the compass he had acquired was technically called a Peiltochterkompass, a type of gyroscopic compass that only registers in thirty-degree increments and works off a master compass. Kevin explained how the system worked. "The master compass zeroes in on the North Star. Each time the aircraft changes its heading, it activates a motor in the master compass which sends an electronic signal to the Peiltochterkompass. That signal changes the headings on the Peiltochterkompass , which tells the pilot or navigator the precise location of the craft. It all sounds complicated, but it works when the craft cannot rely on Earth's magnetic field for guidance." It is a very uncommon device, which Bill Lime found in a salvage yard in Albuquerque. He said it was listed as "classified salvage." There were two types of salvage: unclassified salvage, which could be sold to the public and classified salvage, which had to be destroyed by the military. Bill Lime said that compass somehow escaped destruction and mysteriously wound up in a scrap yard. Bill Lime said there was no mystery, however, just good old underhanded chicanery when a contractor who was to deliver the compass for destruction slipped it off the truck to make some money on the side. That's how it wound up in the salvage yard.

There were two compelling aspects to the story for us regarding Bill Lime's Peiltochterkompass. First, we had a piece of classified salvage that should have never gone to a scrap yard. Second, it finally wound up in the hands of an Air Force veteran who says he knows what it was used for. Lime said that he recognized it because when he was a young boy he saw a flight of UFOs traveling from the direction of New Mexico across the Texas border and they were turning in thirty-degree increments. A flying saucer that he saw in 1953, he said, looked like "two woks stuck together on top of each other." It was about fifty feet in diameter, reflected light from its bright shiny metal, and on the top there was an electrical discharge that produced very bright colors. There was a trail of ions, Bill said, that sparkled and glittered and gradually faded out as this craft took off. "And then it shot off to a point of infinity in three seconds," Lime said.

"Do you think this was extraterrestrial?" Kevin Cook asked. "Or was this man-made?"

"I never knew of any aircraft or machine that wasn't made by human beings," Lime answered. He said that the German rocket scientists were brought to New Mexico where their work continued on projects they had developed during the war. "But for any ship to go as fast as the ships I saw, you would have to know where the heck you were," according to Lime. "So when I saw the face of this device, I could see it was divided up into thirty-degree increments. So I said, 'Wow, this is a navigational device for one of those ships.'"

The *Hunters* team agreed that there was a mystery concerning this device. How did a device that was supposed to be classified salvage wind up in a scrap yard in New Mexico when, at least on the face of it, it was a German compass that looked nothing like a regular magnetic compass but more like a gyroscope? What was it used for? We had to go to Germany to find out the source of this device. Ultimately, we wanted to find out if there was any connection between UFO navigational technology—assuming that there was any Nazi connection to UFOs—and otherworldly craft. One connection between the Nazis and otherworldly thinking was the Nazi search for ancient artifacts, especially artifacts that bespoke an extraterrestrial provenance from which they could summon an unconventional power. That was the reason, I explained in a white-box presentation, the Nazis were fascinated by the Vril Society and the idea of a life force that could turn human beings into supermen. The Nazis were seeking the foundations of the Aryan race in ancient historical legend. They believed that the Vril Society pointed not to an earthly origin of the Aryan race, but to an extraterrestrial one. And that tantalized the Nazis and suggested that an extraterrestrial technology would advance their goal to dominate all civilization here on Earth.

"The German Vril Society was a society interested in what the Vril is. Vril is a notion of a superpower going beyond atomic power, something that has the capacity to do all kinds of things including powers attributed to UFOs," our guest Alan Greenfield said. "At the end of World War I when Germany was in abject defeat, it was an interest to the German military as a source of power. The mediums in the Vril Society said that this capacity was a force to power UFOs."

At this Kevin perked up, skeptically repeating, "Mediums that were doing exactly what?"

"Okay," Greenfield said. "It is generally thought that mediums simply channel the dead. But there is another group of mediums who channel information that's extraterrestrial or related to ultra-terrestrtial beings and they claim that there is a science that comes from these beings and that if we adapt this science, we learn a lot about the technology we have. Of course the Nazis, buying into that, became more and more desperate as the war turned against them. So they wanted to do aircraft in tune with what these mediums had said. They seemed to grasp the shape of these things, which was saucer-shaped or cigar-shaped just as UFOs are seen today. But they could never get the idea of the power that was involved in these things because even though they used the name 'Vril Society,' they never understood what the Vril really was."

I explained that the Vril was a life force, something like the Force in *Star Wars* that makes things work.

Pat then asked Greenfield, "Could what the Vril learned be the reason that the Germans had a twenty-five-year leap in technology over everyone else?"

"Could it be?" Greenfield said. "It almost certainly was a major part of the Nazi advances in technology."

Alan Greenfield was telling us some very strange stuff. The Germans were channeling extraterrestrial knowledge from the planet Aldebaran. But what was it and how did it match up with what Hermann Oberth wrote in *The American Weekly* and with what he told Corso? And we also knew that the Nazis were absolutely obsessed with advancing their science by any means possible. We took this information to our next guest, Michael Hesemann whom we met in Berlin by the historic Brandenburg Gate, where we asked him how the whole story of the Nazi UFO began.

"First of all," Michael told us, "there were disk-shaped craft developed in the Third Reich. And, you know, the Nazis were also developing the nuclear bomb." Hesemann is a very important German historian who has spent decades researching World War II and the events that led up to it, including the rise of the National Socialists and the Third Reich. More important for UFO history, Hesemann interviewed many German scientists in his pursuit of the history of Nazi wonder weapons, including Hermann Oberth himself.

"I interviewed the German Nazi engineer who developed the German Nazi flying disk," Hesemann revealed. "His idea was that the flying disk could deliver the atomic bomb to Allied capitals. So Hermann Göring started a small project to develop the disk-shaped helicopter, and it went into test flights, but it didn't really maneuver sufficiently." But this, Kevin pointed out, was a helicopter with a different shape and it was all conventional technology. Hesemann agreed, saying that if Nazi Germany had real UFO technology, advanced technology, "do you really think we would have lost the war?" Hesemann speculated: "Of course not, because Hitler would have used everything he had to get to final victory."

I asked Hesemann about the Hermann Oberth quote about the Nazi scientists having been helped by people from other worlds. "True, true," Hesemann said. "After World War II, he joined the UFO movement in Germany. He became the honorary president of the German UFO study group and the study group involved contacts and psychics. He, himself, worked with channelers and mediums and received channeled information. He believed it. He believed he came into contact with extraterrestrials through this channeling medium." This statement was a shocker. The father of German rocketry was a trance medium. How early did Oberth involve himself in channeling and could that be one of the reasons the Germans were able to develop the concepts for their advanced technology that put them twenty-five years ahead of the Allies?

I believed there were two major reasons, among many minor ones, that the Germans lost the war. One, they just couldn't develop this advanced technology fast enough to get it weaponized to deploy to win the war. But the second reason is really intriguing. We know that there were German scientists who refused to let the German high command have this advanced technology in the first place. They denied this technology to the military leadership precisely because they feared what a world dominated by Hitler would mean and so they decided that Germany should lose the war.

After our interview with Michael Hesemann and his tantalizing revelations about Hermann Oberth and what the Nazis might have known about extraterrestrials, we decided to follow up with a trip to the Baltic coast to interview the science historian at the Peenemünde Historical Technical Museum, where the Germans first developed the cruise missile, the V-1, and the first ballistic missile, the V-2.

"Peenemünde was the first huge research center in the world for rocketry, for example, compared to Silicon Valley," said Christian Milldorf Vervoft, director of the Historical Technical Museum at Peenemünde and who has studied every aspect of research and development that the Nazis did there. "This research center was needed to build the first rocket that reached space. This was an innovation because nobody before could produce the thrust of twenty-four tons. The Russians and the Americans at that time were only able to produce one and a half tons." According to Christian, while all superpowers during World War II were working on rocket technology—and modern rocket technology itself was heavily developed by Robert Goddard in New Mexico as early as the 1920s—the Germans somehow found a breakthrough that gave them over sixteen times more power than their adversaries. And this, Kevin Cook reminded us, was in addition to advanced computer technology, closed-circuit television, and deployable jet engines.

Kevin asked why was it that the Germans were so advanced, more advanced than the Allies. It was because, Christian explained, German science was dedicated to the war effort, to weapons development, because their aim was to conquer the entire world and everything was subsumed into that effort. When you have a leadership that can focus their efforts like a laser beam on a specific goal to the exclusion of most everything else, those efforts seem to advance faster.

Pat said he always wondered that if Peenemünde was so secret, how did the Allies, particularly the RAF, find out about it. "In June 1942," Vervoft said, "British reconnaissance planes observed the activity at Peenemünde, and in 1943, the first attack by more than six hundred bombers from the Royal Air Force, and seventy percent of what was here was destroyed." But the bombing did not stop the production of the German rocketry program, even though it did stop the mass production of the V-1 and V-2 weapons. The production had to be moved to where it could be hidden from Allied surveillance and bombing. Thus, the facility was put into Mittelbau-Dora, inside a hill in a concentration camp in the Harz Mountains. This allowed for secrecy and the development of unconventional technology. The man in charge of these facilities was SS General Hans Kammler, an engineer who found solutions to some of the darkest Nazi projects.

"By 1943, the war was lost for the German troops," Vervoft said. "They wanted to build the so-called Wunderwaffe, the wonder weapon that would change the war. The Nazis hoped to change and to win." Accordingly, as Germany was losing the war, a group of scientists invested all their hope in one single weapon, the Wunderwaffe, a weapon so effective, so destructive that even in the face of military catastrophe had the capability to turn the tide of battle and vanquish the Allied forces closing in on both fronts. My questions: Was it a super jet, a rocket plane that could fly to such altitudes it was unstoppable as it swooped down upon defenseless bombers and escort fighters? Was it the guided missile? Or was it a flying saucer? Or was it something else, something so powerful that one stroke and the fortunes of war would turn? That was something we would have to investigate.

Kevin said that he found it pretty convincing that the culmination of advanced technology was the V-2 rocket. Everything we had learned from scientists and historians so far had nothing to do with UFOs or extraterrestrial technology other than what Hermann Oberth had said. Therefore, Kevin said, he dismissed an ET connection to Nazi technology, and, "that was all there was to it." But Pat said, "Just because the scientists we talked to didn't know anything about extraterrestrial technology doesn't mean it didn't exist. Things were pretty chaotic at the end of the war." I said I believed that the Germans might have had contact with something that could have confirmed what they believed about extraterrestrials or they at least believed that the stories in the Vedic texts about aliens with powerful weapons and flying craft were true, and they strove to build just such a weapon. And it might have seeded the technology the Germans pursued.

In October 1942, the Germans launched the first V-2 rocket into space. One has to wonder whether that launch, in addition to the test of a powerful game-changing weapon, was also a signal to extraterrestrials that the Germans were making contact. Moreover, I disagreed with Kevin that all the German advanced weapons were conventional. The Wunderwaffe, I thought was something different, a serious German weapon, some called more myth than real, Die Glocke, "the Bell." And to find out more about this weapon, we traveled back to Berlin to talk to Dr. Axel Stoll a geophysicist, an expert in unified field theory, and an author of a book on advanced technology in the Third Reich.

Stoll said, "This high technology was developed during the Third Reich from flying saucers. Special aircraft and much more."

"Have you heard of anything called Die Glocke?" Pat asked.

"Die Glocke is space-time curvation, easier to understand as time travel," Stoll explained. It, for me, was a major piece of the puzzle. If real, if this device was able to alter space-time, it would explain why the Germans devoted so much effort to its development and consider it a wonder weapon to reverse the tide of war. If we could understand how this device worked, we might get some insight into the workings of flying saucers.

"The work is based on electromagnetic fields," Stoll told us. "One hundred million volts and more. Plasma, too. There are so-called electrogravitational fields. This is the propulsion from the flying saucers."

Kevin agreed that, if real, flying saucers could employ electromagnetic propulsion. Moreover, Kevin explained, "If what Axel Stoll says is true, it would support what Bill Lime told us about UFOs traveling within electromagnetic envelopes."

"Die Glocke is very complicated," Stoll said. "It was constructed in the Project Riese." This was the Riese mine in Poland, a vast underground network of tunnels and caverns. Pat explained that Riese meant "giant." Thus, Project Riese was "giant project."

"Riese was the greatest project during the Third Reich. They had flying saucers and atomic weapons," explained Stoll, putting together his interpretation of the amalgamation of alien technology with ongoing research into nuclear fission since the early twentieth century.

My take on this was that the Bill Lime compass and his description of how the flying saucers he saw as a child maneuvered had led us back to Germany, where that compass was built, to Peenemünde, and thence to Axel Stoll and the secret of Die Glocke. We were at the center of exciting discoveries into the possible relationship between ET and human technology. At this point, we all agreed that we had to get on the trail of the Wunderwaffe to find out if there was any evidence that it ever truly existed, even if only in the minds of those who conceived it. We headed into Poland to the Owl Mountains in Lower Silesia where we would visit our next expert Igor Witkowski at the Riese mine complex, allegedly the home of Die Glocke.

Igor Witkowski is a military historian and the first person to uncover evidence that the Bell might have been built and tested in the Riese mine. He led us through the entrance tunnel over the now decaying tracks deep into a cave over two hundred meters into the side of the mountain. The Riese mine itself housed six development and manufacturing facilities. We were entering one of the smallest facilities even though, to us, it looked enormous. This was one factory, but it was connected to other manufacturing sites in the mountains by a spiderweb of tunnels. We walked through cement-block passage-ways into adjoining tunnels, past machine gun emplacements, guard stations protecting the entrances to the complex, and sentry posts. The machine gun emplacement, Pat commented, proved to him that something very secret was going on in the Riese.

As we marveled at the construction of the facility, Witkowski said that there was a difference between the size of the facilities we were touring that day and the original German plans and diagrams for the complex. There was much more than what we were seeing in 2009 than we imagined. The plans indicated that there should have been something bigger than what we were seeing. To demonstrate his point, Witkowski lit a piece of paper and held it up to a small vent pipe above our heads. As it caught fire, an updraft wooshed so hard that it sucked the burning paper right up into it, just like the flame in a fireplace gets sucked up toward the chimney. This was more than a simple vent. It had to open into another large chamber, but one that we could only see on the original charts.

"The paper is going up six or seven meters," Witkowski said. "But there is no outlet up into the ground on the surface of the mountain. So there must have been some cavity up there." Kevin agreed, saying that because the paper was sucked up so fast, there had to be a blanket of cold air above us that created a pressure differential that pulled the paper through the vent. But because we were so far under the surface, what was above us had to be a large chamber full of cold air. Kevin wanted to get into the upper level, but Witkowski said that all the other entrances had been blown up and there was no access to it.

What we found out was that the facility we were in was just a small part of the complex, which was truly vast, like a small city. It was certainly large enough to hold a weapon that might have been key to ending the war in victory. This facility was the central part of the Riese, where, Igor surmised, was the very place where the production of the wonder weapon was taking place before the end of the war. Pat asked whether Witkowski knew what kind of craft was being developed in this complex. But to answer that, Igor said, he would have to take us to another part of the complex where we would see a different part of the mystery. Igor led us outside to a huge structure he called "the Henge," a circular cement structure with a diameter of over a hundred feet, where, he said, the Bell was tested. Although the Henge resembled the basic design of the underlying support structure of a water tower, something that Kevin pointed out immediately, Witkowski maintained that it was too big for a standard water tower. In fact, he said, he had seen nothing else like it.

"It is painted in camouflage green paint," he said. "Water tower or cooling tower structures are not painted like that. And it has an unusually reinforced structure just as if it had to hold something of a huge weight or there were unusually strong forces weighing on it."

"So you think some sort of important craft was tested here," Kevin said. "This was something of a test rig?"

"It could have been used for testing the Bell, Die Glocke," Witkowski explained.

Kevin had the idea to determine whether the Bell or any other anomalous craft could have been tested there. "If the Bell were as powerful as Igor says it was, especially if it were radioactive, maybe we could still find physical traces on or around the Henge," he said. "Evidence that would be present decades later. So what we're going to do is look for radiation signatures and magnetic aberrations in the center of the Henge."

We began digging through the late-winter snowdrifts still piled up on the frozen ground in the center of the Henge. But as thoroughly as Kevin made us dig, we retrieved no results. Kevin remarked, "After almost seventy years, I was not surprised that we would find no results, even though I was hopeful we'd get some magnetic readings or a spike in radiation." But Witkowski suggested that there might not be any physical trace energy readings because, he said, "the Bell used some kind of torsion field physics related with gravity, but quantum physics as well." It made me speculate whether, if quantum physics and gravity were related to torsion field physics, that might involve time travel. "Yes," Witkowski said, and said with a degree of authority, "it was one of the aspects of this device." He described how the Bell's power could disrupt local space-time. Time travel is something many researchers linked to UFOs.

It worked in such a way that inside the Bell, Witkowski said, "there were two metal cylinders with a liquid metal inside which rotated at such a speed around a common axis, a very high speed, and created a very high discharge of electric current." The electrical field was so intense, that the Bell could levitate and, according to what Witkowski said he gleaned from former Nazi scientists he had interviewed, travel great distances in an instant, even traveling through time. It sounded like science fiction, I admitted. "I found a document," Witkowski said, "that revealed that this was the most important research of the Third Reich."

Kevin, however, was unimpressed with the story, especially the Henge, which, he said, still looked to him much like the support structure of a standard water tower and not a secret weapon test facility. To demonstrate his point, he drove us to a local power plant nearby where he showed us a henge, "a concrete support for a water tower," he said. Point made, point demonstrated. But Pat was unconvinced. "Of course, they're similar, Kevin," he said. "We're not saying that aliens built the Henge, nothing like that. The Henge is not an extraterrestrial structure. Both of these are built by humans, so, of course, they look similar, right?"

"Yeah," I said. "And the fact that it's camouflaged; it's supposed to be camouflaged. You don't have a top-secret weapon to end the war and put a neon sign on it, saying 'top-secret weapon to end the war.'"

"So if you have a test rig, you'd disguise it as a water tower support. Is that what you're asking?" Kevin asked.

"Absolutely," I said. "You hide it in plain sight."

Unmoved by our logic, Kevin said, "You remember at the Henge that there was a factory close by. They needed a water tower for the cooling system. And that's exactly what the Henge was. It was a place for that. It's exactly what we're seeing here. Look guys, it's Occam's razor," he said, pounding home his point. "The theory states that the simplest answer is always the best. And it's clear that we have the same thing going on right here. The simple answer is at the Henge there was a factory. It needed a cooling system, a water tower, and the Henge is simply the base of a water tower."

Two points: First, William of Occam was only talking about the sophistry of medieval logic concerning arguments over church dogma. Second, Occam was not making an absolute statement about every argument. So to apply his statement to what might have been a camouflaged structure, constructed according to the same architecture as other standard supporting structures, supporting an energy-intense object that needed to be tested at various levels of power would be to make an incorrect analogy.

Our next stop, as we pushed our investigation further into what facilities might have supported a Nazi space program, was back in Lower Silesia in a town called Bad Solsburg where Igor Witkowski wanted to show us a sanatorium, a health spa, that was really a covert operation that might have connected the secrets of the Bell to other parts of the Nazi superweapons program. The facility looked just like a small village. But in a reinforced white-walled chamber, that Igor said was a pressure tank was a vacuum chamber used during the war to test the abilities of pilots to withstand the increased g-forces of a rocket launch. Dr. Hubertus Strughold, a Luftwaffe medical officer and one of the German pioneers of space medicine, who was brought to the US in 1947 as part of Operation Paperclip, commanded this facility, Witkowski said. It was here Strughold pursued his research into the effects of intense pressure and weightlessness on pilots at the top of Earth's atmosphere.

"Why was there research in space medicine here, at that time, in the 1940s?" I asked Witkowski.

"We know that they were experimenting here with some kind of spacecraft simulator. We know from the testimonies of former prisoners at the concentration camp here that Dr. Strughold was conducting experiments on humans. They simulated altitudes up to forty thousand meters to ascertain what altitude can the human body withstand."

"Forty thousand meters equals a hundred and thirty thousand feet, and if what Igor is saying is true," Kevin said. "Then these altitudes would cause permanent damage if not immediate death. UFO connection or not, if they were using human subjects in these kinds of experiments, then this is another example of Nazi brutality."

However, in my opinion, this was far worse than simple brutality. It was a part of the ongoing human experimentation on Jewish prisoners that Nazi doctors were conducting throughout Nazi facilities as part of Hitler's avowed aim of murdering all of European Jewry. The most extreme example of this was Dr. Josef Mengele's torturous experiments in human resiliency and endurance at Auschwitz. The records of those experiments went to U.S. intelligence and thence to the CIA, where, decades later, they still inflict themselves on our society in the acts of Ted "Unabomber," Kaczynski, a victim of Dr. Harry Murray's psychological experimentation at Harvard when he was only seventeen; Norwegian mass murderer Anders Breivik, who modeled himself on Kaczynski; Sandy Hook Elementary suicidal mass murderer Adam Lanza, who modeled himself after Anders Breivik; and just in 2014, Army Specialist Ivan Lopez, who killed and injured over ten people at Fort Hood, Texas, and who posted that he was influenced by Adam Lanza (Drs. John Liebert and William Birnes, *Hearts of Darkness,* 2014). Remember the book *I'm OK—You're OK* (Thomas A. Harris, 1967) or psychiatrist Eric Berne's *The Games People Play* (1964)? They, too, were based upon experiments conducted in Canada by psychiatrist and CIA contract researcher Dr. Donald Ewen Cameron and neurosurgeon Dr. Wilder Penfield, both of MK-ULTRA fame to test basic neurological responses to stimuli. This stuff has never ended.

Kevin asked about our location, "Although this is a pressure chamber, this entire facility was a sanatorium and back in the forties there were a lot of bronchial diseases. Couldn't this just be a room to treat those bronchial diseases?"

"It could have been such a room," Witkowski said. "But in an interview Strughold said that he carried out his experiments related to space medicine research right here in this city."

Pat was amazed, asking whether we were standing in the room that Strughold used to test subjects for their ability to withstand pressure because Germany was exploring sending pilots into space. And Witkowski revealed that Strughold himself said in an interview after the war that right in this facility, underground and protected from Allied bombers, he was conducting tests on the effects of high pressure on subjects for the purposes of sending them into space on some kind of a manned craft. "It was something strange, something unconventional and something that would contribute to the end of the war," he said.

"You're talking Wunderwaffe?" I asked.

"Yes," Witkowski answered. "It would have been the wonder weapon."

By this point, here's what we'd been able to ascertain: Nazis might have benefited, at least in the short run, from totally unconventional technology. And the Bell, if it existed, fit the description of the wonder weapon that the Nazis were developing. But, of course, so would the V-2, V-3, and V-1—early versions of what today we call the cruise missile. Had any of these weapons been deployed early in the war so as to provide a long-arm strike capability, and possibility an intercontinental strike capability, the war might have turned out very differently, especially if the Nazis had been able to develop a nuclear warhead. Kevin, however, was very skeptical of a Nazi-UFO connection.

"This is very much like every other UFO case we've investigated," he said. "There's a witness whose story we can't confirm independently. Sources who are dead. Information we can't find strict evidence for. There is usually a door that's closed to us or facilities we can't get access to." But Pat was not about to go down that road with him. "Of course, these things are top secret," he said. "And of course there are mysterious stories. But look at the names we're investigating here, Kurt Debus, Oberth, Von Braun. They all went to work for NASA in the United States." At the end of the war, both the U.S. and the Soviets had their pick of German rocket technology. Both sides had their secret scientist partition program in efforts to grab as much technology as possible.

"Pat makes a good point," I said. "At the end of the war the Germans gave their secrets up and by 1947, we had our own rocket program." It was a matter of recorded fact that after the end of the war many Nazi scientists came to work for the U.S. For us to follow the trail of any Nazi-UFO connection, we would have had to follow the lead of these Nazi scientists. And that trail took us to Huntsville, Alabama, and NASA, where we sought information about Operation Paperclip and the American space program. We spoke to aviation historian Mike Schratt who specializes in researching how the so-called black budget covers up clandestine military operations.

"Operation Paperclip started in 1946," Mike began. "It was to bring former Nazi scientists and aeronautical engineers into the United States, and they were actually given political immunity in exchange for technical expertise." Some of these scientists like Strughold, Von Braun, and Kurt Debus were actually war criminals who should have been tried at Nuremburg for the deaths and torture they inflicted on concentration camp prisoners. But retribution for their crimes was washed away because the U.S. was desperate to gain a technological advantage over the Soviets.

Pat told Mike Schratt that we were investigating the possibility that some flying saucer technology came into the United States from Germany. And Mike said that there was a paper trail to reference for this theory from Wright-Patterson Air Force Base air materiel command that tracks how the technology in question was brought from the Third Reich and trickled into the American aerospace industry. The paper trail indicated that from the military air war strategy of the Third Reich, the technology flowed into German industry and from there into U.S. intelligence at Wright-Patt, T-2, the air military intelligence command, and thence into the U.S. Air Force, then the Navy and the Army, and ultimately into the military aeronautical industrial complex. T-2 analyzed all the documents pertaining to Operation Paperclip as well as UFO reports. "In fact," Mike said, "we have some evidence that the British and Canadian designs were procured from German originals. They were working on what was called a VTOL supersonic gyroplane using a radial thrust engine. And that's Project Y."

Pat explained that Project Y was an attempt to create a vertical take-off and landing plane, a kind of space car that was better known as the Avrocar, films of which show how hard it was to corral a flying saucer. But Kevin was more interested in whether any technology from the Bell was transferred to the United States.

"The Bell," Mike said, "which was approximately fifteen feet high, twelve feet in diameter, had two counterrotating drums on the upper section of the body and a central shaft that ran down the center of the craft that terminated in what was called the 'thermos bottle.' And, from the Germans own documents, we know that a chemical called Serum 525 was actually pumped into this vehicle and that represented the plasma vortex that was created by this craft." I asked, looking at Schratt's diagram of the Bell whether there was some sort of lettering around the base of the craft. He acknowledged that and told us that "Back in December 1965, we had an almost identical craft crash in the woods of Kecksburg, Pennsylvania, and it, too, had the same sort of hieroglyphic writing."

Kevin was quick to relate the similarities between the two craft to the interest of the military, and NASA, to retrieve the Kecksburg craft immediately after it crash-landed, almost as if they knew it was coming. The line of reasoning, he said, was that Nazis created Die Glocke, their technology came to the U.S. along with the German scientists, and they created more of these craft. That was one possibility. I asked whether there was any human link between Die Glocke from the 1940s and the Kecksburg object. Mike said, "In fact, the person who was the senior design engineer for the Bell program in the 1940s was a man by the name of Kurt Debus, an electrical engineer and an officer in the SS." Debus, brought to the United States during Operation Paperclip was launch director at NASA between 1962 and 1974. If he was a director at NASA in 1965, and we know he was working at Kennedy Space Center at that time, could he be the human link between the Bell and Kecksburg? If so, it might be evidence that some of the UFOs were man-made, reverse engineered from German technology. Thus, some of what we're seeing up there isn't "them," it's us.

"When you spend four hundred billion dollars per year on classi-fied black-budget programs, you are going to get something for your money," Schratt said.

"And where would you keep those projects?" I asked.

"You would keep those at Edwards North Base Complex and some of them at MacDill Air Force Base, some of them at Wright-Patterson Air Force Base, and the remaining craft are at the remote test site in Nevada." That would be Groom Lake or Area 51.

It was more than curious that many of the Nazi scientists who were brought over wound up either in New Mexico, Texas, and Nevada, all of which are UFO hotspots.

Pat was really impressed by what Mike Schratt had told us and the plans he had shared. "There's no disputing that the Germans were twenty-five years ahead of everybody else." I asked whether it was fea-sible that the Germans were actually contemplating putting a manned craft into outer space. It was not only feasible, Kevin said, it was Strughold, working for NASA, who developed the first pressurized spacesuit in 1958. Dr. Strughold became the head of the NASA space medicine program and played a major role in getting human beings safely into space. "It seems to back up Igor's theory that the Germans were close to putting a man in space." And for Pat, the most impres-sive aspect of our investigation was our visit to the vast underground factories at the Riese complex in Poland. "If they were developing some kind of Wunderwaffe, that would have been the perfect place to do it," he said. "The more desperate they got, the more they embraced secret concepts and ideas. The result? Nazi experimental craft like the Bell." We speculated what the world would have been like had the Nazis been able to launch that craft and send it wherever they wanted to send it, send it with an atomic bomb. What kind of a world would we have today?

Whatever the original source of Nazi technology, we established the link between some aspects of UFO technology today and what the Nazis were working on before and during the war. We established the link, at least on paper, between Nazi technology and early experiments like the Avrocar and our own rocket program. After all, it was Kurt De-bus, Director of the Bell project and subsequently of NASA, who was instrumental in the development of the Saturn V booster rocket that launched the Apollo astronauts to the moon. We know that Von Braun, Oberth, Debus, and Strughold came to the United States in Operation Paperclip and revolutionized conventional aircraft technology. But what else might they have revolutionized? Did they, we asked, bring us the technology of UFOs? It was, of course, pure speculation.

BILL'S BLOG

There have been more than a few studies about the relationship of Nazi technology and UFOs just as there have been many studies, including mine and Joel Martin's *The Haunting of Twentieth-Century America* and *The Haunting of Twenty-first-Century America* (2011, 2013) about the mystical aspects of Nazi philosophy, such as it was, and Hitler's cult beliefs and their relationship to Nazi secret technology. For an excellent overview of this history, see Joseph P. Farrell's *Secrets of the Unified Field: The Philadelphia Experiment, The Nazi Bell, and the Discarded Theory* (2008) and *The SS Brotherhood of the Bell: The Nazis' Incredible Secret Technology* (2006). What I was hoping for in this episode was to avoid the wow factor in exploring the history of Nazi technology and to focus on the science and the physics of what the German Wehrmacht sought to develop absent as much cultism as possible. I also wanted the episode to focus on the facts about the German rocketry engineers we revere so much in America because of their contributions to our space programs after the war and right through the Apollo program. There was no doubt about the contributions of Von Braun, Oberth, Debus, and Strughold, just as there was no doubt about the war crimes these men committed and their escape from the Nuremburg tribunal. Moreover, we should note their reliance upon the work of American rocketry pioneer Robert Goddard well before the start of World War II. For all their developmental accomplishments, ultimately, their technology did not turn the war around in their favor. In fact, Hitler himself was so convinced of the superiority of his aerospace technology that he relied on his existing aircraft to confront the Allied bombers until it was too late to deploy his more advanced jet-propelled Messerschmitts and his experimental rocket plane. Even the German ballistic and cruise missiles, which could have made a big difference in the war, were subjected to Allied bombardment of their development sites early in the war and only got to be deployed after the war was already lost when the German's eastern front collapsed. All of these historical events were the basis of our investigation into whether the Nazis had any connection to UFOs.

What the episode showed was that, indeed, the Nazis had very advanced technology and had possibly created a fantastic device called Die Glocke, also the subject of much conjecture and myth. For example, one theory concerning the time-travel aspect of the Bell posits that even if the device were capable of transporting a small crew back in time, what would that accomplish? Would we start another timeline, leaving our original timeline intact so that we actually changed nothing? Would we cause a catastrophe in our own timeline? Alternatively, there is the theory that the Bell was not a craft or a weapon at all, but a type of nuclear fuel enrichment device to enable the Germans to assemble a nuclear warhead that would devastate London, thus knocking England out of the war and allowing the Germans to negotiate a separate peace that would allow them to turn their full remaining might against the Soviets?

Another possibility involved bombing New York or Washington with nuclear-tipped V-2s launched from submarines. We know from articles in *The New York Times* from November 1944, that Mayor Fiorello La Guardia admonished the air defense command over New York to prepare for such an attack from U-boats. We know also that Admiral Dönitz did launch a fleet of U-boats to attack the United States and that we repulsed them with antisubmarine vessels and aircraft. Perhaps even today, as it existed at least three decades ago, there was a U-boat lying on its side on the bottom of Long Island Sound just off Port Jefferson, Long Island. Was it part of the Dönitz fleet?

The possibilities of all these potential outcomes were in the backs of our minds as we explored the true history of Nazi secret weapons that might, or might not, have been related to UFO technology. But the investigation was eye opening in that we actually visited the very places that would shape our space technology and rocket program for the ensuing fifty years after the war. But in so doing, we revisited the horror of the Nazi Reich, the mass slaughter of innocents, and the imprisonment of nearly an entire population. We actually stood inside an execution chamber and contemplated what an awful world it would have been if the Nazis had developed the weapons they were actively working on as the Allies closed in on both fronts.

Still intriguing was the possibility, although remote, that the Kecksburg craft was actually the Nazi Bell or a device related to or similar to it. Also of interest was the presence of SS officer and later NASA director Kurt Debus when NASA personnel helped retrieve the object in 1965. Leslie Kean and John Podesta are correct when they push the U.S. government and NASA to come clean about their roles in the Kecksburg event. They know far more than they are willing to tell and obfuscate rather than simply tell the truth.

Telling the truth, however, is exactly what led our subject

James E. McDonald, a respected professor of meteorological physics at the University of Arizona to wind up dead. And his story was one of our most popular episodes during season two of *UFO Hunters.*

THE LOST UFO FILES OF
PROFESSOR JAMES E. McDONALD

an an academic dedication to seeking the truth about the UFO phenomena, real or not, a dedication so intense that, during a heightened period of domestic intelligence surveillance in the U.S., the government places the investigator on its radar and eventually winds up being instrumental in the investigator's death? Sounds like a conspiracy writer's nightmare, but it really happened. The investigator and ultimate victim of his own investigations was a meteorology professor, a climate physicist, named James E. McDonald. McDonald was one of the few UFO researchers to testify before the United States House of Representatives, which he did in 1968 as the Cold war, the Vietnam War, and the Civil Rights movement all came to a head. The lengths he went to in his search to collaborate with scientists and potential UFO researchers from other countries, particularly the Soviet Union, brought him to the attention of the FBI, while his wife Betsy's involvement with the Black Panthers and her strident support for civil rights created a perfect storm of what the FBI saw as a form of subversion. FBI files concerning McDonald obtained by the Center for UFO Studies under the Freedom of Information Act were heavily redacted, but make note of McDonald's belief that UFOs "are extraterrestrial and are real."

We set out in the "Lost Files" episode to explore the investigations of James McDonald, interviewing our friend and colleague Stanton Friedman and UFO and paranormal historian Ann Druffel, author of a critical biography of McDonald (*Firestorm: Dr. James E. McDonald's Fight for UFO Science*, 2003). As I wrote on the *UFO Magazine* blog at the outset of our episode's first broadcast:

> Unless there's a change in the schedule, this week's *UFO Hunters* episode on Wednesday night on History is about the James McDonald files, comprehensive records of his research into some of the most important UFO cases since Roswell. McDonald was the senior physicist at the Institute for Atmospheric Physics at the University of Arizona in Tucson, which is where his files are now stored.
>
> In this week's episode, Pat, Ted, and I visit the University of Arizona library and select three cases for follow-up investigation. The cases are: RB-47, which Ted investigated along with our guest expert retired Rocky Mountain Bureau Chief of Aviation Week Bill Scott, who knows his radar and his aircraft; Lonnie Zamora, whose chilling sighting in Socorro, New Mexico, is as compelling today as it was decades ago, and who tells Pat all about it; the Rex Hefflin photographs, which I investigate with the help of celebrated UFO researcher and author Ann Druffel, experts from the Polaroid camera company, and photo analyst Terrence Masson, who joins Ted Acworth in a detailed digital analysis of the Heflin photographs and the military's attempt to discredit them as a hoax.
>
> This episode uncovered so much information that is was impossible to squeeze it into a one-hour program. Stan Friedman explained that McDonald was so meticulous in his research and so detailed in his attention to the facts that the claims of UFO debunkers actually collapsed under the weight of McDonald's arguments. Stanton provided us with an overview of McDonald's congressional testimony

202 ✦ UFO HUNTERS

and his submission of case evidence. Betsy McDonald, McDonald's widow, also described James McDonald's inner demons, his ideations of suicide that he wrote in his journal well before he actually did commit suicide. She also described the couple's involvement with radical politics in the late 1960s, which might have been a casus belli for the Nixon Administration to investigate the couple. And the release of the FBI files on McDonald revealed that he and his wife, because of their sympathies with left-wing and anti-Vietnam War groups in the late sixties caught J. Edgar Hoover's attention.

The story of James McDonald is fraught with all types of conspiracies. At one point, because McDonald had the temerity to present his findings about UFOs before Congress in probably the most comprehensive science-based, case-study document in the history of UFOs in America, the FBI sought to discredit him among his colleagues. McDonald also became very frustrated by the lack of interest the United States government had in UFOs. Of course, McDonald didn't realize that the military was taking a very active interest in UFOs, fighting an air war with them in the 1950s. But on the surface, was "Ho-hum, there are no UFOs." Even then representative Gerald Ford got House Armed Services Committee chairman Mendel Rivers to hold hearings on UFOs in 1966, but was castigated by the director of Project Blue Book, who accused him of staging a political event.

McDonald, because he did not get the reaction from Congress that he wanted, took it upon himself to contact scientists from other countries about their interest or experience with UFO research. He even went so far as to make contact with Soviet scientists and contact the Soviet consulate. This, as far as the FBI was concerned, combined with his and his Betsy's contacts to radical groups of the day, was enough to target him. The FBI then went to McDonald's colleagues to gather information about him, solicit negative opinions about his UFO research, and to see if a case could be put together against him for subversion.

McDonald also raised the hackles of federal lawmakers because of his opposition to the SST, the supersonic transport aircraft, which he, along with other atmospheric scientists, believed could severely harm the earth's ozone layer. He was ridiculed for this testimony before Congress by Massachusetts representative Silvio Conte—in whose district parts of the supersonic transport would be manufactured—for lacking all credibility because he believed in the existence of "little green men" and the flying saucers that brought them to Earth. Of course, McDonald's reservations about the physical impact of the SST on the upper atmosphere had nothing to do with his research into the scientific basis of UFOs, but that was seemingly of no consequence to Representative Conte and others in Congress who, in my opinion, used any smear they could conjure up to bring money into their districts at the expense of the environment and public health. The derision McDonald had to endure at the hands of lawmakers possibly pushed him further into the relentless hopelessness that was at the heart of his suicidal ideations.

There is a conspiracy theory floating about—one that's not entirely implausible—that the FBI finally got to him through his wife. Because McDonald had manifested thoughts of suicide, even written a poem about suicide, the FBI thought that he might put himself to rest given the right set of circumstances. Therefore, and this is only conjecture not an accusation, the FBI or some clandestine arm of government, inserted a dupe into one of the socialist meetings that Betsy attended to attempt to garner Betsy's affections. Perhaps this person wooed her, initiated a sexual affair with her, and when Betsy sprung her wish for a divorce upon her husband because she was in love with this new person, McDonald tried, not once, but twice, to kill himself. His first attempt blinded him and left him wheelchair bound. His second attempt was successful.

Thus, the field of ufology lost one of its greatest researchers and the government put to rest one of its greatest threats to the cover-up of UFOs. True? False? Different scholars have different opinions.

You'll find Ted's investigation into RB-47, the strange object that popped up on radar, was picked up on other radar, and literally flew circles around one of our most advanced electronic countermeasures aircraft of the time, particularly fascinating. Pat's interview with Lonnie Zamora is a real eye-opener. And I think we put to rest the Air Force's debunking of the veracity of the Heflin photos once and for all. This is a real science-based episode, and I think a particularly strong one.

James McDonald, besides becoming a target of the FBI, was also the subject of particularly vicious attacks by debunkers, such as CIA operative Phil Klass and branches of the military, who actually hoaxed their own debunking. In this episode, we set out to explore McDonald's career and to debunk his debunkers by revisiting his research and testing the arguments of the debunkers with modern scientific experiments. The results were astounding. Our episode covered the story of James McDonald and his most important cases: The Lonnie Zamora sighting, the Rex Heflin flying saucer photographs, and the encounter between our RB-47 surveillance aircraft and a UFO. We also sought to explain how McDonald's academic career fed into his interest in UFO investigations. And we explain how his political sentiments; his reaching out to scientists behind the Iron Curtain; his wife's political activities; the nature of the political environment during the Nixon administration's COINTEL program; and the fear that McDonald's research could compromise our nation's most closely guarded secret all coalesced into a type of perfect storm that put him into the crosshairs of government security watchdogs, particularly J. Edgar Hoover. Ultimately, we tried to investigate the nature of McDonald's suicide and how the strange intimate relationship between Betsy McDonald and a visitor to the meetings of the Socialist Party, to which she belonged, resulted in her asking her husband for a divorce, which finally led to his suicide. We ask, was this a setup by those out to eliminate him as a perceived threat and was Betsy McDonald the perfect foil of a dark and ugly branch of U.S. counterintelligence that plotted the death of James McDonald? Following this path made this one of our most interesting and intricate episodes.

THE EPISODE

Near sunset in the Arizona desert in 1954, climate physicist at the University of Arizona, Professor James McDonald, was driving with four other meteorologists when he noticed a strange light off in the distance hovering over the mountains. He pointed it out to his colleagues, but none of them was able to identify it. It soon disappeared without any reaction from McDonald's friends in the car. None of the other occupants in the car could have known that mysterious light in the sky and McDonald's taking notice of it had just changed the course of the history of UFO research in the United States.

Former naval officer James McDonald had become fascinated, both academically and scientifically, with the nature of UFO studies. The more his fascination grew, the more he believed he had to get involved. Over the ensuing sixteen years McDonald interviewed over five hundred witnesses, uncovered important government documents, testified before the House of Representatives, and gave presentations about his research to huge crowds across the country, his academic standing giving him much credibility. As Pat Uskert reminded us, McDonald was one of the first people to take hard science into the world of UFO research and bring it into the scientific community.

Our investigation began with a visit to the archives of McDonald's research at the University of Arizona to find the cases we thought were most illustrative of the types of research McDonald conducted. We planned to reinvestigate them, follow the paths of arguments of the debunkers who tried to discredit McDonald's work, and to see if McDonald's research held up to our own scientific reevaluation. We wanted to bring McDonald's work into the twenty-first century. At the archive we met with Scott Cossel, who led us into the vault where McDonald's special collection was housed. It was a restricted area, but we were granted special access.

Ted, searching through the library stacks, remarked about the extensive amount of information McDonald had amassed and the reams of evidence he'd compiled from his handwritten notes to film and video and to actual artifacts. "There could be some very interesting information here," Ted suggested, and the three of us searched through the files for the cases we found most fascinating and most compelling to reinvestigate.

I focused on the Rex Heflin photos, a series of four pictures of what looked, at first glance, like a flying hubcap floating over an intersection in Santa Ana, California, and caught on camera by an Orange County road inspector, who had never intended to make them public. Ultimately, Heflin found himself caught in a web of intrigue, derision, and a strange group of folks who represented themselves as investigators from the North American Air Defense Command, but whose very presence was downright unearthly. I remarked that these images had become the Holy Grail of ufology. If they're real, they were among the best pictures of a UFO anywhere.

Ted Acworth dug into the 1957 RB-47 sighting, when a UFO reportedly pursued a U.S. Air Force crew for over ninety minutes and seven hundred miles. One of McDonald's most compelling cases, the incident included three verifiable sources: the pilot, a ground radar station, and the plane's state-of-the-art countermeasure technology. The object picked up by the three different sources displayed staggering capabilities, and, assuming it was the same object that all three sources picked up, it still remains one of the most verifiable sightings and encounters in American ufology.

"This one looks pretty good," Ted told Pat, "because it's not just witness testimony. If we can recover more technical data about the radar, and it wasn't just the radar system on board the aircraft but also the radar on the ground because there were active radar installations that actually picked up the UFO at the same time, we may have something." Correlating all this data and talking to experts about the RB-47 itself and its capabilities, Ted believed, would help corroborate what McDonald believed.

Pat Uskert was intrigued by the 1964 Socorro, New Mexico, sighting by police officer Lonnie Zamora, of a strange craft on the ground in the desert. The case involved a shiny capsulelike object that blasted off from the desert floor leaving behind hard physical evidence of its presence. "In the Zamora file there were sketches, photographs, and his own testimony," Pat said. "What I want to do is to use our modern tools and technology to pick up where McDonald left off and see what actually happened that day to Lonnie Zamora. After all these years this has never been resolved." Of course, skeptics have argued that Zamora was the victim of a practical joke perpetrated by students at a nearby college. But Pat believed that McDonald had pointed to physical evidence that would support Zamora's testimony that he saw something otherworldly and Pat was out to test the veracity of that physical evidence and whether it comported with Zamora's description of what he saw.

The files we researched were the culmination of seventeen years of McDonald's research, which he began assembling in 1953 while he was a professor at the University of Arizona. Within the McDonald files are cases originally compiled by Project Blue Book and reopened. His research uncovered some of the first proof that the CIA was investigating UFOs. His documents revealed the possibility that the Air Defense Command, Air Force Intelligence, and the Strategic Air Command were involved in UFO incidents. He concluded that the public was being deceived. His conclusions, tragically, cost him his life.

THE REX HEFLIN CASE

McDonald was fascinated by the Heflin case, a case about which McDonald was originally quite skeptical. But despite that skepticism, he couldn't let it go. Even though he dismissed one of the photographs as not real, the other photos in the series fascinated him and he included the case as one of his most important investigations. Finally McDonald came to believe that all the photos depicted a real event.

The events began on August 3, 1965, in Santa Ana, California, at approximately 12:30 P.M. when traffic investigator for the Orange County road department Rex Heflin was about to take a photo of a tree branch that was obscuring a road sign. But out of the corner of his eye, he witnessed something fascinating. A saucer-shaped craft was moving across the horizon at what he estimated to be a hundred and fifty feet above the ground. He was transfixed and told his coworkers that he pointed his Polaroid 101 instant camera at the object and snapped a series of three shots of the object. As the object traveled left to right across the road, the first photo, taken through Heflin's front windshield, shows a saucerlike object, like a flying disk-shaped hubcap, that appeared to be off in the distance flying above the ground at the edge of the roadway. The second photo shows the same disk taken through the passenger-side window of Heflin's truck. In the third photo, also taken through the passenger-side window, the object looks as if it were flying away from the camera. Within two minutes of the initial sighting, the object disappears, leaving behind a peculiar smoke ring floating in the sky, which Heflin captured in a fourth photo he snapped from outside the truck.

The other interesting incident that occurred during Heflin's sighting in Santa Ana involved the radio in his van, which suddenly was blanked out by electrical interference when the object appeared. After the object disappeared from view, the van's radio came back to life. Heflin's boss offered no explanation for the performance of Heflin's radio, which checked out as perfectly functional after the incident. The only possible explanation for the interference would have been that Heflin had keyed his mike, thus sending out a carrier signal that would have blocked any incoming transmissions. But Heflin said he did not do that. A similar type of electrical interference with an electrical device would occur in September when Heflin was visited by two men claiming they were from NORAD and were investigating the incident. The photos were heavily investigated by all branches of the military.

"James McDonald wasn't the only person fascinated by the Rex Heflin case," I said. "The Air Force, too, investigated it as well as Project Blue Book, and the infamous Condon Committee investigated it. All of those groups dismissed the case as a hoax." For the record, the Condon Committee's findings, mainly the executive overview of Dr. Edward Condon at the University of Colorado, said that UFOs, which were more illusion than real, and an investigation into them was unlikely to yield any serious scientific results, and, in any event, posed no threat to national security. Thus, UFOs were not worthy of investigation by the Air Force. That moved the Air Force to close down Project Blue Book in 1970, their official public inquiry into the nature of UFOs. But none of that satisfied James McDonald, who was convinced not only were Condon's conclusions deeply flawed and showed a blatant disregard for the real evidence presented by some UFO cases, but that more scientific study was needed about the Heflin case in particular.

My follow-up on the Heflin case and McDonald in general took me to Pasadena, California, where I met with Ann Druffel, whose 2003 book, *Firestorm: Dr. James E. McDonald's Fight for UFO Science,* was a serious biography and critical study of James McDonald and his years-long effort to bring the study of the science behind the reality of a UFO presence before the United States Congress and the world's scientists. Ann has kept original copies of the Heflin photographs and has become an expert on the case along with Stan Friedman.

The irony behind the Heflin photos, Ann told me, was that even though most people believed these photos constituted absolute proof that flying saucers were real and visiting Earth, "Rex Heflin didn't think anything about it. He had lent them first to two military sources that wanted to analyze them, and both of these sources returned them," Ann said. Heflin did not think, at first, he'd photographed a flying saucer because he believed the object in the photo was an experimental craft flown from the nearby El Toro Marine base, which was why the military was so interested in the photos. But then, according to Heflin's own files, after a phone call from a man claiming to be from the North American Air Defense Command (NORAD), two men representing themselves as coming from NORAD asked him if they could borrow the photos. Ann continued, "Heflin was used to working with official sources because of his job. He gave them the photos, expecting that they would be returned in a few days, but they never were. All he had left were second-generation copies."

There is another weird aspect concerning the self-announced

NORAD representatives who visited Heflin to take his original photos. Prior to the NORAD representatives showing up at his door, in
September 1965, Heflin received a setup phone call from someone identifying himself as a NORAD officer, asking for a meeting so Heflin
could give NORAD the photos for analysis. The person on the phone
strongly advised Heflin not to talk about his sighting or the photos with
anyone. When the two individuals, dressed in civilian clothes, showed
up at Heflin's house a few days later, Heflin said that only one of them
came to his door. The other stayed in the car, but, strangely, when
Heflin looked at the car, he saw a purplish glow coming from inside the
car, a glow he could not identify, but which raised no obvious suspicions
at the time. As the one representative stood in his doorway, Heflin also
noticed that his high-fidelity receiver inside his house suddenly cut out,
blanketed by some type of interference. At that moment, Heflin did
not connect the interference on his hi-fi with the interference he experienced on his van's radio when the object in his photos flew across
the road.

After Heflin complained that his original photos were not returned
by NORAD, the Air Force made public its review of the photos, officially labeling them a "photographic hoax." Then, absent the originals
and with only copies of the originals to analyze, some debunkers
claimed to see a line just above the UFO indicting some type of wire or
connection to the object. Others disagree, saying these are alterations
or defects seen only in the copies. Without the original photos, there
was no way to be sure. Then, suddenly, other copies of the photos began to spread through the UFO community, copies, Ann said, that had
been altered.

"So if one were paranoid," I suggested, "one could say that there was
some sort of a disinformation program going on with various copies
of the photos that kept turning up." Some conspiracy theorists believe
that the originals of the photos were taken by the men announcing
themselves as NORAD representatives for precisely this reason, se-
questering the originals and distributing copies that had been altered
to debunk the originals and, eventually, McDonald himself. But then,

almost twenty years later, something miraculous happened to Heflin. "One day his phone rang," Ann said. "And a woman's voice said, 'Have you checked your mailbox lately?' And though Rex was puzzled by the message, he went out and saw an envelope there in his mailbox, and there were the three original photos that the so-called NORAD men had borrowed twenty years before."

Ann Druffel is the closest source to the original photographs taken by Heflin. She gave us copies of the originals to analyze, which we planned to do with Terrence Masson and Ted Acworth. Rex Heflin died in 2005 and never wavered in his story that he had photographed an unnatural object, a real object that was very unusual. But the question remained: Did Heflin fake the photos or were these images real? Was this a real object he captured with his Polaroid camera? Our job was to determine whether the line seen in the photos that debunkers claimed was holding up the object was real or simply an anomaly on a copy of the original photo. We relied on McDonald's notes from his files along with Heflin's photos to see if the object in the photos was real. Also, I tested out the theory posed by debunkers that the 1950s Polaroid 101 camera Heflin was using could not possibly have snapped off the first three photos in the twenty seconds Heflin said it took. The entire incident happened too quickly, debunkers have argued. The Polaroid camera, which developed the image inside the camera, was too slow to catch that entire sequence as it was happening. Thus, the photos had to be staged and hoaxed. I would test out the speed of the camera with Ted McClelland, a technical expert from Polaroid, who brought along with him an authentic original Polaroid 101 camera, the exact same model Rex Heflin used in his everyday work for the Orange County road department and that he used to take the series of photographs of the object that looks like a flying saucer.

"As in most Polaroids," McClelland explained. "The photo package goes into the back of the camera." When the back film door is closed the camera is locked tight, admitting no light except through the shutter to expose the film. When the operator clicks the shutter, he or she has to slide the frame out of the back of the camera slot immediately so that the chemicals can process the exposed film frame. The frame includes the exposed photograph so that the actual developing takes place outside the camera, not inside.

Ted McClelland conducted the first test of the camera's ability to snap off three shots in twenty seconds or less. He snapped the shutter while I clicked the time clock. McClelland was able to snap four photographs in seventeen seconds, beating the twenty-second three-photo requirement. This meant that an operator, Rex Heflin, could have caught all three images of the object crossing the road in front of his truck. Therefore, debunkers were wrong about the speed at which Heflin claimed to have taken his photos of the object. This debunking claim is now off the list.

Next up was the sharp focus of the object on the Heflin photographs. Was it too focused, too sharp? Did the sharpness of the object in the photos suggest a double exposure, thus a deliberate hoax on Heflin's part? A double exposure on a Polaroid 101 means that two photos are taken on the same frame of film so that one image is imposed upon another. If this is what Heflin did, he would have had to have taken a first photo of the sky through his windshield and not removed the frame. Then he could have thrown a hubcap into the air and taken that photo on the same frame, which he kept in the camera. Thus, the image of the hubcap would appear in the frame of the sky, thus looking as if the hubcap were flying through the sky so that it resembled a flying saucer. We tested for this, too. Debunkers have said that this is exactly what happened because the big clue was that every part of the through-the-windshield photo was in focus, the object, the background, and the frame of the interior truck windshield. How to explain this?

Depending upon the film stock and the distance from the lens, objects in different parts of the film, foreground and background, can appear out of focus. In motion pictures and in many action photos, especially in sports, the photographer deliberately focuses on a specific object so as to render the background out of focus. This is a function of depth of field: which objects are deliberately kept in focus and which are not? How many times in a movie have we been focused on a background object in a frame and then the operator changes the focus to an object in the foreground, thereby deliberately taking the background out of focus. Heflin's ability to capture a crisp foreground and background led many to believe he had set the shot up as a double exposure.

"Setting the camera lens to infinity and using 3000 ASA speed film, you would be in focus from three feet to infinity," Ted McClelland explained. In this way, Heflin's camera could have kept all the disparate objects in the film in focus at the same time as well as the centerline on the road going off into infinity. Therefore, the camera was capable of keeping everything in focus. This possibility debunks the argument that because everything in the photo was in sharp or crisp focus, it meant that the photos were double exposures. The photos didn't have to be double exposures to keep all the objects in the frame sharp and crisp.

Next debunker argument up was the fourth photo of the smoke ring, which seems to show a smoke ring that lingers after the object, according to Heflin, flew off. Even McDonald had a problem with the fourth photo because the first three photos of the image, taken from inside the truck, show a clear sky in the background. But the fourth image of the smoke ring, taken from outside the truck, shows a cloudy sky in the background. What could have accounted for the difference in the background? McDonald thought at first that these were hoaxed photos because of the difference between the fourth photo and the first three. He couldn't bring himself initially to accept that the photos had actually captured a flying saucer in flight even though Heflin said that he took the photos in succession and that the object in them was real and had left a smoke ring when it flew away.

Ted McClelland explained that the missing part of the difference between the backgrounds probably resulted from the automatic exposure setting on the Polaroid 101, which takes into account the ambient background light and adjusts the image based upon the light. Thus, because the first three photos were taken from inside the van, the camera might have been tricked by the darkness inside the van, which made the automatic exposure adjust to that darkness and overcompensate by opening the lens wider, thus allowing more light to flood the frame from outside the van. That would explain the bright background sky. However, Ted said, "In the last photo, there was nothing to interfere with the automatic exposure and the camera is picking up exactly what it sees." Because, now outside the van, Heflin's camera picked up only the outside light, it took a true image of the cloudy sky that it could not do because it overcompensated for the lack of light inside the van. That would explain the difference in the background between the fourth and the prior three photos. Hence, according to Polaroid expert Mc-Clelland, the mystery is explained and the difference in background is accounted for.

While we have disproven three of the obvious debunker arguments, the fourth debunker argument was the harshest of all. It asserts that the object itself is a fake, a hubcap or something similar, and not a flying saucer. Project Blue Book, for example, labeled the photos as a hoax, calculating that the object in the photos was only nine inches in diameter, twelve feet off the ground, and about fifteen to twenty feet in the distance from the van. McClelland disagreed with Blue Book. "There is no hoax that I saw," he said. "Holding up the negatives and magnifying them as best as I could, I saw no signs of a hoax." There are no strings, no piano wire, no external support for the object over the ground, nothing that speak of a hoax to McClelland's expert eye. However the strongest evidence that the photos were not hoaxed lies in the calculations made by McDonald himself, calculations that Ted and photo analyst Terrence Masson analyzed again, this time employing sophisticated photo metrics software.

Heflin claimed the object he photographed was roughly twenty feet in diameter and about an eighth of a mile from his truck, or seven hundred feet from the lens of his camera. Project Blue Book said the photos were hoaxed, the object was small, a hubcap, no more than nine inches in diameter, maybe only twelve feet off the ground, and close to the camera, perhaps fifteen to twenty feet away from the lens. Using Heflin's and Blue Book's numbers, Terrence constructed a three-dimensional landscape to compare Blue Book's conclusions with Heflin's observation and test his claims. He placed a twenty-foot diameter saucer seven hundred feet in the distance, matching Heflin's description of the incident. If Heflin had hoaxed the photos regarding the size and distance of the object, as Blue Book and many debunkers have said, there would be almost no chance of the three-dimensional model matching the photos because Heflin's numbers wouldn't comport with the image.

"If he was telling the truth," Masson said, "and he was making an accurate eyeball estimation, that object in our simulation has to line up with our twenty-foot diameter object, a hundred and fifty feet off the ground." Terrence punched in the parameters and began sliding the actual photo image of the object to meet the parameters of the 3-D model. Then he cross-faded the model to the Heflin photograph, and guess what, the image comported almost exactly with the model. The debunkers were, in Terrence's words, "not even close." The image and the 3-D model based on Heflin's measurements lined up perfectly, meaning that Heflin was right and Blue Book and the debunkers were wrong in their estimates. The photos were not hoaxed. We had to ask whether this was a simple mistake made by the Blue Book analysts or a deliberate hoax they, themselves, concocted to dismiss the Heflin photo. We believed Blue Book deliberately hoaxed their conclusions so as to dismiss the Heflin photos completely to comport with the Air Force analysis.

"This is just very simple trigonometry," Terrence said. "You just put in the space that's very accurate at the size of the object and the height of the object that Heflin said it was and his estimate and the actual photographs match very, very precisely."

"So you've eliminated the theory," I suggested. "Of someone throwing some stupid thing in the air like a hubcap. You've knocked that out because if it were a hubcap, it wouldn't come up this way." On the screen in that photo-modeling software, a hubcap only a few feet in diameter would have looked very different against the actual photo Heflin took. The conclusion had to be, based on the analysis of the photo, that Heflin had to have been observing something not under his control. And the other tests we performed indicated that the camera was capable of not only snapping off the number of photos during the time sequence Heflin said had transpired, but was capable of keeping all elements of the image in focus if the lens had been set to a distance of infinity. And because of the automatic light exposure control in the Polaroid 101, the ambient light entering the lens while Heflin was photographing the object from inside the truck cab overexposed the sky background blocking out the clouds. Once Heflin stood outside the cab to photograph the smoke ring, the camera adjusted to the background light and captured the images of the clouds. Thus, the debunker arguments were incorrect and the Blue Book evaluation of the photos was not only mathematically incorrect, the Blue Book analysts hoaxed their debunking.

"In my estimation," Ted said. "James McDonald did a really good job collecting relevant evidence for this case. They didn't have a lot of computational power back then and digital image processing was a brand-new technology." In our evaluation of McDonald's work and the Heflin case we covered we were able to corroborate what McDonald said because we had these tools at our disposal and therefore could definitely show by the mathematics of computer simulation that Heflin was right. And once again, debunkers were debunked.

THE LONNIE ZAMORA CASE

The Zamora case is still a hotly debated case fifty years after its occurrence. It was studied, and taken seriously, by the military, corroborated by multiple witnesses and some physical trace evidence on the ground, heavily investigated by J. Allen Hynek, who said it was one of the cases that convinced him that UFO reports deserved greater scientific scrutiny, and, of course, investigated by James McDonald, who included it in his July 1968, statement to the House Committee on Science and Astronautics. The case involved the report of witness, Lonnie Zamora, a sergeant in the Socorro, New Mexico, police force, who said he was in pursuit of a speeding black Chevy late in the afternoon when he saw something that caught his eye and, ultimately, changed his life. It was a flame in the sky that accompanied the sound of a roar, or at least that's what Zamora thought it was at first, as he explained to Air Force investigators from Blue Book. He believed some explosives had gone off in the distance, possibly at a dynamite shack, and went off to investigate, driving along a gravel road in the direction of the sound.

As he approached the area and watched the flame in the distance rise and then disappear, he still believed he was watching an ignition of explosives from inside a shack he knew was on the other side of the incline. His patrol car had trouble climbing the steep rise, but he finally made it and saw a small object shining in the distance about two hundred yards away, he told Air Force investigators. Nothing anomalous, he thought at first, believing the object to be a car that had crashed. He also noticed two figures by the object, one of whom looked at Zamora in surprise. As he got closer, he saw that the object seemed more like an oval or the letter O, he reported. The two people he saw seemed smaller than normal adults, but he thought nothing of it, assuming they were simply that: small adults. He called in a ten-twenty location report to his dispatch and advised that he would be investigating the sound and the flame, thinking that it was a car accident and he would render assistance. Then, Zamora, as reported in Blue Book, once out of his patrol car he heard a loud roar that started low and rose to a high frequency. He saw a bright blue and orange flame from under the object, which had begun to ascend straight into the air, stirring up a cloud of dust.

Zamora retreated from the object, using his car as a shield, but kept the object in his field of vision as it rose. He later told his interviewers that it was an oval-shaped device, shiny like aluminum, and had no portholes or windows and no noticeable access port or door. However, he noticed some form of red lettering that he could not make out and an insignia that he did not recognize. He watched the object rise from his vantage point on the other side of the hill as it continued to rise until it took off out of sight. He radioed a report of the sighting to the county sheriff, who tried to locate the object through his headquarters window, but could not see it. Then Zamora was joined on the radio by state police sergeant Chavez, whom he asked to join him at his location.

While waiting for Chavez to arrive, Zamora walked to the spot from where the object had taken off and later said to his interviewers that he noted an area where the brush was still burning. When Sergeant Chavez arrived, he accompanied Zamora back down to the area where Zamora had spotted the object so Zamora could show him the burned residue. But Chavez found something else, tracks in the dirt as if made by landing skids. Zamora reported that the oval object was standing on a set of what looked like four metallic legs that protruded from its bottom. Other officers on the scene also saw the tracks in the dirt from these legs after Zamora had called in his report. Officers also noted the brush that was still smoldering when they arrived.

Zamora was not the only person who had seen the strange-looking flying oval sitting atop a flame. Other people claimed to have seen the object, one of whom not only saw it, but also saw a police car approaching it. That car was presumably Zamora's.

A formal investigation began within a day after the sighting. Both Zamora and Chavez were interviewed at length by the Air Force and the FBI. Both agencies visited the site and collected physical samples from the soil, including fused sand: sand that had been melted by the application of great heat. It was this fused sand evidence that made its way to James McDonald years after the incident. By the time McDonald learned about the sand from analyst Mary Mayes, who had been asked to analyze trace evidence from the site, the Zamora case was already hotly disputed. The military was debunking the sighting completely while J. Allen Hynek was calling it a vitally important incident. But it was Mary Mayes who grabbed McDonald's interest because she said that the military had given her their assignment of testing the soil for radiation—which she could not find—but did find unidentifiable organic remains at the landing site, burned plants that showed exposure to an anomalous agent that had dried them out completely, and the fused sand. It was the report of the fused sand and possible reasons for its presence that captured Pat Uskert's imagination, too, which was one of the reasons he chose the Zamora case from McDonald's files as one he wanted to examine.

As for Lonnie Zamora, he ultimately became a person of interest for ufologists around the world as well as for debunkers, who claimed he was perpetrating a hoax. Journalists also kept asking him for interviews. Zamora quit the police force, quit talking to ufologists and journalists, and became a gas station attendant, passing away in 2009. But during his years after the sighting debunkers like Donald Menzel from Harvard, whom Stan Friedman said was a member of MJ-12 and debunking was his cover, said that Zamora didn't know what he was looking at or that some students were playing a joke on him and confused him into thinking that he was seeing something otherworldly. Actually, Zamora thought that he had seen a top-secret test craft from nearby White Sands. Debunker Phil Klass said that either Zamora only saw ball lightning or that he himself was perpetrating a hoax to get more tourists to Socorro. McDonald blew holes in both of these accusations, particularly the ball lightning theory. Project Blue Book deemed the sighting an "unknown" even though they dismissed any extraterrestrial origin for the object. The head of Blue Book, however remarked that Zamora was an excellent witness, highly credible, who really did see something whose origin was not identifiable. The investigation continues to this day.

Back in 1968, however, the president of New Mexico Tech in Socorro, Dr. Stirling A. Colgate, wrote a letter to Nobel Prize winner Linus Pauling, in response to Pauling's inquiry about the Zamora sighting, in which letter Colgate said the Zamora incident was a hoax, nothing more than a prank perpetrated by students at New Mexico Tech. Dr. Pauling reportedly had an interest in UFO sighting reports and wanted to know what Colgate thought of the Zamora story. Colgate wrote Pauling that he had firsthand knowledge of the prank and that Zamora had been completely fooled by it.

There are problems with this story, however, not the least of which is that, assuming for the purpose of argument that everything Dr. Colgate wrote is absolutely true, there is no dispositive proof that what the students were hoaxing was what Zamora saw. What if they perpetrated a hoax and Zamora saw a real object? Colgate's letter, although persuasive, is really an example of the post hoc ergo propter hoc fallacy. Just because some students were pulling a prank, probably in the same area where Zamora was patrolling, doesn't mean that it's the cause of the Zamora sighting.

Another explanation might have involved the testing of equipment for upcoming NASA missions because, at least to me, the object that Zamora reported seeing was far too conventional for some type of otherworldly device. The object was an ovoid, capsule-shaped device supported by landing skids or legs and ascended via a type of rocket-propulsion system. Why would extraterrestrials, presumably more advanced than us, rely upon a conventional rocket propulsion system, circa World War II, on such a small device? But, this doesn't provide a clear explanation for the Zamora sighting either because if the Air Force knew that an aerospace company was testing a devise for NASA, wouldn't that have been the explanation in the Blue Book report? And wouldn't J. Allen Hynek have been apprised of this conventional explanation? Hence, the case remains a mystery, a mystery that Pat Uskert set out to unravel.

"It's really hard to emphasize how significant the Lonnie Zamora case is," Pat explained. "It's been a part of every major UFO report since Project Blue Book. This case has never been solved, and that's why we have to look at it."

Pat interviewed local reporter Paul Harden, who recently covered the Zamora incident in the Socorro newspaper and after forty years he found that Zamora's story still held a basis in truth.

"Why are people still talking about this story forty years after it happened?" Pat asked. Harden said that although he didn't consider himself a ufologist at all, he was a historian and the Zamora story intrigued him. He said that he was surprised that so many people in the Socorro area were fascinated by the story Zamora told and the state police response to the incident, which is one of the reasons why he chose to follow up the story. "From a historical point of view, this really happened?" Pat asked.

"No doubt in my mind that the incident happened," Harden said.

"The only thing history can't tell you is what did Mr. Zamora see. I can't answer that."

The Zamora sighting in McDonald's file is one of the most detailed cases he followed. Not only did McDonald note Zamora's specific descriptions of what he saw—the object's size, appearance, speed, and behavior—but the reports of marks in the sand left by the object, as well as fused sand and scorched brush. Numerous witnesses to these traces were on scene within minutes of the sighting. "So immediately," Harden explained, "you have a fair number of law enforcement agents that were at the scene ten minutes or so after Lonnie saw it. They went to the actual landing site." These were law enforcement personnel who understood forensics and could confirm the trace evidence Zamora reported, such as the landing marks in the dirt and that there were burn marks in the brush.

"In fact," Harden said, "in the original newspaper story, they cite how when they arrived at the scene the plants were still smoldering. It was clear," he repeated, "that something happened."

Because there have been so many different opinions about what Zamora saw in the desert and so much contradictory theory about its nature, Pat decided to get the story firsthand from the witness himself. Lonnie Zamora, who had not spoken about the incident for years, had agreed to break his silence and talk to Pat. Pat drove out to the Socorro desert for the interview.

Pat first visited the Socorro Police Department, where he was to meet with the chief of police, Lawrence Romero, who agreed to take Pat to interview Lonnie Zamora at the alleged landing site of the object Zamora said he saw. Talking to Zamora in person, Pat believed, the source, would allow him to get a clearer picture of what the police sergeant actually saw and what he believed had happened. As Pat rode alongside Socorro Police Chief Lawrence Romero, he asked background questions about Zamora and the chief's impression of Zamora both as a friend, police officer, and witness.

"Lonnie is an upfront type of guy, an excellent police officer, and a pillar of his church," Socorro Police Chief Romero told Pat, thus establishing his estimation of the credibility and honesty of the witness and confirming that he did not doubt the veracity of Zamora's story at all. Pat was thrilled at the opportunity to meet Zamora, the subject of so much controversy and debate.

Zamora had been silent about his sighting experience for over a decade before Pat met up with him. But he said he wanted to tell his side of the story again and explain why he believed his sighting was real and not his mistaking a conventional event for something unearthly. Standing with Pat on the bluff overlooking the depression where he said he saw the object, Zamora said that from where he first stood, he could see down on top of the object. "It was sort of an egg-shaped object about thirty to forty feet wide," Zamora remembered. "I didn't know what it was until I started moving toward it. Then I realized it was something I'd never seen before. I thought it was some kind of Air Force experiment, I thought at the first."

Maybe Zamora thought it was a military aircraft, Pat suggested. And Zamora agreed. "But it was investigated," Pat said. "And they found out there was no such aircraft."

The odd shape and structure of the object that Lonnie Zamora described was similar to NASA's lunar module. In fact, Air Force investigators theorized at first that what Zamora saw might have been a test of this same vehicle. But further analysis quickly proved this theory wrong. A flying, working model of the lunar module was not ready until 1965, a year after the Zamora sighting. However, what had landed in the Socorro desert had left physical evidence of its presence.

Pat, Chief Romero, and Lonnie Zamora then made their way down the slope from the bluff to the site itself, where Pat asked, "Now you're saying there were actual indentations from the craft?"

"All around here," Zamora said. "In fact, there is one right here."

"This is one of the original indentations?" Pat asked, pointing to a spot on the desert floor. "Yeah," Zamora said. "Right here. And there's another one right over there where the rock is. And another one there and one more right here." Zamora outlined the area where the object had sat. "There were four," he said.

"Right after the craft lifted off these indentations were fresh?" Pat asked. And Zamora agreed, saying they were "real fresh."

Interestingly, the indentations are not the only traces of physical evidence left by the object. According to Zamora, bushes were burning and rocks were smoldering after the object had lifted off from the site. "Where were these bushes exactly?" Pat asked Zamora, who pointed to four clumps of bush. But there was one that was burning so hot, Zamora said, standing over the burn spot, "that you couldn't get near it."

"Do you think this fire was directly related to the fire you saw?" Pat asked. Zamora agreed, but said that the evidence was quickly confiscated by Air Force investigators, who arrived soon after Lonnie had reached the site and then made his report to his supervisors. But McDonald revealed that it actually wasn't the Air Force that had collected the debris and took it away. It was the FBI. And adding to the mystery of this incident, the FBI, according to McDonald's file, didn't want anyone to know they were working on the case. The FBI agent, D. Arthur Byrnes, had accompanied Air Force Captain Richard T. Holder to the site and, according to Captain Holder, requested, as indicated in McDonald's notes, that "no mention be made of the FBI's interest in the case." The reason for this request has never been revealed.

FBI Agent Byrnes and Air Force Captain Holder were excited about the event and the trace evidence at the scene, Zamora told Pat. When Zamora tried to ask questions of the investigators, however, they refused to answer and, according to Zamora, "They wouldn't let me ask them any questions and told me to keep it quiet for a while." But James McDonald wanted to break the silence about the incident and doggedly tracked down specialists who had been brought in by the government to investigate Zamora's sighting.

McDonald's files indicated that Mary G. Mayes from the University of New Mexico was enlisted to analyze plant material from the site. In her interview with McDonald, Mayes described the location and reported seeing a twenty-five-to-thirty-foot patch of fused sand at the site where Zamora said the object was sitting. According to Mayes, a small area of desert had turned to glass. This prompted Pat to set up a test to determine how that sand was fused into glass and whether the fused sand might shed some light on Zamora's story. Pat collected some sand at the site for testing purposes, separating samples from different areas and labeling them based on from where they were retrieved. Pat wanted to find out how much energy it would have taken to fuse the sand from the site. Could the sand have been fused naturally? Might the prank that New Mexico Tech president Dr. Colgate described to Dr. Linus Pauling have generated enough energy to fuse the sand into glass? Patrick Morrissey, a glass blower who agreed to work with Pat Uskert, would be able to provide the answers.

"Morrissey, with over thirty years of experience in working with melted glass, might be able to tell us how sand fuses into glass," Pat said. And in order to demonstrate the level of heat required to fuse the sand, Pat brought along his samples from the Socorro site. Describing the Zamora incident to Morrissey, Pat explained, "You know there are various theories about what happened. One of those theories is that something landed and fused the sand into glass with incredibly high temperatures. Another theory is that there may be hoaxers who fused the sand. So what I'd like to learn from you is what does it take to fuse sand into glass?"

Morrissey took Pat's sand samples and set them on a fired clay base that could withstand the intense heat of a "glory hole," the furnace where glass is melted so that the artist can form it into shapes. While the sand was heating, Pat continued his questioning.

"Let's say," he said, "that these hoaxers came out with some equipment. Let's say a blowtorch. Could that work if a hoaxer brought out a blowtorch and tried to fuse sand?"

"A blowtorch puts out a pretty good flame," Morrissey explained. "But that would not really melt any glass at all. It's just not hot enough."

"So basically you're saying that you would need an oven to melt glass," Pat said. And as Pat and Morrissey watched the flame inside the oven, they could see the sand start to change color and start to bond. But, Morrissey cautioned, the bonding of the sand didn't mean that it was changing into glass, at least not at the moment. Then, after twenty-five minutes and the temperature in the oven reached 2,100 degrees Fahrenheit, the sand sample from the Zamora site was ready to be examined. It had completely melted and fused, meaning that it would have taken heat at 2,100 degrees Fahrenheit or above and applied for at least a half an hour to fuse the sand into glass. "So the hoaxer scenario?" Pat asked.

"Would be very hard to believe," Morrissey said.

In Morrissey's professional opinion, Pat went on to explain, the demonstration debunked the student practical joke explanation put forth by college president Stirling Colgate. And Pat's finding lent even greater credibility to Zamora's experience.

THE RB-47 INCIDENT

This incident took place on July 17, 1957, at 4:00 A.M. local time when our nation's most advanced electronic surveillance aircraft, the RB-47, flying on a training mission over the Gulf of Mexico, near the city of Gulfport, Mississippi, picked up a strange target on radar that kept moving around the plane in ways the crew could not easily explain. As the plane turned west, heading for Texas, the pilots also saw a strange blue pulsating light in front of the plane whose origin they could not explain. On the number two radar monitor, the radar officer, or "Raven," detected a signal he could not explain. For the next ninety minutes and seven hundred miles, the aircraft's electronic intelligence apparatus, ground radar installations, and even the pilots in the cockpit observed what many ufologists believe, including James McDonald, was a strange object tracking the RB-47, one of our Air Force's most important aircraft. The signal on one of the radar scopes picked up a target on the right side of the aircraft, which quickly climbed up scope—meaning that it was moving along the right side of the RB-47 toward the nose—then even as it intermittently disappeared from the scope, it crossed the front of the plane and showed up on the scope covering the left side of the plane and seemed to climb down the scope. It seemed to be tracking the aircraft as it flew north-west and even appeared as a hanging blue light in front of the plane, where the pilots observed it from the cockpit. Because what the crew picked up on radar was also picked up by ground radar, it thus made this incident a multiple-witness event.

The science and technology behind this story was tailor-made for MIT physicist Ted Acworth, who had worked for NASA and was an expert in metrics. Against the background of Ted's reinvestigation of the case is a controversy concerning whether this is one of the best UFO cases ever reported or whether this is the most misunderstood case of an encounter with an unidentified object. The RB-47 electronic sur-veillance and countermeasures aircraft either was followed by a UFO, which the crew said they visually tracked as well as tracked on their ra-dar, or whether what they saw and picked up was an American Airlines flight, which is what Blue Book reported. Skeptics and debunkers, in-cluding the late Phil Klass, argued that the electronic counterwarfare officers on the RB-47 actually picked up ground radars and mistook them for another aircraft. The Condon Report said this case was unex-plained. McDonald believed this was a real UFO case with an anoma-lous object, and he included it in his case file. UFO researcher and filmmaker Paul Kimball has also included the RB-47 incident as one of his ten best cases.

The contention, in order to oversimplify a complicated case of con-flicting interpretations of electronic and visual data, circles around whether a well-trained crew of electronic warfare countermeasures could distinguish between the pattern of ground radar stations trans-mitting a signal that the ECM officers, also called "Ravens" or "Crows," said was following them in an unconventional manner, or an object that was following them. Also, the issue continues, could the cockpit crew be confused about an object that crossed the plane's flight path, reappeared on the other side, then followed them across a few states, and then disappeared. The radar signal also appeared to the crew to wink in and out, for which the radar operators had no explanation. The radar target was also picked up by ground radar. The highly technical and well-researched investigations, even including the one by Phil Klass, are persuasive. However, even the most technical analysis of the plane's flight path, capabilities, functionality of the ground radar and the atmospheric conditions that could have lengthened the ground radar signals, as well as the actual object that the pilot and copilot visually observed, do have a level of conjecture to them that is way less than conclusive because of the high implausibility that all the events would have to have if they happened in a sequence described by even the most well-meaning skeptics. Accordingly, could the *UFO Hunters* shed any more light on the case? Could we resolve any of the controversy? This question had become Ted's challenge.

Ted's guest was Bill Scott, our aeronautical expert, former NSA officer, retired Rocky Mountain Bureau Chief for *Aviation Week,* and my coauthor along with retired naval officer Mike Coumatos of *Space Wars* and *Counter Space* (2008, 2009). Ted met Bill at the Castle Air Museum in Atwater, California. Bill knew the specifications and mission of the RB-47, especially its electronic warfare countermeasures capability, and what the ECM officers were tasked to do in the "bubble," the radar pod in the RB-47's bomb bay. The RB-47 was the backbone of the U.S. Air Force surveillance mission. It was specifically outfitted not to carry weaponry, but to carry sophisticated radar and analysis equipment for electronic intelligence gathering. It was the functionality of this equipment and the analytical abilities of the Ravens that lie at the heart of what the crew actually saw and experienced.

Ted introduced his conversation with Bill Scott by explaining that, "Professor McDonald was very interested in this case because of all the technology involved." He continued, "Technology can usually involve hard evidence, and that's what McDonald was looking for. The RB-47 in 1957, when this incident occurred, had the most sophisticated listening technology on the planet." The RB-47 was the reconnaissance backbone of the USAF, specifically configured for its recon and surveillance mission, scrubbing for electronic intelligence such as the capabilities of enemy radar and tracking targets. Therefore, when the crew picked up something they thought might be anomalous, it caught

McDonald's interest because of the real data that he could focus on to evaluate the nature of the event. As Bill Scott said, "The plane would fly along the borders of the Soviet Union and listen for the radars transmitting along the ground. We're talking about technology in the 1950s, but the RB-47 was the state of the art and critical to our national security."

"This crew was on their way back from a training mission, all six of them aboard," Ted said. The crew was comprised of three electronic intelligence officers, a navigator, and a pilot and copilot. "This was the end of their training. They were about to ship out so that they were probably at the height of their expertise, just finishing up an extensive training program in the States before their deployment."

Bill Scott agreed. "At the time, this was our frontline fighting force, the Strategic Air Command. These ELINT [electronic signals intelligence] operators would have been very well trained because the fate of the country was in their hands and in the hands of the pilots who flew these airplanes."

"How about the ELINT equipment?" Ted asked. "How long had that been out? Was there any chance that this equipment was malfunctioning or it was such a brand-new technology that there's some question there? Or is this tried and true hardware?"

"I would say it was probably tried and true hardware of the time," Bill Scott answered. "So maybe it was not cutting edge, but very well maintained."

According to Professor McDonald's report on the case, despite this being the most advanced equipment in service, the officer who first spotted the object on the ELINT thinks the equipment is malfunctioning. But, Bill Scott said, they had one of the other operators double-check the equipment and try to fix the signal on a different set of antennas on the RB-47. The ELINT crew established very early on that the equipment was functioning perfectly according to specifications. In other words, there was no perceivable malfunction.

In a short while, however, the crew, according to McDonald, was about to get visual confirmation of what they had seen on their scopes just as the RB-47 headed toward Jackson, Mississippi. At that course change, one of the pilots spotted what he thought were the landing lights of another jet coming in fast. As the single blue light closed rapidly on the RB-47, the pilot, Colonel Lewis D. Chase, alerted the crew that they should prepare themselves for sudden evasive maneuvers. But before he could do anything, Chase and his copilot saw the light instantaneously change direction right in front of them and flash across their flight path. Then it blinked out. James McDonald interviewed the cockpit crew, obtaining firsthand eyewitness confirmation of what they saw. McDonald tape-recorded those interviews.

"I'm looking at it as a pilot at night," Colonel Chase told McDonald. "Seeing a light source that I interpreted as an airplane. But then suddenly it's flying in front of me so fast that I couldn't respond."

"Did it suddenly blink out or did it take off at an appreciable velocity?" McDonald asked Chase.

"No, just gone," Chase responded. "Just disappeared."

"That was quite an intercept you were flying there," McDonald suggested. "That is really very strange."

Ted commented that these were trained aircraft pilots, United States Air Force officers. "These guys know what aircraft look like." Nothing in the United States military, we believe, had the ability in 1957 to blink out. In the McDonald report, Colonel Chase, claimed that the object moved at a velocity that "he'd never seen matched in his flight experience." Ted suggested that for the crew to be really shocked at what they saw says a lot. It begs the question, as some skeptics and debunkers have argued, that the cockpit crew only had a sighting of a falling meteor that crossed their path and then disappeared, which would explain the velocity and the object's blinking out. "You add to that," Ted said, "in addition to the visible sighting you had the technology back in the bay, which was the most sophisticated technology listening system, listening to radar." It was our most advanced electronic intelligence and counterwarfare equipment in our arsenal. Combine that with a well-trained veteran crew and you have a mix of expertise and technology that would have normally recognized the playing of ground radars around the RB-47's antennas and a meteor falling through the sky. And, by the way, did anyone else see that meteor? Did the falling meteor show up on the ground radars that the RB-47 was supposedly picking up? And did the meteor simply burn up or did it hit the ground somewhere? All things to be considered if there was a conventional explanation for this incident, a conventional explanation that one of our country's most important climate physicists could not figure out, why are there so many ifs that defy the measure of plausibility?

There were no images of the radar scope target tracking in McDonald's files. However, Ted Acworth referred to McDonald's notes to analyze the object's maneuvers around and across the flight path of the RB-47 and pursued the case further with Bill Scott. Scott was adamant that in 1957, the year of the incident, "you didn't have an aircraft that could jump from eleven o'clock to two o'clock instantaneously and then just blink out." Assuming, just for the sake of argument, that the target on the RB-47's Ravens' radar scope was a craft and not the plane's radar picking up signals from ground radar emplacements, this target was a completely anomalous flying object. However, because there are no actual images of the targets on the RB-47 scopes that remain today, Ted and Bill Scott recreated the event on paper by, first, replotting the actual course the RB-47 took on the night of the encounter in the hopes of understanding what actually took place in the early morning summer darkness in July 1957.

The aircraft crossed the gulf coast, picked up a radar target on the scope covering the starboard side of the plane, and then, Ted marked on the map, "the aircraft turns west toward Dallas and that's when the pilot has a visual sighting. Were they trying to evade the object?" he asked Bill Scott.

"They started accelerating and decelerating to see if they could lose the object," Bill said. As the pilots watched the object in their path, the radar operators at Duncanville said they also had an anomalous target on their screens that corresponded to the position of the object the pilots were seeing. "When the light blinked out," Bill Scott said, "the pilots reported that the light disappeared, the ground-based radar at

Duncanville said they lost the object as well. Also the ELINT operators on the RB-47, the Ravens, said they lost the target from their
scopes." Scott surmised that the correspondence between the visual
sighting and the radar sightings is significant. It seems to eliminate a
falling meteorite as the explanation for the visual sighting. But things
got even more interesting when the object reappeared visually and,
again, turned up on the Duncanville radar and the ELINT scopes on
the RB-47. Everything associated with the appearance of this target, the
visual sighting, the ground-based radar hit, and the ELINT tracking on
the plane's scopes were all seeing this light-target at the same time and
confirming each other's tracking of the target, thus confirming that
they were seeing the same thing visually as well as electronically so
as to discount ground radar as the source of the signal and a meteorite
as the visual sighting.

After the crew had made their turn toward Texas, heading for their
home base, Colonel Chase requested and received permission to pursue the target that appeared on their scopes. The object, they confirmed
visually, was at a lower altitude so the pilot dived toward the object and
suddenly, the object stopped right in midair, another clue that it wasn't
a meteorite. The plane overshot the object and then the crew started a
left-hand turn to get back to where they could see the object. "At this
point," Ted asked, "they were running low on fuel, right?"

Bill agreed and Ted said, "That's when they decided to break off the
pursuit and head back for home."

"So they took off to the north and headed back to Forbes Air Force
Base in Kansas, and that's when the object stayed with them," Bill said.
And the object stayed with the RB-47 almost half the way back to
Forbes, disappearing from the radar tracking over Oklahoma City
when it suddenly vanished. The ninety-minute chase of an object that
both tracked and evaded the RB-47, bouncing from one radar scope
to another and turning up on ground radar, left the plane's crew and
ground-based personnel dumbfounded as to the nature of what they
encountered. None of them had an explanation for what had just occurred.

"When you string together the various descriptions of the flight maneuvers of this object," Ted asked Bill Scott, "would you say that these are explainable through conventional aircraft?"

"In 1957, you don't have an aircraft that can just blink out both in the electromagnetic spectrum as well as in the visual spectrum," Bill said. "And I would say that we didn't have anything back then and don't have anything like that now."

However, despite all of these anomalies and events that defied conventional explanation, Project Blue Book dismissed the event out of hand even though it involved the Air Force's most advanced electronic counterwarfare weapons system. Blue Book said that the event was really a misidentification of the near collision between two commercial DC-6 airliners near Salt Flat, Texas. But they gave no explanation for their conclusion except to say, "It was definitely established by the CAA that the object observed in the vicinity of Dallas and Fort Worth was an airliner." However Blue Book's conclusion is as implausible as it is unlikely. The RB-47's flight path didn't come within four hundred miles of Salt Flat, Texas, where Blue Book said the DC-6 airliners were. And Professor McDonald used the reference in Blue Book to comment on the Air Force's poor methods of investigation. We now suspect, of course, that the public Blue Book was simply a way to satisfy the public with conventional explanations for unexplainable UFO events. The RB-47 incident? Blue Book categorized it as "Identified."

"I feel there must have been something out there, something going on," Ted said to Bill Scott.

Bill Scott agreed. "It sure looks like something was out there. I don't think we know, and, here it is, fifty years later, and we still don't know." But even if we still don't know conclusively what happened during the RB-47 incident, James McDonald never agreed with the Blue Book conclusion because nothing they said comported with the crew's own observations, and the case remained "Unidentified."

Had James McDonald's investigations into UFO phenomena been able to utilize today's computational technology, his investigations would only have gotten stronger. But McDonald posed too much of a threat to the government's cover-up of UFOs. And his zeal in sharing his information not only with other scientists and with Congress, but with scientists from the Soviet Union posed an even greater perceived threat to the guardians of the secret. He ran afoul of J. Edgar Hoover and the FBI, the CIA, and the military. His suicidal tendencies that he wrote about in his journal provided the perfect opportunity, at least in my opinion, for those faceless persons behind the veil of clandestine operations to eliminate what they saw as a threat by setting up Betsy McDonald to become involved with someone they planted in her Socialist Party meetings. And her announced intention to divorce James McDonald pushed him right over the edge. His suicide in 1971 was tragic, as his personal life finally overwhelmed his fascination with and study of science. And, as Stanton Friedman has said on many occasions, including on UFO Hunters, "We lost one of the greatest UFO investigators who ever lived." McDonald brought real science, real analytics, and conservative logic to the study of UFO phenomena, and his work, despite the strenuous efforts of the debunkers, remains unimpeachable.

BILL'S BLOG

The "Lost UFO Files" episode was one of my favorites in the *UFO Hunters* series because it was an amalgamation of everything I believe is legitimate and substantive evidence of the reality of UFO encounters. It combined personal observations by credible witnesses, multiple-witness observation, photographic evidence, physical trace evidence, government denials to the point of implausible interpretation of evidence and the disregard of relevant facts in the cases, hoaxing actual evidence, and an overreaction of debunkers to the point where their explanations of the events were beyond implausible. Moreover, the McDonald case itself involved a government reaction so severe that in my estimation it resulted in McDonald's death. In the late 1960s, McDonald's pursuit of explanations for UFO phenomena, especially his reaching out to the Soviet consulate at the UN, was perceived by the government, particularly the FBI, as a real threat. Betsy McDonald's hosting members of the Black Panther Party at the McDonald home was also perceived by the FBI as subversive. And McDonald's 1968 testimony before the congressional Committee on Science and Astronautics might easily have been perceived by the military as threatening because McDonald's testimony challenged official explanations debunking UFO incidents. Thus, the McDonald case combined real science with evidence of debunker hoaxing along with a sense of political conspiracy to undermine national security. At least that's how the government might have perceived it. And the end of the McDonald story was indeed tragic and ended the career of an individual who was probably, in Stan Friedman's opinion, one of the most important, meticulous, and scrupulous investigators of UFO phenomena who ever lived.

In this episode we got the chance to interview Betsy McDonald, and I was impressed with what I perceived to be her blissful naiveté about her relationship with the person to whom she had become attached to the point of asking her husband for a divorce. Did she put two and two together—assuming for the sake of argument there was a two and two—that her relationship and her husband's suicide were somehow related to his UFO research and his contact with the Soviet consulate? No, she apparently did not. But after thirty-five years, the unhappiness of the moment fades away. I believed she was set up by the government cooperating individual to push her husband into a suicide so as to end his threat to the UFO cover-up. But that's just my opinion.

The other aspect of this episode that was so appealing to me was its reliance on the science underlying the cases McDonald studied and how we were able to present that science in such a way as to debunk the debunkers. For example, in the Heflin photos, wannabe debunkers argue that because items like the van's side-view mirror, the circular object in the frame, and the window frame are all in focus at the same time means that the object in the frame has to be small and close to the camera. But the Polaroid 101 expert we worked with to evaluate the Heflin photos said that if Heflin had set his lens to a distance of infinity, all of the objects would still be in focus. This was very important because debunkers seized on the focus issue to assert that Heflin had hoaxed the photos.

The other major argument was that the fourth photo of the smoke ring against a cloudy sky proved that the photo was hoaxed because the background sky was different from the first three photos. But, again, our expert showed that the automatic exposure of the Polaroid 101 would have compensated for the darkened van cabin interior by admitting more light into the lens so as to render the background sky lighter. Once Heflin stepped outside the van to get a shot of the smoke ring, the camera readjusted its automatic exposure and depicted the cloudy sky.

Finally, the major argument over the size of the object in the photos, whether the size of a hubcap or a larger object, was resolved by Terrence Masson's utilization of 3-D photo modeling software to account for Heflin's estimate of the object's size, its height off the road surface, and distance of the object from the camera as opposed to the military's calculation of the same metrics. The result was that the military had hoaxed its own argument.

Similarly, in the RB-47 case, in which classic debunker Phil Klass argued that the plane's ELINT crew had been unable to understand the difference on their scopes between an object in the sky tracking the plane and ground radar they were picking up, we showed that because the radar was moving along the scopes in conjunction with ground radar observations and visual observations, the crew could not be accused of a misidentification of the nature of the target. Also, debunkers seized on the possibility that the pilots in the cockpit only saw a falling meteor and not a flying object. However, the relationship between the visual observation and radar tracking from different positions on the ground as well as in the air, debunked that debunker argument as well, especially because falling meteors don't stop in midair.

Some of our strongest evidence for a legitimate UFO sighting came in our evaluation of the Lonnie Zamora case where New Mexico Tech president Stirling Colgate said there was no real UFO, only a practical joke, a prank, played by students. That argument, perhaps made especially for Linus Pauling, was easily debunked logically as well as by evidence. Let's say, arguendo, that Dr. Colgate was absolutely correct in revealing the nature of the prank to Dr. Pauling. So what? He didn't prove conclusively that the prank was what Zamora saw. The sighting and the prank could have taken place at the same time, but Zamora saw the object while only the students saw the prank. None of this accounts for our evaluation of the physical evidence. Even though the indentations on the desert sand and the burning bushes could have been made by pranksters, how about the glass made from fused sand at the landing site? Professional glass blowers will tell you that it takes over 2,100 degrees Fahrenheit in an oven to fuse sand into glass. Moreover, a glass blower's oven must heat slowly to reach the necessary temperature, sometimes requiring twenty-four-hours to reach the right temperature. Were these pranksters out in the desert for a day or more to melt the sand into glass? Sure, they could have melted sand from the desert in a glass blower's furnace off site and then transported it to the desert so Lonnie Zamora could find it. But how elaborate and expensive a prank was this? When you ask who made the indentations, the burning foliage, and the glass on the desert floor, placing it in such a way as to fabricate the evidence of rocket exhaust heat, you have to accept that the pranksters knew in advance that Zamora would be chasing a speeding car when they set off the launch. Seriously? This fails the plausibility test even before we reach the logical test that demonstrates the fallacy of arguing that a "can" or even a "probably" necessarily becomes an "is" just because the arguer wants it that way.

Paving the way for the success of the McDonald files episode was the excellent work of filmmaker Paul Kimball, whose appearance on the show had to be edited out because our format was that any expert had to appear in an interview with one of the *Hunters*. Paul's appearance was planned for Ted Acworth, whose flight to L.A. from Boston was delayed because of weather. Even though producer Scott Goldie interviewed Kimball and said that it was one of the most informed explanations of an unconventional event he had ever heard, it had to be cut because it was an expert scientific interview scheduled for Ted, who was held up by East Coast weather. The other expert who informed our research was Brad Sparks whose evaluation of the RB-47 case provided a strong rejoinder to Phil Klass's historic debunking of the incident. This healthy debate about the RB-47 case was one of the highlight episodes of the entire *UFO Hunters* series.

The three cases we covered from the McDonald files indicate that James McDonald's analysis was on point, logical, and backed up by scientific evaluation of the physical evidence. It showed that the debunker arguments were frivolous, lacking in evidentiary analysis, attenuated, and devoid of clean logic. We focused this episode on debunking the debunkers. And we succeeded.

"UFO SURVEILLANCE"
BROOKHAVEN, LAWRENCE LIVERMORE,
AND THE JOHN FORD AFFAIR

This is the story of reported mysterious UFO crashes in Suffolk County, Long Island, and outside of Oakland, California; exotic particle beam experiments taking place at nearby Brookhaven and Lawrence Livermore national laboratories; brush fires near both labs possibly started by local authorities to cover up the UFO crashes; disputed charges of attempted murder filed against a court officer, John Ford; and Ford's commitment to a mental institution because he sought to expose the corruption and the nature of the Brookhaven UFO crash itself. This is a story of how the CIA, the Israeli Mossad, and local police all became involved in one of the most convoluted stories of UFO encounters of which I have ever heard. But this was ultimately a UFO story with a victim, a victim who today, eighteen years after his commitment still lives in a mental institution, partly because his psychiatrists assert that his belief in the existence of UFOs is a mental disease.

"Free John Ford" was a chant that we encountered when we landed in Suffolk County on Long Island to cover the story of the alleged UFO crash at around 7:00 P.M. on November 24, 1992, at Southaven County Park in Shirley, New York. This was during our third season, and it brought us smack into contact with an individual who claimed to be a nonofficial cover officer for the Central Intelligence Agency and who had crossed our path to give us some information about the story we were investigating, as well as a dire warning about stories we had already investigated: Area 51 and Dulce.

THE JOHN FORD CASE

John Ford was at the center of the Southaven Park incident. Ford, now confined to a mental institution in New York's Hudson Valley north of New York City, had been a court officer in Suffolk County as well as in New York County, when he founded Long Island UFO Network and started investigating what he said was official corruption in Suffolk County's Republican Party administration, some of it, he alleged, involved New York's organized crime families. Why his case became a rallying cry for Long Island UFO investigators involved not only his investigation into the 1992 Southaven Park incident, but his investigations into other alleged UFO incidents in the Suffolk County area as well, including a forest fire, which he claimed was deliberately set by the folks he was investigating for corruption who were covering up evidence of a UFO crash. What made his story, and the story of other Long Island residents so intriguing was the proximity of Southaven Park to the Brookhaven National Laboratory and the claims of some area residents, who witnessed emergency responder units in the area on November 24, 1992, including fire apparatus from Brookhaven Laboratory. That claim piqued our interest because the Brookhaven apparatus cannot leave the laboratory facility unless called upon for mutual aid or to respond to an emergency that involved the Brookhaven Laboratory. We wanted to interview witnesses to the aftermath of the alleged crash, review video that had been taken of the impact area, and revisit the issues in the John Ford case.

First, this is the John Ford story as told in his own words on my radio show, *Future Theater* (www.futuretheateer.com). Ford's statement was compiled and edited by Robert Morningstar and the Ford material for the radio show was assembled by Alfred Lehmberg, both respected longtime UFO researchers and authors.

Ford first popped up on the radar of U.S. intelligence services and law enforcement when he was in college and asked by the New York Police Department to keep his eyes on an acquaintance who was suspected of spying for the KGB. John says that he was targeted by the KGB, operating on American college campuses, because they were trying to lure politically conservative students into their orbit. Ultimately Ford was recruited by another friend to work as a cooperating individual for the CIA, monitoring KGB college campus activity. As a college student, before he began his professional career in law enforcement and unbeknownst to his parents and close family, John Ford, like my favorite counterspy Herbert Philbrick, led three lives. He writes:

It all began in my college days. I was a college student during the Vietnam War when the college campuses were aflame and there were radicals on both sides of the political fence. I was an outspoken conservative student leader on my college campus and led the fight on my college campus against the radical leftist organization Students for a Democratic Society and the Black Panthers. I also was involved in Conservative Party politics off the campus too. I was widely known on campus and off.

Little did I know that my activities would attract outside attention. I learned the following years later from my friend John who was in a position to know the truth.

I worked after school at Macy's Jamaica branch store in Queens, New York, about eight blocks from where I was to live in Queens. While working there one night after school the personnel manager for the store brought a new sales girl to my department to work with me and the other salespeople. She immediately singled me out and over a week began to flirt with me until I began to notice her and finally worked up the courage to ask her out. After the movie we went to her parents' home, which was close by the movie theater. Both her parents were out visiting friends, leaving us alone in the apartment.

One of the things I noticed the moment I entered the apartment was a floor-to-ceiling mirror in the living room. It appeared unusual and also quite unique. After a short spell the girl attempted to seduce me and made no attempt to conceal her intent. I did not take her up on the invitation and left shortly after.

Little did I know that I was the intended victim of a KGB "honey pot" operation. The girl, her parents, and the personnel manager were all KGB agents assigned to compromise me and blackmail me into working for the KGB as a spy.

I would later learn that I was a victim of a nationwide operation by the KGB to recruit conservative youth leaders as potential spies should they enter government service. In the 1930s they did the same thing with young liberals to turn them into Red agents.

Remember Alger Hiss, Owen Lattimore, and Lauchlin Currie?

The Russians realized that the voting patterns were changing in the sixties and seventies, drifting to more conservative issues and political leadership. They wanted to recruit spies so they could once again infiltrate our government.

During my senior and junior years in college, I started working for the NYPD photographing radical student leaders and their demonstrations on campus. I was working for the police unit known as Special Services for a detective friend of my best friend in college. He recruited me to work for him. The detective's name was John Judge. Little did I know this would lead me to a career in law enforcement and also to a secret career in another one. It seemed that the honey pot operation and my work for the NYPD attracted the attention of another spy organization.

During my years in college, I made a very close friendship with another conservative activist who will be known as "Walter." We became very close friends over the years. Little did I know that he had another side and a very sinister one.

In my senior year I made a friendship with another gentleman by the name of John who was working for the ATF in the treasury department, catching gunrunners and gathering intelligence on campus radicals. He knew of my work for the NYPD and got me interested in joining the New York City Auxiliary Police. Little did I know that he worked for the CIA also and was sent to recruit me for the CIA. Later on he would orient me toward a career in law enforcement and later train me to do covert operations for the CIA.

It appears my friend Walter had a double identity and was in fact a deep-cover, deep-penetration Soviet agent for the KGB. I was re-cruited to keep tabs on the Red bastard and report on his friends and activities. I would do this for some sixteen years and at great risk to myself. My mother, my father, my brother, and my sister knew nothing of my secret life nor did the rest of my family. It was a well-kept secret.

Not only did I do this operation, but I also was used for covert air operations and paramilitary operations. Again I could not reveal any-thing of what I did.

I was also used for covert surveillance and monitoring as-signments on KGB operations in the New York City metropolitan area.

After I graduated college, I continued my operations again with my old college buddy, Walter. I was also used for the other activities as I described.

In 1973, I joined the court system as a court officer and was as-signed to Brooklyn Criminal Court at Schermerhorn Street in Down-town Brooklyn. In July 1974, I was promoted to senior court officer and assigned to Brooklyn Supreme Court on Adams Street in Down-town Brooklyn, just six blocks from the Criminal Court House. In January 1975, I was transferred to the Dangerous Drug Division of the supreme court located in the Brooklyn Criminal Court House. [As the] CO of the drug division I would later learn was the Mid-Atlantic Regional Director for Covert Operations for the CIA. It was no mistake that I was assigned there.

In 1978, New York State assumed direct administration of the courts county by county. The same year the Dangerous Drug Division was reorganized with the Violent Felony Division of Brooklyn Supreme Court.

In 1979, I moved my mother and myself out to Bellport, [Long Island], after my father's death. In 1982, I won a transfer to Suffolk County Supreme Court and there I remained until I retired in 1993. In 1987, Richard Stout and I met and became friends, sharing a interest in war gaming and military scale modeling and also the subject of UFOs.

1987 was the same year I did my last job for the CIA and became inactive. My friend Walter had been deactivated by us and rendered useless to the KGB by our operations. In 1987, I attended his wedding as my last surveillance duty and reported on who attended the affair.

In 1988 Richard Stout and I began researching UFOs on Long Island and talked about forming a research organization to report on activity on Long Island after being urged on by researchers such as Dick Ruhl, Phil Imbrogno, John Lear, and Linda Moulton Howe.

In January 1989, Richard and I agreed to form a new organization with Richard giving it the name of the Long Island UFO Network. It was the same month as the animal mutilation wave hit the island. In April, Richard and I had our first UFO sighting and after appearing on *The Joel Martin Show* on which we reported our sighting and announced the formation of LIUFON the next month.

With the formation of LIUFON, the hotline never stopped ringing. Long Island UFO Network began reporting on the activity on Long Island and made history. We attracted national and international attention and little did we know we attracted the attention of other nation's intelligence services.

In 1993, I retired from the courts because of a line-of-duty back injury that resulted in a permanent disability. In 1995, my mother died of metastasized lung cancer leaving me devastated at the personal loss. I made up for the loss by concentrating on my UFO research and investigating the Southaven Park incident of 1992.

In January 1996, I was contacted by Joe Zuppardo to come to his home and meet a close personal friend of his who wanted to join LIUFON and get involved in investigating UFOs.

So one night I went to Zuppardo's address and met his childhood friend, Joe Mazzuchelli. He appeared to be a nice guy and we struck up a friendship. That night I drove him home and he promised to come by my home and sign up as a member, which he did a few days later. He also took an investigator's application and applied for a position.

After meeting him he became a frequent visitor and it was nearly impossible to keep him away. He showed an impassioned appetite to learn all he could about UFOs. He attended our regular meetings along with his buddy Sal Marino, who was a longtime friend who he brought to meet me at my home.

Then one weekend in March of 1996, he came to me asking if he could borrow my old pickup truck to move his girlfriend's belongings from her old boyfriend's house up to his uncle's place in Port Jefferson where he was going to store it in his basement. He had the truck for a week and came to my house on a Wednesday night asking if he could keep the truck for a few more days. He also told me he had a friend by the name of Rocket who lived near Southaven Park and had gone into the park after watching the UFO crash and made it to the crash site minutes after it had impacted on a fire road in the park.

He saw what was left of the craft and mentioned that there were a lot of park rangers and police around the site. Joe said his friend was willing to talk to us and he would meet with me at the Manorville Diner in Manorville on Route 111 on Friday morning.

That Thursday night, Joe took my truck and drove up North Ocean Avenue to get to the LIE to visit Joe Zuppardo. He was followed by four big men in an official Suffolk County motor pool car. They cut Joe off as he entered the service road to the LIE and forced him to the side and dragged him out of the truck, beating him severely about the face and the body. Before they left they told him stop investigating things that "are not your business."

The next morning I was awakened by an early morning telephone call by Joe warning me not to keep the appointment with Rocket and to stay all day at home. Not to venture outside. He told me what happened and told me he would be over to my house to return the truck and show me what happened.

That afternoon he came to my house and showed me bruises and lacerations about his face and body from the assault. He related the series of events and told me what they had done and said. I said it sounded like it may have been meant for me, not for him. He agreed with me that this was a possibility but for what reason was beyond us. I photographed his face and body capturing both the bruises and the lacerations. That afternoon we both went to the scene of the crime and photographed the area.

Ford wrote about the history of UFO crashes on the east end of Long Island in another statement to *UFO Magazine,* talking about crashes and retrievals dating all the way back to the 1980s.

When Richard Stout and I formed the Long Island UFO Network Inc. (aka LIUFON) in 1989, we did not anticipate the public reaction we would have. That first year alone saw LIUFON inundated with over 129 reported cases, followed by another ninety-six reported cases in 1990. In the organization's succeeding years, we would see an average of fifty to a hundred cases per year. We had grown from an initial membership of twenty-five in 1989 to over 180 members by 1996. We were constantly besieged with reports and requests for membership. When we held our first conference in October of 1989, we were mobbed. When we held our last conference in 1995, we were sold out. The public supported us. Unfortunately, the politicians did not.

Little did we realize that LIUFON's research was attracting attention not only from the general public but from the intelligence community of our nation and foreign countries as well.

It began in October of 1989. With good evidence and eyewitness testimony, we followed through on an investigation of a major UFO incident reported on September 28, 1989. Based on eyewitnesses and photographs of the incident, we had reason to believe that the United States government had intercepted and shot down a UFO over Moriches Bay in Center Moriches [on Long Island]. Our investigation proved our suspicions to be valid and the case put LIUFON on the map.

With the aide of eyewitness testimony, government informants and physical evidence, we were able to establish that there had been five UFO crashes on Long Island since the 1980s. In summary, they were as follows:

1982, February, Montauk—a wedge-shaped UFO crashes on a beach out at Montauk, Long Island. During the night, it is airlifted by helicopter to West Hampton AFB. It is flown from there to Wright-Patterson AFB the next day.

1989, September 28, Moriches Bay—a UFO is shot down over Moriches Bay. It involves the interception of one of two Hudson Valley Boomerangs. The object in question is recovered under the guise of dredging operations and brought to Brookhaven National Laboratory for study.

1992, November 24, Shirley, Southaven County Park—a large mother ship, three hundred to five hundred feet in diameter, explodes over Yaphank. A two-man escape vehicle crashes in the park. Bodies are recovered and wreckage is spread over wide areas of Yaphank. The vehicle's main control room is sent to Brookhaven National Laboratory. The incident is covered up until LIUFON breaks the story.

1993, May 23, Shirley, Southaven County Park—a wedge-shaped object crashes on a fire road, adjoining the park's shotgun range, causing a large brush fire. The public is evacuated from the park by both the county police and the FBI. The Yaphank Fire Department is called to extinguish the fire. We do not have information with regard to the object's recovery or disposition. We were alerted to the crash by eyewitnesses in the park and by a Yaphank firefighter.

1995, August, Riverhead—this is one case that we honestly don't know a hell of a lot about. The principal witness, Steven Ferare of Riverhead, discovers the crashed ship outside of Riverhead in a wilderness preserve. Both the U.S. Air Force and the FBI secure the crash site and intimidate the witness into silence. We found out about this incident due to information given to us by two of our members, as well as Patty McDonald, who heard the original story relayed to her by Mr. Ferare while purchasing a used car from him. Subsequently, we had located the general area of the reported crash site and were preparing a field investigation when I was arrested. This was the reason why the East End forest fires were started. The fires had served as a cover for the crash site's recovery while corrupt politicians exploited the situation for their own ends.

Ford explained to me over the phone from the Mid-Hudson Forensic Psychiatric Center, where he says he's being held against his will, that he believed his investigation into the field fire and his continuing probe into the activities of the Suffolk County administration were coming together and that higher powers in either the New York State and federal governments were pushing hard for a cover-up to the Southaven Park UFO crashes that they even went to the extreme of inciting county officials to commit arson to cover up any trace evidence of the crashes. Ford believed that, in light of the attack on Mazzuchelli, local Suffolk politicians and office holders had been instructed to make sure that Ford's investigation went nowhere and that he would be punished for it. He wrote:

Mazzuchelli stated that at the request of the United States government, Gaffney ordered the woods adjacent to the UFO crash site to be burned so as to cover up the crash retrieval. Gaffney had asked John Powell to help with setting the forest fires. It was Powell and Gazzola, using their political flunkies, who exploited the whole situation for personal gain and profit by setting fires in populated areas as well. Now they had set their sights on coming after me which, in their eyes, would be executed simply as an extension of the exploitation already being fed to the news media during this timeframe.

Against the background of these Long Island crashes, Ford wrote, and because of his investigation of them, he was solicited by Israeli intelligence to provide some evidence of the history of UFO encounters in the United States because the U.S. government had not been forthcoming with the Israelis after the Israeli Air Force had an incident with a UFO in 1989. Again, he wrote:

> I was told that Israel had been planning to contact me because of my leadership in the field of ufology. Israeli fighters had downed a UFO over the Negev Desert in 1989. When the United States government refused to give Israel any information on UFOs and the alien presence, Israel began to form an international coalition to expose and overturn the U.S. government's UFO cover-up. Other nations had detected the alien presence on our planet and wanted answers to their questions. As such, I was being asked to join the effort and bring LIUFON into this coalition made up of forty-one nations, intelligence agencies, and international research organizations. They had dozens of other researchers in their ranks and they wanted me to lead the effort in the United States.

One of the reasons for the Israeli interest in him, Ford told me, was his work with the CIA and NYPD intelligence years before. Ford believed that his name had been entered into a database of covert nonofficial operatives that could be trusted. In fact, he wrote that even before the Mazzuchelli beating, his former recruiter from the CIA and a friend had warned him to be careful and to "avoid alarming the local political authorities with my UFO research. His warning carried the tone of an ominous threat."

What John Ford wrote was only the start of a series of events, which culminated in his being charged with attempted murder of John Powell, the former head of the Suffolk County Republican Party and the Suffolk County executive. John Powell has since died. After Joe Mazzuchelli was worked over by individuals driving a Suffolk County car who probably believed they had stopped John Ford, the story was picked up by Long Island journalist Jerry Cimisi, again, writing for *UFO Magazine*. Cimisi termed John Ford a political prisoner because of his pursuit of the truth about UFOs. Cimisi, who also appeared on our Brookhaven episode of *UFO Hunters*, wrote:

> For a number of years I was a reporter and editor at a weekly paper in the Hamptons, on the east end of Long Island. My first contact with John Ford was in the autumn of 1988. He had just established the Long Island UFO Network (LIUFON). I met with John and wrote about his organization. His contention was that Long Island was a hotbed of UFO activity. This coincided with what someone else told me around the same time: "Go into any bar on the island, and you'll find someone with a UFO story to tell."
>
> In subsequent years I wrote about John Ford and LIUFON a number of times. There was a UFO seminar he put together in the spring of 1989, the Moriches Bay incident at the end of that year, then the Southaven Park crash in November 1992. In April 1994 John led me on a day's excursion into the woods north of the park, where he showed me what had plainly been caused by large vehicles which had pushed into the woods to put out a fire, the aftermath of which I could still see, almost a year and a half later. There were pits in several places, with fire-blackened rims, where John was convinced debris from a UFO had been retrieved. In the spring of 1995 LIUFON sponsored a daylong conference on what may have occurred that late autumn evening at the park and its environs.

Throughout my reporting on John Ford and LIUFON, I always tried to give the story straight: what John said, what others said, and whatever facts I could track down in the matter at hand. I think John appreciated that I handled my reportage with none of the journalistic rolling of the eyes that marked so much of the media's reporting on UFOs, plainly giving the public the unmistakable message: Well, this is an interesting story, but of course it can't be true—and people who believe it are nuts.

And then, in the spring of 1996, I gave John Ford a call. I hadn't spoken with him for some time. When he picked up the phone there was immediately something desperate and at the same time direct in his manner. He said there were people out to get him, in fact trying to kill him. My first thought was that he was being outright paranoid. Then he closed the conversation with, "If something happens to me, you'll know what I said is true."

Six weeks later . . . It was June 12, 1996. The evening news gave a teasing blurb: UFO researcher from Bellport arrested on suspicion of attempted murder. So before I saw the film of John in handcuffs being led from his house I knew that "something" had indeed happened to him.

Many readers know the outline of the story. John Ford, along with Joseph Mazzuchelli, was charged with conspiracy to kill three local politicians: Suffolk County Republican Party chairman John Powell, county legislator Fred Towle, and Anthony Gazzola, chief investigator for the town of Brookhaven, by putting radium in their toothpaste and or on their car seats. My reaction to the charge was: either John Ford had lost his mind or this is totally unbelievable nonsense.

Ford contended he used radium to calibrate his Geiger counter, which he would take with him to check for radiation when investigating alleged UFO crash sites.

Was John Ford set up? The authorities based their warrant on a police informant that had been wired, one Kenneth Koch, who was allegedly approaching Ford about buying a gun from his collection. The evening news made much of the numerous guns in Ford's house (implication: they were illegal), as well as a magazine, *The Freeman*, to which Ford apparently subscribed. So John Ford, of LIUFON, besides being a UFO nut (the *Newsday* headline was "Lost in Space"), was a militia nut, with an arsenal of guns at the ready to attack the proper bastions of authority. But it turned out that Ford's gun collection was wholly legal, and the magazine, whose name was unfortunately the same as a western militia group the government was after, was merely an established conservative publication.

Some facts before we return to the recorded "conversation" that led to Ford's arrest. Preston Nichols (yes, of Montauk Project fame) visited me near midnight at the paper, that summer of '96, his large form tapping carefully at the glass front door, holding a copy of the warrant for John's arrest.

"I went to John's house three days later to get John's birds," said Nichols, "and I found the warrant taped on the refrigerator. Look at the date."

The warrant was dated June 14, 1996—two days after Ford had been arrested. Nichols concluded that John had been arrested without a warrant and that the police had secured one two days later. Would that make the arrest of John Ford illegal, null and void?

I spoke to Ford's lawyer, John Rouse, about this. Certainly this could be a useful document in a trial. Rouse did not think so. "They are just going to contend it was a typographical error. They'll have a detective testify under oath that it was secured on the correct day." It was not until years later it was pointed out to me that a detective involved in the case would not be the one for a court to question; instead it would be the judge who signed that warrant who would have to testify under oath as to its actual date.

In my first conversations with Rouse he claimed he would forge ahead with a trial that would not only exonerate John Ford, but show Suffolk County DA James Catterson for the despicable person he was. But ultimately, as John Ford himself related to me, "Rouse convinced me I would be found guilty, that my best bet was to accept a not competent to stand trial deal. He said I would just be in jail two or three years."

That, as everyone knows, was eighteen years ago. Ford was held at the Riverhead Correctional Facility on Long Island until the later part of 1997, and then transferred to the Mid-Hudson Psychiatric Center, in New Hampton, New York, where he has been ever since. Had Ford gone to trial, been convicted, he would have been out in a few years. Mazzuchelli, whose odd story, and his con man–like influence on John is too long to tell here, was convicted and in prison for two years.

The radium that was alleged to be the murder weapon was assessed by Brookhaven National Laboratory's Radiological Assistance Program (RAP) team. A year or so afterward I had a conversation with a member of the RAP team who told me that the potency of the radium made it hardly a weapon of immediate murder. Maybe if you exposed someone to it for twenty years they might get cancer. The lab's media officer, Mona Rowe said, "After all this happened, the joke around the lab was that if Ford put radium on someone's car seat and they had prostate cancer, he might cure them."

So there you have it: John Ford was going to sneak into the bathroom windows of his victims and lace their toothpaste with levels of radium that *might* cause cancer in two decades. Hardly the modus operandi of a true killer.

The incriminating wiretap revealed that John Ford had spoken about lacing Gazzola's lasagna with radium, and other such threats that any listener could hardly take seriously. If I said to someone I'm going to the White House and punch the president in the nose, would anyone take that as a serious threat?

Some very pertinent information about Ford's alleged victims: Suffolk County Republican Party chairman (who began his climb up the ladder by working at the Brookhaven town dump) would be himself arrested and convicted (in 2000) for accepting bribes (for allowing companies illegal access to the Brookhaven town landfill) and being involved in an illegal chop shop. Powell died of a heart attack in 2012.

Suffolk County legislator Fred Towle would also go a similar route: In 2003 he pled guilty to receiving a bribe and a scheme to defraud. Because he cooperated with authorities, thirty-three other charges were dropped. Towle's inside information was "invaluable" said Suffolk DA Thomas Spota in getting the goods on a number of other corrupt politicians in Suffolk, and especially those in Brookhaven, which is not known as "Crookhaven" for nothing. Towle spent a brief time in jail and reemerged to own a weekly newspaper, *The South Shore Press*.

Ford's other alleged intended victim, Anthony Gazzola, apparently stayed on the right side of the law, at least in terms of the tenor of the times in Crookhaven—although his son and namesake, Anthony, Jr., an employee of the Brookhaven highway department, was recently charged with selling prescription drugs while on the clock, according to one report.

James Catterson, who vigorously prosecuted John Ford, lost a fourth term bid for Suffolk DA in 2001 to present-day DA Spota. In speaking of that election, a *New York Times* article related that many saw Catterson "as a quick-tempered bully who used the powers of his office to batter enemies and others who got in his way," and that with his defeat he "finally seemed to pay a price for what a widening ring of critics saw as his free-swinging ways." Catterson died in 2007.

Oh, yes: Ford's erstwhile attorney John Rouse himself became Brookhaven town highway supervisor and, in 2012, was elected to a county judgeship.

Thus was the political and legal system that arrested and put away John Ford in what has been an unending incarceration.

It's my contention that the arrest and imprisonment of John Ford had as much to do, maybe more, with local politics, than any truth about UFOs. John was active in local politics. He had broken from the local Republican Party, feeling it had not adhered to its original

LUE255

values. There were those who told me he was considering a run for local office on the Conservative ticket. There were those who said he was gathering some telling dirt on those in power. Apparently, at least with Powell and Towle, there was more than enough "dirt" to go around, enough to finally come to light. John Ford's "craziness" over UFOs might have been a useful excuse to put him away.

But any way you look at it, from the politics of "Crookhaven," to the alleged crashes and cover-ups of UFOs, John Ford is a political prisoner. An article I read recently about Mid-Hudson Psychiatric Center described it as a holding place for the mentally ill who are violent. John Ford has not had one violent incident in all the years he has been there. In phone conversations over the years John has told me that he is continually being reviewed and kept on at Mid-Hudson as being a possible danger to others if he is let out.

John himself might find grim humor in the following possible exchange: Some ominous inmate says to John, "What're you in for?" and John replies, in that every earnest and factual way he has, "Radioactive toothpaste."

In 2007 a TV producer who tried to put together a documentary on John's case and the Southaven Park crash (the producer was fired: more grist for the conspiracy mill) said to me, "John Ford is like the Nelson Mandela of UFOs."

It is to be hoped that John Ford will not match Mandela's twenty-seven years in prison. Seventeen years is enough of a price to pay . . . for what seems to be no crime at all.

Against the background of the mysteries surrounding the Ford case, the alleged cover-up by means of arson, and the rumors of Brookhaven Laboratory downing a UFO, *UFO Hunters* began its own investigation into the Southaven Park incident, looking not only for evidence of the crash, witnesses to the events following the crash, and any video that might have been taken of the cleanup. We would not be disappointed.

THE EPISODE

The incidents of UFOs over Long Island caught our attention, first from the story of John Ford, but also from video taken by a resident on the south shore of Connecticut toward Long Island that showed a series of orblike lights circling over the North Shore of Long Island Sound. This reminded me of the 1992 Southaven Park incident in Shirley that had captured local newspaper headlines and about which local residents were still commenting on even fifteen years later. Southaven Park was an incident in which a craft was said to have crashed in a wooded area, starting a fire that was so intense, but whose origin was so highly classified, that local fire responders were told to stay out of the park and only the Brookhaven National Laboratory fire units could control.

Local residents had seen Brookhaven units at the park, which was a big no-no because Brookhaven fire apparatus could only respond to fires inside the laboratory complex, unless called upon for mutual aid. Their presence outside the laboratory complex, by itself, meant that something significant had occurred five miles south of Brookhaven National Laboratory. And that's significant because high-tech energy facilities, like Brookhaven and Lawrence Livermore in California, had long been suspected of both attracting alien interest and even tracking alien craft.

Brookhaven had a long history of cutting-edge research, Kevin Cook pointed out, not only continuing experiments with high-energy particle colliders, but they were the first to have a peacetime nuclear fission reactor. Brookhaven, along with Lawrence Livermore, was among the leading energy research facilities in the United States. Their research into particle beams, lasers, fusion, and directed energy meant that if there were alien craft over Long Island seeking sources of energy, Brookhaven would have been high on its surveillance list.

Pat speculated that the history of UFO encounters has a lot to do with our research into high-energy development from the 1940s when UFOs were spotted over the Hanford nuclear research facility in Washington and then at White Sands in New Mexico, Oak Ridge, and

Roswell. It was as if, Pat suggested, that for years we had been sur-
veilled by some off-planet culture who were listening to our signals
and noted, with concern, that we had discovered nuclear power, a force
that could destroy far more than an enemy in wartime. The bombing of Hiroshima and Nagasaki became the tipping points. They
decided to make their presence more obvious, probably prior to an
intervention. "Now they're here to stay and to make sure we don't do
it again."

Kevin speculated that because Brookhaven was known for engaging in experiments with particle beams far in advance of what current
lay science believed was possible, it just might be that if there were
an alien species hovering around planet Earth, that species might be
surveilling Brookhaven. Perhaps, if there was any truth to the Southaven Park crash, it might have been an alien craft that somehow got
hit by a beam from Brookhaven. After all, Kevin speculated, if we were
far enough along in particle beam physics, perhaps we could be pos-
ing an even greater threat to any extraterrestrial neighbors than we
were with nuclear weapons.

It was long past the time, we agreed as we drove along the Long
Island Expressway out to Suffolk County, that we had to surveil them
instead of waiting for them to surveil us. Our first stop was at Port
Jefferson for a trip on the Port Jeff ferry across the Long Island Sound
to the Connecticut south shore and the area around Bridgeport where
our first witness, a local resident, had been videotaping strange lights
circling in the skies over the Brookhaven area.

THE LONG ISLAND LIGHTS

We met up with Mark, who asked that we never use his last name, on
the beach where he said that despite his years-long filming of the lights
he could not identify, no one seemed to be interested in the images he
was capturing. Mark was careful about plotting the positions of what
he taped: compass headings, angles of inclination, and areas on the Long
Island map over which the objects looked like they were hovering.

"Originally they were appearing in the Smithtown Bay area near Sunken Meadow State Park," Mark said. "They seemed to be stationary for long periods of time, at first, staying almost motionless for hours, and then sometimes they would change position. These things don't strobe. They're just steady lights. They almost look like signs, they're so consistently lit." He continued describing the lights by saying that it seemed like they were in a dance when they moved. He also said they flew as if they were in a relay by the way they changed places.

"What do you consider your best footage so far?" Pat asked.

"Over the Norwalk Islands," Mark answered, noting a small group of islands off the Connecticut shore. "They were hovering so low above the horizon, they were moving sideways from behind the island."

"Have you ever gotten a good enough view of them to make out a shape?" Kevin asked.

"Through binoculars," Mark said. "I could see it looked like a lozenge-shaped craft with two headlights in it."

If this were a surveillance operation, I suggested, the pattern of the flying lights, their circling over a specific area and seemingly hovering in place, would be a consistent pattern for surveillance. They didn't seem in a hurry to leave the area. We needed to get more information on these lights to see if they, first, were real craft, and next, if real, were they keeping a vigil over Brookhaven or were they something else entirely.

"Why do you go out so much to see the lights?" I asked Mark.

"I want to figure out what they are," Mark said. "If they're drones, if they're some kind of experimental things, fine. Whatever they are, I just need to know what they are."

Kevin remained skeptical. "There are so many airports over Long Island; I just want to see if there's a correlation." And he, along with the team, took Mark's videos to analyze them with our photo specialist, Terrence Masson.

"Most UFO videos turn out not to be UFOs at all," Kevin said. "But they ultimately display conventional features. The other aspect of most UFO videos shot by nonprofessional photographers is that they are spotty and jumpy, sometimes out of focus as the camera struggles to adjust automatically to distance and poor light. Mark's video, however, is different. There are hours of footage meticulously supported by data."

Terrence Masson agreed, saying that Mark was "very diligent about recording his shooting location and keeps very good notes. I would call him a very reliable witness." Terrence also pointed out the steadiness of the camera, the sustained focus on a particular point in the sky instead of a jumping around from one point to another. Terrence was also impressed by the consistent performance of the floating lights that Mark captured and that there were a very large number of lights.

"What's consistent about this footage," Terrence said, "is that their motion is almost stationary. It's very, very slow. What's freaky is that when you speed these things up at many times the playback speed, they dance and fly all around in repeated patterns, follow each other, very wild behavior."

Terrence sought to establish a pattern of how he analyzes footage like this. "The first thing I do when I look at footage like this is to try to establish sight lines. Where's the shooter? Where's the angle of shooting? What's the aspect ratio? What's the coverage?" Terrence displayed a map on his computer screen that laid all these parameters out. He plotted six different locations on the Connecticut shore that he was able to isolate and then correspond these locations to Mark's shooting direction. The result, as if this were a ballistics analysis from a CSI investigator, was a chart of line-of-sight vectors plotting what Mark's specific target areas would have been to enable him to capture the lights on film from his different shooting locations. Simply stated, over what locations were these lights flying?

"The next thing I did," Terrence said, "was to plot out the locations of all the local airports. Six out of the seven sight lines are basically bull's-eye to Republic, JFK, and La Guardia airports. And you can see the light pattern actually corresponds to a figure-eight pattern or a corkscrew very consistent with a lineup of planes coming into an airport." Terrence hypothesized that Mark was picking up the circling and landing patterns of planes coming into area airports.

"Is every video taken line of sight to airports just like this?" I asked.

"No," Terrence said, demonstrating how, in the remaining piece of footage from Mark, lights that looked stationary in the air when speeded up seemed to be queuing up into a pattern one after another so quickly, they almost turned into a horizontal line. Light after light seemed to stop and dip down below the tree line, followed by other lights doing the same thing. This piece of footage, unlike the previous pieces, was not sighted along a line going to an airport. It was sighted along the Connecticut coast more than directly across the sound. "We can't identify them with any of the characteristics we used to identify any of the other footage," Terrence said. "So they are left unidentified."

Mark's video, therefore, showed that craft that could have appeared to be about twenty-five miles from Brookhaven National Laboratory could suggest that there might have been a set surveillance routine. Thus, given Brookhaven's long history as a leader in breakthrough energy research and perhaps an even longer history of UFO surveillance since the final years of World War II, you'd expect some sort of purported incidents or encounters. And we had one that we set off to investigate.

THE BROOKHAVEN AND SOUTHAVEN PARK INCIDENTS

There was a widely reported crash of some kind of object in Southaven Park near the Brookhaven National Laboratory campus in November 1992, a crash whose resulting fire and retrieval efforts were witnessed by a number of local residents even though the local municipal authorities in Suffolk County denied anything unusual ever happened in the park.

One eyewitness to the events on the night in question, Denise Kisowsky, said that on the evening of November 24, 1992, "We saw a mysterious light light up the entire sky. It was about seven o'clock at night and, being November, it was full dark. All of a sudden it was lighter out than when the sun was just setting. After that we noticed that lights in the area and in the surrounding homes went out. There were some gentlemen standing out front and they seemed to be pointing to the direction of Southaven Park." The skies stayed light for about ten seconds, Denise said, but it was a flash, "enough for you to go, 'What's going on?' I actually said to my husband, 'They just bombed New York.'"

She continued, "Ever since that evening we've heard a lot of stories about what might have happened in Southaven Park and things that had happened around that area." Denise's story indicates that if there were an incendiary event, such as a crash, in the Southaven Park area, her story of seeing a flash and an area power outage might corroborate the events at the park.

"I know that we lost our lights," Denise said, indicating it was at the same time as the flash. "And I know that our other neighbors around us lost their lights, too. But when they contacted the utility company, there was no record of any problems with the lights in this area that night." Even though Denise had personally experienced a power outage and witnessed her neighbors' power go down, the utility denied that anything had happened. In her opinion, the utility company was not telling the truth. "Through the whole thing," she said, "there was something that was being kept from the public." Denise told us that she even saw power utility company repair trucks in the area working on the lines. But the company sent a letter to their subscribers saying that nothing was amiss. "Whoever wants to give you an explanation," Denise commented, "they can give you ten different explanations. But they can't explain that light," referring to the flash she and her neighbors saw.

"Finally," Pat said after our interview with Denise, "we have some information that something strange happened that night and there was an incident in the park."

Kevin, Pat, and I met up with Steve Iavarone and Tony West, both members of the Long Island UFO Network and longtime investigators, who had been researching the Southaven Park incident. They led us into the park itself to get a sense of what had happened there and what evidence, if any, still remained, even though the park was locked down after the incident.

Steve told us that that the park, at first, was more of a debris field than an actual crash site because debris had rained down on the area from an object that might have broken up in flight. "Eyewitnesses," Steve said, told him that, "something that was falling out of the sky had a cylindrical shape and was rotating, turning from blue to white to green. As it came over the park, it made a right-angle turn and it fell apart." It spread debris all over the park woods.

At this point in the investigation, Pat summarized, we had Mark's strange light, or maybe a craft, that did not seem to be a conventional plane circling one of the Long Island airports, but, rather, seemed to be surveilling the Brookhaven area. And we had what was described as an actual craft breaking up in midair over Southaven Park after coming in from the southeast, which is only a few miles from Brookhaven. Then we had Denise's story of a flash of light from the park that lit up the area like daytime, also from a southeast direction, and a power outage in her neighborhood, which the local power company, LILCO, denied took place. Was there a connection?

Who, Pat asked the Long Island UFO investigators, would normally respond to a crash in Southaven Park? Steve answered that the local fire department would normally respond. And they did respond. They were the first people on the scene to put out the fire. Then the Suffolk County police arrived and started to close down the park. They kept local residents and lookie-loos away, Tony said, but allowed Brookhaven fire apparatus to enter the park, while the other firefighters were kept outside the park. They couldn't get in, Steve said, because the Suffolk County police turned them away.

"Forty minutes, approximately, after that," Steve continued, "these guys in black jumpsuits came over and the Suffolk County police told them to leave the area, and they left immediately."

I found this to be a significant twist in the story. There seemed to be no reason a local fire crew should have been turned away from what was a forest fire to which county police had been dispatched. Who was putting out the fire and what else, if anything, was going on in Southaven Park? One thing is clear, there is no reason a fire crew from

Brookhaven National Laboratory should have special access to that fire site unless something else was going on, something that the public was not allowed to see.

Witnesses who drove to the park, but were not allowed access, told Steve Iavarone that they saw debris from the area being carried out on flatbed trucks, vehicles that looked like military trucks with, Steve said, "a kind of canvas covering wrapped around it." Steve said they closed up the debris field at the park within two days, widening the roads leading out of the park on the second day to get the flatbeds in and out. They actually had construction crews working the area, Steve said, something they discovered only after the crews had left the area.

"There was a fireman," Steve told us, "who was filming the cleanup events at the park, videotaping all of the activity. About a week later, that videotape was anonymously left in Steve's mailbox. We didn't know who he was, but it was clear he felt we should know what happened."

Steve pulled the video, which he'd transferred to a DVD, out of the car so Pat could run it on his laptop.

The video, shot in poor light, displayed a big chunk of debris that looked as if it were still smoldering. The camera operator zoomed in on it, a metallic object that was aglow. In the next sequence we could see two people pulling a body bag along the ground and then placing what looked like a humanoid figure against a tree and moving what Pat thought was a Mylar blanket around it. Obviously, we had no provenance regarding this video, but if it were real—which is what it looked like—then it might be the only video recording of a UFO retrieval that ever made it out of the world of black projects. It might be the first recorded video evidence of an actual UFO operation in American history.

Citing the lack of provenance and the anonymous nature of the videographer, Kevin was still skeptical. Without more information, he asserted, we just couldn't tell whether this was a hoax or not. He suggested that we had to get some corroborating testimony from first responder teams in the area who could verify the story that Steve and Tony told us.

We interviewed the crew chief, Greg Miglino, Jr., at the South Country fire emergency squad, who told us that on the November date in question in 1992, they were called to respond to a report of smoke and fire in the area of the park. That department would have been the first responder for any fire emergency at the park. Greg told us that he was in one of his marked vehicles when the call came in and he started heading toward the park. The park police and the Suffolk County police, Greg said, made it known that the fire at the park was started by campers who were careless with their campfire. Once that was announced over the radio, Greg said, he released the squad from responding and they returned to headquarters. But Pat was skeptical about this explanation.

"It's November," he said. "Nighttime temperatures are in the thirties. This is not the ideal climate for nighttime camping." The explanation simply didn't ring true for him. "However," Pat asked, "what if there were some kind of Hazmat emergency or radiation emergency? Who would roll on that?"

"Either Suffolk County emergency," Greg said. "Or maybe Brookhaven's own emergency units." We asked Greg why Brookhaven. "Brookhaven has a small nuclear reactor that they use," he said. "They used it for many years for testing, and their fire department is explicitly trained in responding to radiological emergencies."

Next stop, Brookhaven National Laboratory, where we had a meeting set up with one of Brookhaven's leading scientists, who told us that Brookhaven was run by the United States Department of Energy for peacetime and scientific research. We explained that we were investigating a significant amount of UFO activity that took place on Long Island and specifically in the area around Brookhaven. And we stated our hypothesis that somehow UFOs were drawn to the airspace around the laboratory because of the exotic high-energy experiments, specifically the facility's use of nuclear power. Whoever was navigating those craft could keep an alien eye on what the lab was doing. And we asked what the laboratory's take might be on that speculation. We were told that there were no reported UFO sightings over the lab and that the data gathered by the lab did not indicate the possibility that UFOs actually existed.

Brookhaven has several particle accelerators on site for the purpose of researching the behaviors of particles that make up the nuclei of atoms and the forces that hold the particles together. We asked whether the energy that's released in the collider could be detected from Earth orbit. The short answer was "no" because any particles that could escape the collider would decay very rapidly. However, some of the particles could travel long distances and with sensitive or exotic equipment the Brookhaven facility would look somewhat brighter than the surrounding area, indicating an energy release. Might the released energy, we asked, give off a kind of signature that UFOs might be able to pick up. Our answer was a qualified "yes"; if an entity were able to pick up the types of energy released by the particle collider by using very sensitive detection equipment. Hence, we speculated, given the possibility of ETs, they would have been able to detect Brookhaven's signal.

We were invited to visit the Brookhaven Fire Department to meet with the fire chief, Chuck LaSalle, who, had his fire crews responded to the fire in Southaven Park, would have been on site that night and would have been a witness to any emergency activity. Inasmuch as witnesses along the perimeter of the park on the night of the fire had reported seeing Brookhaven fire apparatus on scene, LaSalle, we hoped, would confirm everything we had heard.

"There was nothing that happened," LaSalle told us. "Nothing at all." He said that he had the log for that night, which would prove that the fire department did not leave the station on the night of November 24, 1992. "There was nothing unusual, no unusual calls, and the Brookhaven fire equipment never left site that night for any reason." He handed the logbook to Kevin Cook, who confirmed that there was no mention in the logbook of any activity on the night in question and no indication that Brookhaven firefighting equipment ever left the laboratory complex. We asked LaSalle whether the lack of any notation meant that there was no fire at Southaven Park or whether it only meant that the Brookhaven Fire Department never left the station. LaSalle said that he had no idea what did or didn't happen in the park.

"I have no knowledge about any fire there. I can tell you that we did not participate in any way either as a primary responder or for mutual aid in any shape, way, or form in Southaven Park."

But Pat was not satisfied with the answer. He asked, "If you were involved in some capacity that involved national security that required your silence, something you would not be able to speak about, would you deny that anything had happened?"

"I would have to say yes," LaSalle answered, indicating he would deny his unit's participation in any event that, because of national security required his silence. "But even if something happened that was a secret, if you know firehouses, secrets get out. And for this story to have been kept secret for seventeen years, that would really have to have been a secret."

"If there had been a fire at Southaven Park sixteen years ago, what would you recommend we look for there in order to discover evidence?" Kevin asked.

"Sixteen or seventeen years is going to cover a lot," LaSalle said. "And you still could have the fact that there were other brush fires there during that period. So charred areas might not give away the fact that there was a crash there or something like that. Maybe you can look at the tops of trees for damage."

But I asked him again, this time off camera, whether, if Brookhaven had responded to a fire at the park and had been told straight out that this was a matter of national security that required not only his silence, but a complete absence of any record of the event, would he flatly deny that anything had ever happened and not make any log entry. He said yes. I pushed further, asking whether he would simply say he couldn't talk about it, neither confirming nor denying, or whether he would simply say nothing had happened. And, again, he said he would deny anything had ever happened. And that was my answer.

Following Chuck LaSalle's advice, we returned to the park to look for the types of crash or destruction evidence he described. This time, we brought along historical archeologist Garth Baldwin to look at the land formations for any anomalies that might have resulted from a fire after a crashed vehicle. Garth said he wanted to inspect any land formations that seemed out of place, evidence of new growth amid old growth, paths that might have been carved into the brush, and evidence on tree limbs, and tops of trees that could have been sheared off. Essentially, Garth was on the lookout for unnatural land formations, distortions to the landscape that could not otherwise be accounted for.

He pointed out that there was new foliage less than seventeen years old, new growth that did not fit into the background of existing growth, and trees that looked like they were five to ten years old where there were groups of older trees. He also saw plenty of crushed limbs in the treetops, not only broken limbs that might have fallen off during ice storms, but limbs that were actually crushed by some opposing force. Kevin also asked Garth to look for signs of a fortified road, a road that might have had to have been structurally supported to carry the weight of a military-type flatbed truck that, Steve and Tony said, made its way into the park and transported out the crashed ship. Kevin also noticed that among the groves of older, taller, oak trees, there were younger trees only five to six feet tall that seemed anomalous for that area.

As we stood in a clearing among dense foliage, Garth Baldwin remarked that it looked like we were standing in a place where someone or something had cleared out the area. It couldn't have been a fire, he said, because there was no charring or evidence of burned debris on the ground or even tree stumps. It was something else. It certainly could have been an area of road, parts of which had since been overgrown, he speculated. As we made our way deeper into the park, turning over patches of soil as we went, Garth pointed out that there was gray sand underneath new soil, which indicated to him that we were standing on a "traveled surface." Maybe it was a road cut through the brush. Then we came to a number of soft spots in the soil, which Garth explained as resulting from compaction from something heavy on the surface. Then he pointed to some of the taller trees, which showed clear evidence of scarring. One tree, in particular, he showed us, had been sheared off, and had since died. But the shearing clearly came from an impact. He said that the way the trees were topped off was consistent with an object coming from the air, through the trees, and lopping off the tops. He referred to the falling objects as "shrapnel" that hit some trees and not others. He could tell that, he said, because where the trees were topped, there was splintering in their upper trunks as if an object had smashed into them and bounced off. Even where live trees had been topped, new limbs had started growing though the original lower limbs that still bore scars from an impact.

By the time we had completed our inspection of the park and the interviews with witnesses and with Chuck LaSalle at Brookhaven, there were more questions than answers. The evidence itself did not definitively point to a UFO even though it showed that there was some unknown impact event that had taken place in Southaven Park, an event that might have resulted from the types of objects in Mark's videos of flying objects in that area that did not conform to conventional aircraft. Kevin also said that the Brookhaven Fire Department log looked "legit." If they were going to cover up their response to the Southaven crash, he said, "They did a hell of a job." Pat mentioned that we still had to factor in all of the eyewitnesses we spoke to who said they saw Brookhaven apparatus at the Southaven Park site. I suggested that a parallel investigation of similar anomalous lights over Lawrence Livermore Laboratory in California might shed some more light on Brookhaven. Unlike Brookhaven, however, Livermore was conducting research in high-energy weapons-grade lasers. It was time for a trip back to California, and warm weather.

THE LAWRENCE LIVERMORE LABORATORY UFO INCIDENT

In the hills overlooking Lawrence Livermore National Laboratory, we spoke to Dr. Jack Kasher, a former NASA physicist and a professor of physics at the University of Nebraska, who had worked at Livermore for eighteen years studying the microwave physics of the effects of nuclear weapons.

This work, Jack Kasher told us, was very highly classified. "As time went on, the security surrounding this research became tighter and tighter." Half the research Kasher conducted was in pure physics while the other half was in weaponizing lasers and the energy they projected. At Livermore, they were doing work on nuclear powered X-ray lasers that were the foundation of the Star Wars antimissile program. If Livermore had concentrated that much on weapons research, Pat speculated, it was likely that they might have become a target for alien surveillance.

Kevin posed the theory to Jack Kasher that once the United States started working on nuclear weapons back in the 1940s, extraterrestrials began observing facilities where this nuclear research was taking place. NASA's Jack Kasher plainly answered, "They did." He continued, "Over in Russia, for example, a nine-hundred-foot saucer hovered over a Russian missile silo for hours. And then you have Malmstrom Air Force Base where the UFO was over the base." That object managed to disrupt the communication between the missile launch officers and the missiles themselves, hardwired connections that were supposed to be impenetrable, shutting down the missile launch controls and resulting in a "no-go" status, according to Captain Robert Salas, who was an eyewitness to those events. "It's not just a question of whether you think UFOs will surveil, they already have several times," Dr. Kasher said.

"Do you know of anything at Lawrence Livermore labs that might throw off some kind of energy signature that could be detected from space?" Pat asked Kasher.

"We had done some fusion experiments here," Kasher said. "These might have been attractive." Kasher also talked about the effectiveness of lasers as a weapon, saying they would have to be very powerful. "I don't know how well defended a UFO would be but it would be worth a shot if we felt the UFO was some kind of a threat to us."

"Would aliens consider lasers a threat?" Pat asked.

"If what we are speculating about is true," Kasher said, "then they would certainly watch what we're doing with technology that they might perceive could be a potential threat to them."

Pat's conclusion was that if Brookhaven's particle beam research were somehow responsible for bringing down a UFO, or causing it to break up in midair, then the laser weapons research at Lawrence Livermore might have caused a palpable threat that needed to be closely watched. To follow up on Pat's theory, we met with software engineer and radio producer Olav Phillips, a witness to a UFO flyover at Livermore Laboratory.

"There was an illuminated object that shot across the sky over the Bay area," Olav said. "There were reports from people across the area who witnessed the event and reported that it actually made a course correction as it came in from the coast and then broke up when it came inland." Olav Phillips was one of the first UFO investigators to report this event, a supposed UFO crash on August 6, 1998, over Livermore, California. But there's more to this story, as Olav explained it. "We had a source that saw lasers coming out of Livermore." Late that night multiple witnesses told Olav and his investigative team that they saw a bright light flying in a straight line and then making hairpin course corrections after it crossed the coast. That fact alone indicated to us that it couldn't have been a meteor because meteors don't make abrupt directional changes. Then hours after the initial sighting, a very strange thing happened at a tire dump just seven miles away from Livermore's test area.

"Did anyone come up here to investigate the area as a possible UFO crash site after the event was reported?" Pat asked Olav.

"Everyone wanted to come out here," Olav said. "But because there was a tire fire associated with the event that made the whole area 'toxified.'" The tire fire burned for two and a half years, and the site wasn't cleaned up for over five years. By that point, any possible traces of a crash of an anomalous craft would have been long obliterated.

We asked Olav, "It takes very little effort to start a grass fire. But to start a tire fire requires a lot of sustained heat building up deep in the stacks of tires. This sounds like it might have been started deliberately." Olav said that the tire incident bothered him, too, because it was all too perfect. Witnesses saw a UFO over Livermore and laser beams shooting up from the lab. Then there was an alleged crash and then a tire fire that destroyed any evidence of the event.

"It was the perfect cover," Pat said.

"Even if it wasn't started as a cover," Olav said, "it became the perfect cover."

"At Brookhaven," Pat said, "we had video evidence of anomalous air activity over the area that Terrence Masson said he was unable to identify. Now at Livermore," Pat continued, "we might also have some video that suggested UFO activity in that area as well." Pat met with Al Murphy, one of the premier video analysts in all of California, who had previously worked at Lockheed's Skunk Works on classified projects and specialized in figuring out what's truly happening on a video and how movement can be determined. We presented to Al Murphy a video taken by an individual named "Pablo," who did not want to give us his real name and who did not want to appear on camera. Pablo told us he was twenty miles away from Lawrence Livermore Laboratory when he took the footage. Al reviewed the video.

"The first thing I notice," he said, "is that it was shot with night vision. I can see there is an object here very high up and very far away and it looks like a sequence of lights moving very fast. The geometry of the lights is different and they kind of move with respect to each other. And if you look closely you can see stars behind the lights."

The lights seemed to be moving in a roughly triangular formation against a starry sky.

"The array of lights indicates to me that it is a formation and of a single craft," Al said. "It's a format of something that we don't know what it is."

"Are helicopters an option?" Kevin asks.

"No," Al answered. "I don't think helicopters are an option."

Pat was inclined to dismiss any hint that this was a conventional craft in the video, saying it makes no sense that an aircraft would be flying so brazenly over restricted airspace. He asked Murphy whether he thought that the lights seemed "unconventional."

"I would say it's unconventional for these lights to fly in such a close formation," Murphy said.

And Pat concluded, "We are looking at a formation of UFOs that are flying in close formation over Lawrence Livermore lab." He said that it was time to find out what was happening at Livermore and what's happening now.

It was time to call in our friends from the FLIR corporation, the folks who manufacture the forward-looking infrared camera that we used in investigations in previous episodes and one of the pioneering inventors of thermal imaging technology. This time, the FLIR folks brought in their surveillance vehicle, a tricked-out camper with an array of advanced infrared camera surveillance equipment. Walking us through our nighttime sky watch over Livermore was Roy Momberg from FLIR who explained the science behind the cameras and the truck's equipment. The science behind the FLIR camera is that the device doesn't register the image of conventional light in the visible spectrum. It registers heat signatures of objects against the ambient heat of the surrounding environment. Hence, we would not be looking at car headlights if a car drove through the frame. We would be looking at the heat of the engine, heat emanating from the chassis, and, of course, heat from the exhaust.

"If aliens or extraterrestrials are operating craft outside our visible spectrum," Pat asked, "will this camera be able to pick up that image? Would this camera be able to pick up aerial vehicles flying over Lawrence Livermore?" And Roy assured him that anything that put out a thermal signature would appear on the FLIR.

"With the tool that I have here, I can spot an airplane across the approach corridors twenty-five to thirty miles away," Roy explained. And Kevin agreed, further suggesting that if an alien craft were flying through Lawrence Livermore airspace, the lab itself would have the technology to detect it and "it would most likely possess just the right weapon to destroy that craft."

Roy said that the way the cameras were pointed, we would be able to see the heat signatures of aircraft coming in on approach vectors to

Oakland airport. At first, Roy captured a blob of light on the camera's video monitor. But as he zoomed in on it, the image became a cylinder, prompting Kevin to remark that it looked like a flying saucer. However, Roy said that from the flight pattern and the proximity to the Oakland airport approach corridor, he was sure we were looking at a commercial airliner. If one were to differentiate between the heat signature of a conventional aircraft and an alien craft, we would have to analyze the flight pattern, how the heat signature moved across the monitor. Roy said that, simply stated, unless the image on the screen was making extreme maneuvers not consistent with the aerial capabilities of a conventional aircraft, you could not tell what the nature of the image was except to be able to determine that it was flying.

But suddenly, one of the lights on Roy's FLIR monitor made a strange maneuver. He zoomed in on it and said it was a "go-fast," moving at a higher velocity than a plane approaching an airport. He surmised that it might not be a plane at all, but an object far in the distance going very fast. "So it couldn't be one of ours," Pat said to Kevin. "The problem with this image is that it's moving exceedingly fast and its flight pattern and characteristics don't seem conventional. We could be onto something here," Pat said as he took over the controls of the camera and moved the joystick to zoom in on the object even more. "This is like playing the ultimate *UFO Hunters* video game," Pat said. He speculated that if there was anything up there, he would be able to capture its image with the FLIR system he was operating. But as he zoomed in, Roy was able to determine that the object had a conventional tail structure. "Looks to me like a small corporate jet, a private aircraft," he said. A false alarm, but fun.

Ultimately, Pat concluded, the only images he believed that fit the bill of unidentified craft were Mark's videos of lights over Brookhaven and Pablo's video of a triangular formation of lights over Lawrence Livermore. "The craft in those videos," Pat said, "could definitely be doing surveillance over those labs."

The takeaway for me, was the two videos taken over labs on different sides of the country were too similar to one another, given the nature of the areas in which they were flying. The forest fire in the Southaven

Park area after that witnessed UFO crash and the tire fire at Livermore after high-energy laser tests and a witnessed UFO flyover didn't seem coincidental. At both Brookhaven and Lawrence Livermore National laboratories, two high-energy research and development facilities, we have reported UFO crashes and resulting suspicious fires that destroyed any evidence that may have existed. Not only did the fires cover up any evidence—evidence that might have been subsequently removed—but the fires also served the purpose of keeping onlookers away while Hazmat and emergency response teams did their work. This could suggest that UFOs perceive facilities like this, as well as Hanford, Oak Ridge, Los Alamos, and Roswell in the 1940s, as a threat to them and thus meriting surveillance operations.

On the other hand, it seemed highly possible that if there were UFOs over these areas and in light of the possible UFO that pursued the Air Force RB-47, the case that James McDonald investigated, these alien craft had technology so sophisticated that they would be able to figure out exactly what was going on at the two national laboratories and be able to avoid any accidental or deliberate energy discharge that could bring them down. Much the same could be said for FLIR camera surveillance. A really good ET would know what was watching the skies and be able to stay away.

Ever the skeptic, Kevin argued that because there are thousands of UFO sightings every year, one or two of them, just following the laws of chance, would be bound to be associated with a forest or brush fire in the area. Does that mean there's a cover-up so profound that officials would set fires just to hide the evidence? "You can't take bits of information and concoct fantastic stories around these events," he said. "After looking at all the evidence, I'm not convinced that there's widespread UFO surveillance over our most important energy research facilities. There are tens of thousands of UFO sightings in the U.S. and laboratories such as Livermore and Brookhaven are located near busy airports and population centers. So it's only natural that witnesses might think they see UFOs over these labs."

But Pat was even more skeptical about what Kevin had said. "If the government wanted to cover up UFOs, it wouldn't be hard. Force witnesses into silence, make sure log entries are missing, and deny, deny, deny. We have to focus on eyewitness accounts, people making videotape and taking photos, and test the evidence for credibility." He said that we received two sets of videotapes that neither of our experts could explain away as conventional images for these objects in the sky. "When you map out these videos with all the background explanations, it all adds up for me. There is alien surveillance over our national labs."

We were faced with two parallel situations where something was reported to have crashed over or near highly sensitive government high-energy research installations, one of which was actively involved in weaponizing lasers. But it was what happened after the reported crashes that was so suspicious and bothered us. There were two strange fires that not only kept residents away, but which allowed recovery teams to remove any evidence.

Our episode showed that in both instances of fires after the reported crashes near highly classified energy research facilities there exist two videos taken by people separated by over 3,600 miles. Two people who did not know each other, who captured formations of lights that our video analysts and experts could not explain. Just like our videos over Area 51, we might have just caught UFOs on videotape in places where the government doesn't want them to be. And when they were knocked out of the air, we speculate, any evidence of the crashes was destroyed by suspicious fires. Kevin may have been correct in his insistence upon co-incidence, but Pat raised the appropriate questions. Something is certainly not right, and LIUFON's John Ford, confined to a mental institution where he says he is being forcibly medicated into a semi-somnambulistic state, has paid the price for it with his freedom.

BILL'S BLOG

THE MAN IN BLACK. DARK BLUE, ACTUALLY.

We were filming on the ferry dock at Port Jefferson, Long Island, waiting for the boat to take us across Long Island Sound to Bridgeport to meet Mark and see his video, shooting what are called OTFs—"on the fly"—which are interviews with the subject looking off camera; interviews you've seen countless times on reality television and even on some news shows. I was on camera when out of the corner of my eye, I caught a satisfied-looking sartorial gentleman holding an unlit Churchill cigar and smiling at me. He was, as Tom Wolfe might have described him, a "man in full." I could see that he was trying to catch my attention, subtly but persistently, until we finished the shot and I gave him a wave as I walked over to the craft SUV for something to drink. He followed me, caught up, and said, "Can I buy you a cup of coffee? Love to talk to you for a minute."

What the hell, I thought. Why not?

We walked across the ferry dock to a coffee shop where he introduced himself. In a bit, you'll know why I'm not repeating his name even though he's written two articles for *UFO Magazine,* one of which is not directly about UFOs, but more of a conspiracy story about John Lennon, the alien egg, Mark Chapman, William F. Buckley, Pencey Prep, and J. D. Salinger. There's a UFO in there I guarantee, but you'll have to read the magazine article to get it (*UFO Magazine,* V. 24.1, Issue #154, October, 2010). The story he told me when we sat down for an afternoon cuppa joe was about a mysterious off-the-books black-bag job he was ordered to do regarding the retrieval of an ancient alien artifact from Egypt, which he delivered to Father Malachi Martin.

"Great show," he said. "That's the good news. You guys stepped on some majorly big toes back at Area 51 last year. That's the bad news. That camera stunt up Tikaboo Peak and the surveillance cameras you guys set up over the base got a lot of people really angry. The Delta Force sentries that back up the other security personnel there loved the episode. They were laughing all over the place. But the bosses were fuming. And that episode in Dulce you just shot. If you weren't getting canned for Area 51, you would have got canned for that. You guys are going to be off the air next year, but at least you had a good run."

That was a lot to swallow and hotter than the coffee that was scalding my tongue. I made some lame comments about the McDonald's coffee lawsuit, but he cut me off by saying, "I own this place." Okay, now how do I get out of this?

"I'll cut right to it," he said. "I'm a nonofficial cover officer for the CIA. I was in Delta Force, did my stint in federal law enforcement and the Secret Service as a currency investigator, and finally was offered a job at the CIA." I knew CIA guys, one of whom was my former partner in an ill-fated Internet e-book venture, and another was former station chief Chip Beck, who also wrote for *UFO Magazine* on dark energy research. Without mentioning any names, I indicated I had known CIA guys.

"They probably were attaché case carriers," the sartorial

stranger said. "Not black-bag guys." He told me he had a great UFO story for my magazine, but first he wanted to make sure that I understood the message and would keep it to myself. Then he said, "You're on the right track with Brookhaven. These guys you spoke to could never tell you what's really going on because the agency would be all over them, seriously and painfully. They don't fool around. I know. Here on Long Island is where American intelligence services were founded all the way back during the Revolutionary War. George Washington had his own spy ring. Today, the research at Brookhaven is run out of SUNY Stonybrook. That's where the agency has a lot of clout. You'll never get the truth from any of these guys on camera, but you're right about the UFO cover-up. It runs so deep that there's probably no way to reveal it. Its tentacles go all the way back."

He had my attention. I felt that something hinky was going on at Brookhaven. Too many smiles, too solicitous, and that logbook popped up very suddenly as if LaSalle, who gave me a knowing smile as we left, had known in advance exactly what we wanted to see.

My CIA coffee companion and I chatted about nothing in particular for a few more minutes and then he got up. "Will contact you later about that Malachi Martin story, but if you want some lunch or breakfast on me, just drop my name to the guy behind the counter and it's all taken care of."

And he left. Just like that. Brookhaven was keeping a UFO cover-up, all right, and that was probably the case at Lawrence Livermore as well. And I knew all about goings on in Suffolk County because I used to live there. Therefore, I wasn't surprised about either the CIA connection the stranger talked about or the OSS connection from World War II. I knew about the scuttled German U-boat off Sandy Point with the missile-launching gangplank on its foredeck. It had been lying on its side on the bottom and became a sport for locals to dive for souvenirs until the Coast Guard came in and stripped away all the good stuff.

The boat's probably still there to this very day, crewless, of course, encrusted with all kinds of sea skeletons, and hiding the secret of what Admiral Dönitz was planning when he sent missile-carrying U-boats to bomb American East Coast cities before the end of World War II in 1945.

And in the wake of this stranger's polite exit from his own coffee shop, I was left to wonder about John Ford. When he appealed to his psychiatrists to get out of the mental institution, he reports that they argued that because he was one of the directors of a UFO research organization, he was being delusional and, therefore, too mentally ill to be let loose on the public. Everyone knows that UFOs aren't real and that anyone who believes they're real is delusional. If you're delusional you're a threat to yourself and others. If you're a threat to yourself or others, you belong in an institution. So take these little pink pills, buddy, toddle off to your room, and after we plug you into this machine, you'll forget about your problems. When you wake up, you'll have forgotten a lot more than that.

John Ford's only appeal at this point is to get a court order for his release after seventeen years of an indeterminate sentence, which he has recently done. According to Ford, the state, seeking to keep Ford confined to the mental institution, has argued, again, that Ford's belief in the existence of UFOs is delusional and that because he is delusional he is a danger to himself and others, the legal standard for confinement. Further, according to Ford, the prosecutor argued that LIUFON is a murderous organization. However, if the court so orders that Ford is no longer a danger, he's a free man. But for now he rots away in a mental institution because of his beliefs—a twenty-first-century *Homo sovieticus*—deemed too unstable to pollute our sane society with his belief that not only did Brookhaven National Laboratory cause a UFO to break up in flight, but that after it crashed in Southaven Park, Suffolk County officials, working under the instructions of some powerful group to which my sartorial new friend belonged, started a dangerous fire to cover up the remnants of a UFO retrieval during which Brookhaven's own fire equipment helped put out the fire of the burning spacecraft and the bodies it contained.

Crazy, right?

"THE GREYS CONSPIRACY"
THE STARCHILD AND THE LATE LLOYD PYE

In this episode we sought to return to a theme we covered in season one, the alien abduction phenomenon. Was it real or were the self-described abductees simply delusional? This time, we wanted to see if there existed any real physical evidence, not just of abductions, but of an alien presence. We'd managed to recover metal shards, pieces of anomalous material that abductees said had been implanted in their bodies by aliens. We had actually covered an implant removal surgery hosted by Dr. Roger Leir, who died in 2014, and reviewed videos with him of prior implant surgeries. But now, we decided, we would explore the science behind an actual piece of physical evidence, what had been described by its investigator and custodian as an alien skull.

THE STORY

What is a "Greys conspiracy"? Is it an ongoing cover-up of what the government knows about alien abduction and contact activity? Is it a conspiracy to cover up the true origins of the human race? In ancient alien theory, there are stories about how an advanced race of extra-terrestrial beings, called the Anunnaki in ancient Sumerian writings, came to Earth and manipulated the DNA of the hominid species they found here to create a race of native workers to mine the precious minerals they needed. The stories of creation and the interaction between human beings and advanced otherworldly races have been memorialized in various religious texts and poetry from *Gilgamesh* to the Vedic texts to our own Judeo-Christian Bible. And some of the apocryphal books of the Bible are even more explicit about the intervention of extraterrestrials in human history.

Many of today's abductees and contacts describe both benevolent and malevolent extraterrestrial species, entities who help humans develop in ways that do not destroy the planet, and entities who see humans only as a species who can further their own ends. Usually those ends involve some form of hybridization of the species to create a quasi-alien species that can thrive on planet Earth. The stories of these contactees' self-claimed experience abound. And then there is the physical evidence of giants in the earth, crystal skulls, and skeletal artifacts that apparently challenge the conventional stories of evolution.

The stories of physical evidence of an unconventional history of human evolution or of interaction with nonearthly species rarely make it into the mainstream media. They are laughed off as the ravings of delusional individuals or of hoaxers, like Chaucer's Pardoner seeking to sell bones to gullible individuals. But what is the science behind claims of contact and discovery of anomalous skeletal remains? What are the debunker theories? And what are the debunker theories that lend themselves to debunking? These are the questions we pursued in the investigation of the conspiracies about alien contact and physical trace evidence of that contact in this episode.

THE EPISODE

In early January 2009, we set off for subzero Vermont, wearing three layers of clothing to keep us from going numb and watching our breath condense into tiny ice crystals right before our eyes. Our investigative strategy, as we moved slowly across frozen roads, was to look for a big picture behind the stories of alien abduction and contact. To look at the individual cases as we did in season one, but also to see if the common denominators we found in the individual cases might serve as a background for a larger portrait of the phenomena. Was there, as UFO researcher Jim Marrs has often characterized it, an alien agenda? And was the government in on it?

Pat's approach was to go over every minute detail from every abductee or contact we interviewed because if the details that spread across the different cases could be fitted together like puzzle pieces, the image of the puzzle might emerge. Among the things we wanted to ascertain were where do all these stories of abductions come from and why do all the reported images of the Greys look essentially the same? Was it cross-pollination, which both skeptics and debunkers have argued explains the similarities in the descriptions, or was there truly a race of Greys that do the bidding of some other extraterrestrial species?

Kevin's opinion: They all came out of the movie, *Close Encounters of the Third Kind*.

The problem with that explanation was that the first modern description of the Greys came from Betty Hill in 1961, over fifteen years before *Close Encounters*. But Kevin still clung to his belief that the image of the Grey alien was a mass-media creation, possibly based on the image of the large-headed alien in *Outer Limits* from 1963. Regardless of the thousands of cases of contact with Greys, Kevin said he was still struggling with the idea of human contact with UFOs, much less the Greys who supposedly navigate them. Pat urged him to take baby steps in his belief system.

"Yeah, but it's still a big step," Kevin said.

We have had descriptions of Grey aliens for over forty years, starting with the Roswell incident. Then there was the *Outer Limits* TV series, *Close Encounters*, and the infamous *Alien Autopsy*. But the real description, revealed under a hypnotic regression conducted by famed psychiatrist Dr. Benjamin Simon, was the Betty and Barney Hill incident from 1961 in which they revealed they were captured and abducted by smallish humanoid beings, who were ultimately called "Greys." This was the description that stuck through the ensuing decades and informed all subsequent descriptions of extraterrestrials: large heads, grayish complexion, four and a half feet tall, long, spaghettilike arms, thin legs, no nose, a slit for a mouth, and large, compelling, black eyes. Who are these Greys? we speculated. And why are they here?

For our first answer, we interviewed Miriam Delicado, a longtime contact, who'd reported numerous encounters with different extraterrestrial beings, particularly the Greys. She described an incident in October 1983, when she was driving with friends along a dark road in northern British Columbia when suddenly, "out of nowhere, these lights appeared behind the car." She could see them through the rear windshield.

"It was almost as wide as two lanes," she said and told us she thought at first that they were the headlights on a big truck. "The lights started popping on and off. The girl driving the car started to get really afraid. Then I said to her, again, out of nowhere, 'Pull over the car. It's not you they want. It's me.'" Miriam admitted to Kevin that she really didn't know why she thought that or told that to her friend who was driving, but somehow that thought was in her mind. Kevin, however, thought that her story was "far-fetched."

"She was in a car with three other people," he argued. "None of them saw what she said she saw. None of them experienced what she experienced and none of them remember what happened."

But Miriam was adamant that her memory of the event was entirely correct. "I was just about ready to lean over and grab the steering wheel from her," Miriam said. "My friend did not pull over. Then, suddenly, her head tilted over to the side and she just pulled the car over. Something must have been guiding her because all of a sudden she became very quiet."

Pat was incredulous about this, too, as Miriam continued her story.

"Once the car was in a stopped position, nobody in the car was moving at that point. They were in suspended animation is the way I describe it."

You could see the looks of absolute disbelief on the faces of Kevin and Pat. But for me, I had heard hundreds of stories describing the same sort of phenomena where the elements of the stories all match up: a person claiming to be an abductee or contact seeing how people around them simply seemed to be switched off before the abduction event began.

"In front of the car," Miriam continued, "these short Greys were walking toward me and they were about three and a half feet tall. They had enormous types of heads with round black eyes. There were no features on them that distinguished one from the other. And then I start hearing a voice in my head. And it was, 'Okay, get out of the car. We will not harm you.' My hand started reaching for the door handle and I was thinking, 'Why am I doing this?' I got out of the car. They walked toward me and they took me by the hand."

Kevin's incredulousness at this description increased with every new detail as he repeated, "They actually took her by the hand? What would tell me if it happened or not? It's in the details. The details would allow me to make some sort of determination." So he asked Miriam, "When you touched the Grey's hand, did it feel soft and fleshy or was it a bit more solid?"

"It was solid," Miriam said. "They were really cold. And it wasn't like warmth from a person or an animal. It was just cold."

"Wouldn't a normal reaction be to run for your life?" Pat asked. "Or pull yourself away from little beings that are dragging you into a ship?"

"Absolutely," Miriam said. "But there was no conversation except for the voice inside my head saying over and over again, 'Do not be afraid. We will not harm you.' Which did actually calm me down." All of this sounded to Pat as if it made sense, if we speculated that the beings Miriam described had the ability to convey their intentions through telepathy.

"They just took me by the hand," she continued. "And they led me down the highway. And when I looked up, I saw a very large craft about forty or fifty feet across, and right at the doorway were these two tall blond-haired blue-eyed aliens. Nothing like the Greys. Nothing like them whatsoever. These short Greys that had been with me just let go of my hand and I walked on board the craft with the two tall blonds."

I asked, "What was the relationship of the Greys, who took you from the car, to these tall blonds?"

"I would say that these Greys were their helpers," Miriam said.

She indicated that there was not just one species of ETs called Greys, but another species, at least one of which had somehow employed the Greys to work for them. The Greys, as Miriam described the ones who she said took her, seemed servile and almost robotic in their mission. But Kevin would have none of this. Even more incredulous than before he remarked, "There are multiple species of aliens visiting the planet? This is completely new to me and I'm not quite sure what to think of it right now."

"When we walked on board this craft," Miriam continued, "they sat me down on this chair and in front of me came a screen out of thin air and then they started showing me all these different images. These were images of catastrophes on the planet: earthquakes, solar flares, war, and I'm being shown all of these what I believe were timeline events and paths that humanity could take. And it was explained that if we could come together as a species we would be able to avoid any and all of these events."

"What was the purpose of all this?" Pat asked. "What were they trying to do?"

"It was explained to me," she continued, "that they are the caretakers of this earth and that their purpose in being here is to help enlighten us and make us aware of who we are and to make sure we do not destroy ourselves or our planet."

Pat speculated that it sounded to him like they were bringing a benevolent message and that they were trying to help us. "It doesn't sound to me like these are beings that wish us harm."

"I believe that some of these Greys can be trusted," Miriam said. "And some of them you absolutely should not." She said that the Greys she encountered were here to help us. "But there are several different types of Greys, and I know one in particular has a very dark agenda."

That menacing statement was enough to set us off to investigate the 1996 story told by Bill and Peggy Foster in Yadkinville, North Carolina, whose abduction tales were far less benevolent than Miriam's, spooky even. They said that they were abducted by Grey alien beings, who performed medical experiments on them, memories of which still haunted them over ten years later. They said they recovered details of their experience under hypnotic regression.

But the problem with these stories, like the one told by the Fosters, Kevin asserted, is abduction witnesses have no tangible evidence to support their stories. Of course, that doesn't explain alien implants, which we investigated in our first season and witnessed a live alien implant removal during that episode. But, absent any physical trace evidence, or corroborative witness testimony, all we have to go on is the respondent's own story.

"My life would have been a hundred percent simpler without knowing anything about it," Bill Foster told us, referring to the alien abduction event he said he experienced.

"I wouldn't wish it on anybody," his wife Peggy said. "I would like to forget the whole incident."

Kevin, Pat, and I were privileged to review the videotapes of the Fosters' hypnotic regression sessions during which they recounted stories of what they said happened to them aboard a spacecraft after they were taken by Greys. They described specific medical experiments. We listened as Bill Foster, lying prone on a couch and ostensibly under hypnosis described his emotions as he reacted to what he said was an alien putting his face next to Bill's. He described different entities, one Grey taller than the others with larger dark eyes. Recounting the experience, Foster said, "It feels like I'm looking into eternity."

Pat commented that in his opinion, Bill was describing a very "profound experience, looking into the eyes of a being that's visiting this planet. That's huge."

The hypnotherapist asks Bill what happens when he looks into the creature's eyes. "It really relaxes me," Bill responds on the video, admitting that the entity had a tranquilizing effect on him.

Bill's description of the large head and large eyes comported with descriptions heard hundreds if not thousands of times before related by self-described abductees telling their stories. Even Kevin remarked that the tranquilizing effect that Bill Foster described seemed to him to be a form of telepathy, which, Kevin said, he had also heard before. "It's what everybody says happens," Kevin said.

Peggy Foster, during her session, seemed to be in pain, her face contorted and her head moving from side to side and asking, "Why does it hurt so bad?" Her psychological experience seemed to be very different from her husband's. Where Bill Foster said he was calmed down by seeing the entity standing over him, Peggy said she experienced pain and anxiety. She seemed to cringe in terror from what she said was the alien's touch. She recoiled at her memories of an event in which she said control was taken from her by entities who seemed to her unearthly. In Pat's opinion, "This is the best evidence we have that something traumatic happened to these people. Absent physical evidence of a Grey or a piece of a craft," Pat said, "we have to regard these recovered memories as evidence."

Peggy Foster's description of her experience was in sharp contrast to what Miriam said was her benevolent experience. Miriam expressed a level of calm when she said that the creatures she saw told her that they meant no harm. Thus, here's what we were able to discern: Miriam told us the Grey aliens were helpers, but from what Bill and Peggy Foster told us, the Greys are performing serious medical experiments, some of them, apparently, quite sinister and painful. Is this contact only a current phenomenon or is there any evidence of contact and an alien presence among humans dating back to ancient times?

Our investigation took us back to Southern California and to a meeting with old friend and star of *Ancient Aliens,* publisher of *Legendary Times* magazine, and reddit personality Giorgio Tsoukalos. He posed the rhetorical question that he then answered, "What if there were real evidence of alien contact dating back to ancient times? We have all these accounts from ancient cultures, such as the Sumerian culture, that powerful unearthly beings descended from the skies and made contact with human beings. These were the Anunnaki. Translated into English, Anunnaki means, 'those who from the heavens came.'"

The evidence is right there in the Sumerian cuneiform: the big-headed creature, the rays coming out of it, and an indication, such as wings, that these creatures had the capability of flight. Pat disagreed with this, arguing that there was only limited evidence to support the ancient alien thesis. But Giorgio had more evidence to present, as did I. The images of beings in strange craft hovering over the earth, images from Medieval as well as Renaissance art, descriptions of fire-borne chariots in the Bible, and woodcuts from the fifteenth century depicting flying craft of different shapes firing weapons at each other in an aerial battle were all suggestive of images the different artists had seen. And we hadn't even gotten to the descriptions in the Indian Vedic texts of flying craft firing death rays at the earth. Unearthly beings interacting or encountering human beings has been referenced in almost every culture across the world, including our own Native American cultures.

Giorgio showed us a photograph of figurines that were discovered in Africa. "Here we see a similarity between modern depictions of Greys and these figurines with the big slanted eyes and the enlarged head," he said. "These statues are always in correlation with stories of beings that descended from the sky."

Kevin was as unimpressed as the child who said that the emperor had no clothes. "These don't really look alike, if you ask me," he said. "These African sculptures do not represent the Greys in any way, shape, or form." But Giorgio showed him photos of a lizardlike sculpture from Sumeria, which Kevin agreed looked more like a modern Grey. And then he produced photographs of prehistoric cave art that looked even more similar to our modern description of a Grey. Kevin had to agree, saying, "Yeah, that's kind of eerie." He continued, "Ancient cultures have all had myths and stories about beings that they called 'gods' that come down from the skies. But what we need is real physical evidence, the kind you can hold in your hand and test scientifically, that Greys, which might be interpreted as gods, were really present on Earth and really interacted with humans."

And Giorgio, in response, pointed us to the Starchild Skull, which many believe is the physical, skeletal remains of a Grey. "The Starchild Skull is a very fascinating find. We don't know yet whether this is a misshapen human skull or whether or not it is a hybrid being because in many, many ancient texts it is written that these gods did intermingle with our ancestors."

I have to say that during all my years doing research in UFOs, one artifact that kept coming up was the Starchild Skull and one name was associated with that artifact, my good friend, Lloyd Pye, now the late Lloyd Pye, a researcher who specialized in cryptozoology and in alternative explanations of evolutionary events. Before we filmed this episode, I'd never held the Starchild Skull in my hand, but I knew that it was found in a cave in the Copper Canyon region of northern Mexico in the 1930s by a teenage girl who was vacationing with her family. It's been speculated, from the shape of the skull, that it's of alien origin, possibly from a Grey. This, I believed, could be the greatest single find to date in the history of UFO research. Therefore, our next stop in our travels was to meet Melanie Young, the owner of the skull in El Paso, Texas, and, as a medical professional in the field of neonatal care, is one of the most qualified people to speak about the nature of the artifact.

THE STARCHILD SKULL

The artifacts themselves were in a nondescript metal case. Melanie showed us the first skull the teenager had found, the skull of a normal human who lived around 1000 C.E. This skull was found on top of the ground. Then we were in for a shock when she pulled out the Starchild Skull and all three of us drew a collective breath of awe. Holding it, staring into its eye sockets, marveling at the extreme lightbulb shape of the cranium, Pat and I had to stretch our imaginations to contemplate whether it was an entirely different type of humanoid creature.

Or was it simply a biological anomaly or the skull of a child who suffered from hydrocephalus? Just looking at it, however, gave all of us shivers. The possibility that it could be an alien artifact was huge. And looking at the two skulls, one of which was clearly human, together put the differences between them into a stark relief.

"Do you know how old this is?" Pat asked Melanie while he turned the artifact over in his hand.

"It was carbon dated at nine hundred years old," Melanie Young answered, describing the site of the artifact find. "The normal skull was resting on top of the ground while the deformed hand of the skeleton of the Starchild Skull looked like it was reaching out from under the ground. The child who made the discovery dug under the deformed hand and found the skeleton. She picked up both skeletons and took them back to the village. But there was a hard rainstorm and everything got washed away. And the very next day, this is all she could find."

Kevin raised the question that in a rainstorm that washed away items lying on the ground, he would have expected that the flatter bones would have been left by the flood and the rounder bones, like skulls, would have washed away. "But, if this story is true, then what happened was exactly the opposite."

Melanie Young said that the skull came into her possession from a friend, who got it from a friend, who was the original owner of it, gave it to Melanie because of her expertise in neonatal nursing and anatomy. "When I saw it, and told the owners that this was totally out of this world, they were like, 'Take it; don't bring it back.'"

"This is obviously extremely bizarre," Kevin said. "Is it possible this is some kind of deformity?"

"I've never seen anything like it," Melanie said, and in response to Kevin's asking about the number of skull deformities she had seen, she said, "I've seen every kind of deformity you can think of and nothing looks like that."

Kevin reminded us that folks who had looked at photos of the Starchild Skull had commented that it looked like the skull of a child who had suffered from water on the brain, a hydrocephalic skull, the result of a disease that affects infants and causes a misshapen skull. But Melanie, asserting her experience in dealing with deformed skulls of infants said, "If it were hydrocephalic, the skull would be bulged out. But only one side would be bulged out or the back only would be bulged. It wouldn't be symmetrical like this skull is. A hydrocephalic skull is asymmetrical while this skull is completely symmetrical. Moreover," Melanie pointed out, "if this were a hydrocephalic skull, the bones wouldn't be connected the way they are in the Starchild. There would basically be bone connection at the rear of the skull."

"Was there any other conventional explanation for the shape of this skull artifact?" Kevin asked.

"I don't have one," Melanie answered. "I can't find one."

"We've come this far," Pat said. "And now have to explore the possibility that this could be the skull of a Grey." Pat said that to his eye, it looked different from a conventional human skull. "It looks big and bulbous and fits the description of what some people say alien Greys look like. I'd like to get more information on it."

"Lloyd Pye is our lead researcher," Melanie said. "And he's done a lot of work with hominids and has so much knowledge on different species and how the humans have evolved. He is the guy to talk to."

Lloyd Pye, who had worked as a military intelligence specialist and had more than thirty years studying cryptozoology, was our next visit, and Pat put the ball right into play by asking him what the significant aspect of this skull was for UFO research.

"The Starchild can provide proof that is undeniable, the Holy Grail in this field of UFO alien research." Lloyd answered. Pye was the primary expert on the Starchild Skull and had spent more than ten years investigating its scientific basis. He said he believed the Starchild Skull "stands a very good chance of being the smoking gun that everyone is looking for in the field of UFO and alien research."

With a piece of real physical evidence in his hand, Kevin sought to determine what the evidence pointed to. "What I want know," he said, "is not only what the specialists and the medical doctors think, but what kinds of tests have been done and what, exactly, were the results?"

"Let's start with this," Pat began. "Can you walk us through the differences between the Starchild Skull and a normal human skull?"

"The eye sockets of a normal human are at a depth of about two inches. The Starchild's are not even one," Lloyd began. "There are no sinus cavities in the Starchild Skull as there are in conventional human skulls. No upper sinuses at all. When you turn the skulls over on their sides, you notice that in the human skull the chewing muscles that connect the jaw to the upper cranium cover a wide area. In the Starchild, it is much reduced so we have a much smaller, much reduced lower face."

This, to me, was very interesting because the development of the human jaw muscles was a major factor in the development of human civilization, particularly as it was related to the discovery of fire, the cooking of food, and the development of spoken language. Early humans ate their food raw, which required powerful jaw muscles, like those of canines. But with the discovery of fire, humans began to cook their food, particularly meat, meaning that jaw muscles could evolve to be more flexible because cooked meat was easier to chew. More flexible jaw muscles meant that humans could access a wider range of points of articulation in their vocal apparatus, thus allowing for a wider range of sounds and the ultimate development of language. Language meant that human beings could form broader social hierarchies, turning hand gestures and grunted vocalizations into actual commands and specific warnings, thus enabling hunting parties to communicate with each other at night. This, in turn, enabled smaller family units to form larger clans and clans into tribes that would soon evolve from nomadic hunter-gatherers into farmers and establish territorial boundaries. This was the process of the evolution of human civilization over a hundred and fifty thousand years. But what does this history mean for the smaller jaw muscle arrangement of the Starchild Skull?

For one thing, it meant that the Starchild did not need powerful jaw muscles to eat or even to vocalize. It meant that there might have been another way for the Starchild to receive nutrients, if it received nutrients at all. And as for language, if the Starchild was not capable of producing a wide range of sounds or phonemic vocalizations, might it have communicated in a radically different way? Of course, this is all speculation.

Lloyd Pye pointed to another huge difference between the Starchild and the human skull. "There are red fibers running through the matrix of the bone," he said. "The red fibers were found by scanning with an electron microscope. No skull of any kind of primate, or of any animal bone that we know of, has those kinds of fibers. They seem to be unique to the Starchild."

"Although I've never seen a Grey myself," Pat said, "large head, large wraparound eyes, and a small slit for a mouth. This skull fits in with that description."

Lloyd Pye continued, "If you turn the skull over and look on the inside, you feel here." He pointed to where the spinal column would have connected to the base of the human skull. "You feel that ridge of bone that would hold the cerebellum in place. With the Starchild, because there is clearly such an expanded brain pressing down on that spinal structure at such a steep angle, we should have a spreading of this bone structure connectivity, but we don't. So we have a very different kind of brain in this skull, whatever it is. And if you stick your finger inside the foramen magnum"—which, Lloyd explained, is essentially the hole in the bottom of the skull that serves as the connecting point where the spinal cord passes in order to plug into the brain—"you'll find something interesting. The nature of the foramen magnum, its aperture, indicates how the brain is supported by the spinal column and, accordingly, the size of the brain." In the Starchild Skull, the balance of the skull itself is very different from a human skull, "kind of like a golf ball on a tee," Lloyd explained. The spinal column looks to be half the size of a human spinal column and it's centered up under the neck. Therefore, when one sees how the neck is connected to the skull, it's clearly not a deformity because the skull, essentially, was built that way.

"We've had the DNA of the human tested fully," Lloyd said. "Completely recovered, fully human, no problem. But in 2003, we found that the Starchild was very different. While we could recover its mitochondrial DNA—the DNA from the cytoplasm in the cell structure surrounding the nucleus—inside the cytoplasm are little chips, like raisins, in which there is DNA that comes from its mother. The nuclear DNA, which contains the DNA of its mother and father, we could not recover. That means there is something very different about that DNA from the father, which differentiates it not only from the Starchild's human companion in the cave, but from all other humans. There is something very different about the father."

Pat wanted to know if the skeletal human companion of the Starchild was the entity's mother. But Lloyd Pye said that, for sure, he now knew from the genetic testing, that the human skeleton and the Starchild skeleton found together in the cave were not genetically related.

Now Kevin had perked up because there was real biology and genetic testing underlying theories concerning the Starchild artifact. He was impressed that, at least as of 2003, the preliminary testing suggested that the Starchild's mitochondrial DNA was human. "However, nuclear DNA recovery should have proven that the father was human as well. But it didn't. That means that the tests were inconclusive. The mother was human but the father is simply unknown." He asked Lloyd, "To your knowledge, is there any reason that the father's DNA is not recoverable? Are you saying that this was not a human father?"

"If the father had been human," Lloyd said. "All indications are the father's DNA should have pulled up very easily with the primers that were used. But it didn't. So we can only conclude that there is something very unusual about the father."

What neither Lloyd nor the *UFO Hunters* knew at the moment, but what Lloyd would find out years later, were the results of two successive genome recoveries. The first, Lloyd would explain on our *Future Theater* radio show, was that the mitochondrial DNA did, in fact, turn out to be human. However the nucleic DNA, from the mother and the father did not match any DNA in the National Institutes of Health database of all human DNA. This was a stunning fact because it pointed to, in lay terms, an in vitro fertilization with two nonhuman parents and a host human mother. But there was no in vitro fertilization in 1000 C.E. It wouldn't exist until the twentieth century. So how did that happen and why were the donor parents not human? Then Lloyd said on the radio that there was another follow-up genome recovery—and these things are quite expensive—and in that genome sequencing, it turned out that the mitochondrial DNA itself didn't match any of the DNA samples in the NIH database. In short, the DNA showed that this Starchild creature was not human.

Pat remarked that one of the problems concerning recovering more background about the skull was that it was incomplete. A large portion of it was missing, particularly the maxilla and most of its facial structure. "Would you mind," Pat asked, "if we took this to Los Angeles and had a specialist in facial reproduction see if he can reconstruct this entity's face so that we can see what this might have looked like when it was alive?"

"I would be as anxious to see what it might have looked like as you are," Lloyd said. And with that, we packed up and left Florida for Los Angeles.

Part of our plan for the Los Angeles experiment with the skull was to look at other aspects of its construction. For example, because the skull had a larger cranium area than a human skull, did it mean necessarily that it had a capacity for a much larger brain? This matches what we heard about the Roswell Grey who had, according to Lieutenant Colonel Philip Corso's statements about an alien autopsy at Walter Reed (*The Day After Roswell*, 1997) a large multiple lobe brain. To test out the brain capacity theory, Pat, Kevin, and I went to our laboratory facility in Hollywood where, with exact reproductions of the Starchild and the human skull, we set up our first Greys experiment, conducted by Kevin.

"With these two skulls," he said, "we want to measure the volume of the craniums' interiors to see if the Starchild had a larger capacity than the human, and if so, by how much. We know that a normal human brain is thirteen hundred to fourteen hundred cubic centimeters.

There's a scientific test to measure brain capacity. That's simply to fill the cranium's interior up with birdseed." And that was the experiment we set out to do.

I poured birdseed through a funnel into the human skull Kevin was balancing while Pat poured his bag of birdseed into the Starchild's cranium. "This is the bottomless skull," Pat said as he kept on pouring and pouring and pouring. Finally he had filled the Starchild Skull to the top and it was time to measure the respective capacities. Kevin's human reproduction skull held 1,250 milliliters, which, he said, was a lot of birdseed. "I don't think there's more birdseed in the Starchild," he said. But Pat's Starchild held two hundred milliliters more than Kevin's. The human skull might have looked larger, but the Starchild Skull held a greater capacity.

"This is a huge difference," Kevin said. "We're talking about fifteen percent more brain capacity here, which would completely bulge out a normal skull. But with all that said, I'm still not convinced that this is alien."

But why did the Starchild Skull seem to hold more brain material than a normal human skull? This was no accident of nature nor was this a brain or skull deformity. But this was a designed skull inside which its brain should have had more functionality than the accompanying adult skull found in the cave. "This skull exactly conforms to the Walter Reed autopsy on a little Grey that they retrieved from the crash at Roswell. Now the difference is that this might have had three lobes because it has human DNA," I said to Kevin and Pat, relying on information that Lloyd had told us at the time. "The army autopsy essentially confirmed this. It was in black and white."

"Black and white, as in documents," Kevin said, challenging the very basis of what happened to the alien debris after it was removed from Roswell. "There is no proof that such an autopsy ever existed," he said.

But I told him he was dead wrong. The Pentagon didn't confirm it because to this day, the Pentagon hasn't confirmed there was a crash at Roswell, much less an autopsy on the recovered alien bodies. But they never denied it. "Not one refutation came out of the military," I said to Kevin. "They never objected to anything we said in *The Day After Roswell*."

"But they never confirmed it either," Kevin said, remarking that I keep throwing *The Day After Roswell* on the table. He said, "But what exactly happened at Roswell is still very much debated." Kevin also brought up an interview Pat and I conducted with a member of an Army Air Force crew that cleaned up the wreckage of the downed alien craft at Roswell. This was the late sergeant Earl Fulford, an eyewitness to the UFOs over the base in July 1947, and the removal of material from the debris field after the crash. But Pat broke in, reminding us that we were arguing over facts concerning a skull that wasn't even complete and about which we only had limited knowledge. His plan was to go to visual effects artist Robert Lindsay, an expert on skulls, jaws, teeth, and facial reconstruction to see what he thought it would look like. Would it be more human than alien or more alien than human?

Robert's first step was to reconstruct the lower jaw from scratch to give context to the rest of the skull. Next, Kevin explained, Robert had to attach the tissue depth markers to the skull to determine how thick he should apply the tissue under the skin. Next he would attach muscles and sinews to the skull and then the flesh. Once that's in place, he would be able to fill in the eyes on the model. And lastly, Kevin said, he would attach skin to give the skull a face. But remember, we cautioned, what Robert Lindsay creates wouldn't necessarily be what the Starchild might have looked like in real life. It would be a Hollywood special effect artist's vision of what he saw in the skull. Meanwhile, however, while the reconstruction was taking place, we pursued a conversation to figure out whether it would be possible for just such a life-form to evolve on another planet. And that took us to the Harvard-Smithsonian Center for Astrophysics in Cambridge, Massachusetts, and a meeting with scientist and *National Geographic* author David Aguilar, whose 2007 *Planets, Stars, and Galaxies: A Visual Encyclopedia of Our Universe* is a graphic and colorful introduction to astronomy and our celestial neighborhood. David's specialty was speculating scientifically on what kinds of life-forms might exist out there on other planets, what they might look like, and what was the scientific basis for making that determination.

David told us, "We are talking to NASA, we're talking to the Origins of Life Initiative here at Harvard, we're actively searching for life in the universe."

Kevin told him that we had been researching the nature of what aliens might look like, specifically what Greys might look like and how life might have evolved on other planets.

"What shapes, what forms, what evolutionary pattern they might take, that's the big mystery today," David said.

We had some clues to the mysteries that confronted David and his colleagues, clues, albeit testimonial, through the descriptions of Betty and Barney Hill, whose 1961 abduction story was widely publicized in newspapers, magazines, books, and on television. Betty Hill had revealed that after she and Barney were taken aboard a spacecraft, she was shown a star map that depicted a double-star system, called Zeta Reticuli, in a specific point in the sky, a star system that was the home of the aliens who had abducted her. Why did the aliens reveal a detail like that to Betty? We asked David about this.

"I remember that," he said. "They saw the map inside the ship and they put it out there and it wasn't until later that they were able to go back and say 'Oh my gosh, this looks like the system we're talking about.' But then in the infinity of space there could be a thousand locations that look just like that."

Pat added that "We've actually contacted witnesses who say they've seen beings from another planet and we've got some sketches here to show you." These were the sketches our artist created from descriptions provided by Bill and Peggy Foster. We projected the sketches on a large screen in David Aguilar's conference room. "Does this sketch look like something that could have evolved on another planet?" Pat asked.

"Of course, life will evolve differently on other planets, in other environments," David said. "And there's no reason we would necessarily have humanoids. The chance of finding humanoids that look something like us, like you might see on *Star Trek,* are so unbelievably small. You're gonna get intelligent creatures, but they're not going to look like anything we would relate to an intelligence." Pointing to the image of the Grey projected on the screen, David said, "This creature comes from another planet, perhaps a small red star. These may not be eyes at all. They could see in the infrared spectrum. And the bright lights we see on this planet could really mess with their eyes so this whole idea we see here," he said, pointing to the large black wraparound eyes in the sketch, "might not even be lenses because they might just be blocking out light. The head is big, but the problem I have is that you can't support it on this neck. These small, little, thin, frail creatures look like they come from a world that has less gravity than the earth because if they came from a planet with less gravity, this gravity would really be tugging on them and would really slow them down. With less gravity they would grow more elongated, thinner, and we know that as a principle of what happens in different environments. Obviously the nose being so small and the ears being small, these are not important senses anymore for these creatures. If they've evolved this way, they've evolved without these senses. There are other senses that creatures use that we don't use. Radar with bats; there are fish that can sense proximity and octopi that can sense other creatures as far as ninety feet away just by the electromagnetic waves that are around them. This creature could certainly have these types of senses. We simply don't know."

Kevin commented that he couldn't imagine a creature that thin and frail being hostile to anyone, let alone carrying out abductions. It looked like it could barely move in our environment. But David had another answer: "Maybe these are genetically engineered specifically for this task and function like robots. They just send them out like androids to do whatever they're doing." In other words, David was saying, the Grey creatures people have described could simply be just drones sent long distances to perform specific tasks. It is a story that we'd heard from many witnesses. And this is exactly what Philip Corso said the Walter Reed Army hospital autopsy revealed about the Roswell Greys.

"There's no telling what could be possible," David continued, "but since we don't have anything in our hands to look at and compare, we don't know. I'd love to bring one of these guys into a real lab and have everybody take a look at it."

At this point, Pat brought up the Starchild Skull. "David, you said there's no evidence of extraterrestrial life right now. We think we may have something here." And he handed David Aguilar the Starchild Skull.

"What am I looking at?" David asked.

I explained that the skull was found in a cave in northern Mexico and has been carbon dated to be nine hundred years old. I pointed to the eye sockets. "Look at the eye sockets. Look at the shape of the head. And look at the neck."

"I'm curious," David said. "Any DNA samples from this?"

"The mitochondrial DNA is human," I said. "They did a nucleic DNA test and could not sequence the father's DNA from that nucleus of the cell."

"Are you saying this was a cross with an alien or just a human with a terrible deformity?" David asked.

"That's one theory," I said. "It's a hybrid."

"Prove it," he said.

And five years later, Lloyd Pye would prove something: This was no human.

After our meeting with David Aguilar at the Harvard-Smithsonian, we flew back to Hollywood to see how Robert Lindsay had reconstructed the face of the Starchild Skull. As Kevin said, he hoped that the reconstruction Lindsay created might help us prove or disprove conclusively whether the Starchild was some form of an alien. But regardless of what the facial reconstruction might reveal, I believed, the existing science behind the Starchild Skull was the key to unlocking a mystery about the Greys, whatever that mystery might be.

Robert's reconstructed model was fascinating. It retained the basic shape of the head, of course, the same very small nose and ears, although they looked more human than anything else, and a very small slit for a mouth, but with human-looking lips. Pat said that he was amazed because to him, the model looked truly like a Grey. Witness descriptions of the Roswell Greys' faces indicated that the creatures looked more human than not, even though the eerie aspects of their shapes told them these creatures weren't human.

"What experience do you bring to accurately creating this face?" Pat asked Robert.

"I am a technician that knows something about jaws and muscles of the face and how they are constructed." And that was why he represented the face the way it was, more human than not. Sure, there was artistic interpretation that could take him either way. But his background helped him create the way this creature's mouth looked, its chin looked, and how its teeth met.

"The lower jaw is missing," Robert said. "The whole front piece is missing and so I had to redo all that. I made it as close as I think possible to what it would look like anatomically. And I added the muscles accordingly with no alien in mind. So this is more like it would look from the features I envisioned."

"When I first saw this face on the skull," Kevin said. "I thought alien. I took a little further look and I saw a real human face behind it. And if you add hair and change the skin tone and put regular eyes in it, I'm seeing a human being with a slightly misshapen skull. This is indeed beautiful," Kevin said to Robert, "but it is your creative interpretation."

"Sure, you can never be for sure," Robert said, "because there are many different variations that are possible."

"What do you think about this skull that you're holding?" I asked Robert.

"It's weird," he said, "because it's very symmetrical. And you guys had the hypothesis that it had this disease, that it was hydrocephalic. But it's symmetrical and looks not like it was an accident."

"Can you offer up any explanation as to why you think this skull might be shaped like this?" Kevin asked.

"There are two opinions," Robert said. "Either it's an anomaly or it's some kind of hybrid."

Bingo.

When we first spoke to Lloyd Pye and he presented his theory of the Starchild, he gave the impression that this was some type of crossbreeding between an extraterrestrial and a human being. However, looking at that representation, it looked too human. Thus, the skull could be the artifact of a human having been bred with a hybrid.

I said to Robert, "Everyone thinks that a hybrid is simply an alien crossed with a human being. But it's actually not. Because some of the stories that we've heard, and some of the stories told to us by author and researcher David Jacobs of Temple University (*The Threat: Revealing the Secret Alien Agenda*, 1999), are that the extraterrestrials are interbreeding hybrids with humans through succeeding generations to create entities that look more and more human." I could see Kevin freaking out.

"So there's a hybrid of a hybrid," he said. "And a hybrid of a hybrid again, and again. It could be one-quarter alien, an eighth alien, a sixteenth of an alien, or even one sixty-fourth of an alien. Is that the theory?"

"Yes, Kevin. It's enough of an alien that if they were taking over planet Earth, all they would need is part alien because it's what's inside there that counts." And I pointed to the Starchild Skull. "Not what's outside here."

"Now we're there?" Kevin said, this time even more derisively than usual. "Taking over planet Earth?"

"That's one theory," I said.

But Kevin was not impressed. He said that all we really had was a skull that looked very deformed. However, when facially reconstructed, it looked very human. Thus, the alien-human hybrid theory was simply a way to argue for the extraterrestrial hypothesis by couching it in human terms. But I think the theory still holds because over years and years and many generations of interacting and crossbreeding hybridization, these creatures are coming into conformity with what the aliens were looking for. It was a designer hybrid, improved from generation to generation, but retaining its extraterrestrial intelligence and any psychic abilities. When one looks at this Starchild creature and compares its looks with a theoretical plan for hybridization, live creatures like this could be walking among us today. What better way to invade a planet without destroying it? Simply replace some of the human DNA with alien DNA and inhabit the planet. Even Pat had to admit that although the hybridization theory was just that, a theory, it did give us a window into what the Greys might look like in the flesh. Kevin, however, was unconvinced because, as he laid it out, there was just not enough evidence to support it.

For my part, I looked at the evidence of abductees, such as the Hills, and of contactees like Miriam, and the cultural evidence presented by Giorgio Tsoukalos. Comparing that with the physical evidence of the skull and the science behind its testing, and I believed that the Starchild represented the best physical evidence we have to date, especially with the subsequent DNA testing, that what abductees and contactees have said has a ring of truth and that what Giorgio argued about the ancient alien theory makes a lot of sense.

BILL'S BLOG

This episode focused on one of my favorite topics, stories of alien-human contact and interaction, and presented the story of what I do believe is the Holy Grail of alternative history, the Starchild Skull and what it means. I was also able to strike a balance in this episode between the stories of personal testimony of alien contact and the dark side of alien abduction with the hard science of researching the biology of what I think is a true alien artifact. It's this personal drama laid against hard science that has always excited me on the show. And in this episode we also followed the path we've taken in the episodes of two prior seasons, taking the arguments of debunkers and skeptics and using good physical science to either prove or disprove what the debunkers say.

That's exactly what we did with the Starchild Skull by subjecting the debunker arguments behind it to the process of elimination. For example, the first debunker argument against any anomalous theory concerning the skull's shape was that the person—call it the Starchild for the sake of conversation—was simply a hydrocephalic child who died from the condition. But neonatal nurse Melanie Young, whose expertise during her medical practice working with hydrocephalic newborns, said she had seen hundreds of infants who were born with hydrocephaly and could tell just by looking at the Starchild Skull's symmetric shape and the way the bones had knitted together in the back of the cranium that this was not a hydrocephalic child. Then came the successive genome sequencing, which revealed that the skull's DNA did not match any known DNA in the NIH database. So much for the debunker arguments.

Perhaps the most direct comment about an alien presence on Earth came from David Aguilar at the Harvard-Smithsonian Center for Astrophysics, who said, pointedly when we presented the theory about the Starchild Skull, "Prove it." He was right. How do you prove it? You do that by taking every argument that the skull was that of a deformed human child and laying out the DNA sequence. No human DNA, no human. And as for the sketches of the Grey alien that came from descriptions provided by the Fosters, that, too, was worth a conversation with David Aguilar, who, without further physical evidence, was able to speculate on the nature of the creature's original habitat. Even better, David independently suggested a theory that had become popular in ufology circles, which was that the Greys were androidlike in their biological fabrication. They were "grown" and programmed to perform specific missions from navigating a craft to identifying and capturing potential subjects for medical experimentation and breeding. Sounds gruesome, but what if there's truth behind it?

One of the quandaries that bedevil most serious UFO researchers is the possibility of cross-pollination among the various stories of alien contact. For example, the stories told by Bill and Peggy Foster were so remarkably similar to the stories told by Betty and Barney Hill that you have to wonder whether the experiences are actually the same or, under hypnotic regression, are the Fosters repeating what has been the long publicized story told by the Hills. We simply do not know whether the pattern of alien encounters is so similar from witness to witness that the stories have the same archetypal structure, which is what Dr. Jonathan Mack at Harvard discovered, or have stories of alien abduction so penetrated our cultural zeitgeist that if you are abducted you will retell the same story. None of this is meant to disparage any legitimate stories told by honest witnesses. However, as the Hills' psychiatrist Dr. Benjamin Simon said, he could not dismiss the possibility that the image of an alien creature was part of our culture and that image was easily transferable through a type of suggestion from one person to another.

The other aspect of this episode that was interesting to consider was the possibility that certain species of ETs, as described by contactees, are benevolent. Miriam described her ET contacts as "helpers," stewards of a sort whose concern was for life on this planet and the survival of the planet itself. Why? What's in it for the ETs? One theory is that because they seeded life on this planet, we are their experiment, their colony, whose existence is important to their species. Another theory, sometimes called the "inner Earth theory," suggests that ETs already live here. They live under our oceans as USOs (unidentified submerged objects) or they live inside our planet and have a huge stake in the survival of the planet and the life that exists on its surface. These theories might explain why contactees like Miriam report ETs, those who look like us and are called "Nordics," display scenes of future destruction as a warning, almost like the Ghost of Christmas Future from Dickens', A Christmas Carol warning that if humanity does not take better care of the planet, if humans neglect their stewardship because of their own greed and self-gratification, the very thing that sustains their health will be destroyed.

No investigation of the Greys would be complete without taking a look at the historical context for alien visitation. And there is no better person to provide that context than the lead host of History's *Ancient Aliens* Giorgio Tsoukalos, who has since been meme-ified on the Internet. As the publisher of *Legendary Times* and a colleague of the legend himself, Erich von Däniken (author of *Chariots of the Gods*, 1984), Giorgio delivers a wealth of comparative culture-based information on the widespread similarities of images of large and elongated-headed deities, who, in creation stories, came to Earth from the stars to provide benevolent help to prehistoric cultures. How did these similar stories spread? Or did they not spread but were implanted separately by repeated visits from ancient aliens? That became the intellectual basis for the television series spawned by *UFO Hunters*.

No retrospective on this episode would be complete without an encomium to the late Lloyd S. Pye, who challenged conventional evolutionary theory and biology to present his own views on cryptozoology.

LLOYD PYE: AN ENCOMIUM

Lloyd Pye, cryptozoologist, researcher of human origins, curator of the now celebrated Starchild Skull, and guest on *UFO Hunters* and *Future Theater*, lost his battle with leukemia in 2013 after a period of intensive therapy to stay the aggressive onslaught of the disease. Lloyd was indefatigable to the end as he pursued alternative therapies to a form of cancer where the conventional therapy can be devastating, too.

For over fifteen years, Lloyd Pye, whose first book, *Everything You Know Is Wrong—Book One: Human Evolution* (1997), was consumed by the search for the origin of the strange humanoid skull, a nine-hundred-year-old artifact that had been discovered by a teenage girl in a cave in northern Mexico early in the twentieth century. As reported in *UFO Magazine* (June 2007) by Sean Casteel, the strange-looking Starchild Skull had been given to Pye by Ray and Melanie Young for the purposes of researching its nature. Pye was absolutely taken by the anomalies of the skull, its shape, the position of its eye sockets, the density of its bone, and the alignment of where its spinal cord would have connected with the skull's base. The skull, although humanoid, was all wrong, and not even hydrocephalus, a condition known as "water on the brain," which results in an inverted bell-shaped skull, could explain all the anomalies.

Lloyd pursued his research into the biology of the skull and finally determined, through series of genetic analyses, that the skull's DNA didn't match any human DNA in the National Institutes of Health database. Was this an alien hybrid? Was this an alien? Lloyd was determined to find an answer. But along the way, detractors, some from the UFO or quasi-UFO community derided both Lloyd and his efforts, dismissing the skull as simply deformed and nothing else. Television reality series production companies—not ours—took every opportunity to debunk Lloyd's research even when their debunking fell well short of the actual science that Lloyd had demonstrated. What some of these television shows concocted was nothing short of outrageous, but Lloyd Pye persevered.

The UFO community will miss Lloyd Pye's dedication to scientific research, his scholarship, his humor, his good-natured willingness to engage in debate, and his honesty. Maybe someday we will learn the true nature of the Starchild and maybe Lloyd Pye, in some other reality, will take notice. But for the present, we honor the memory of Lloyd Pye, one of the true heroes of ufology.

"UNDERGROUND ALIEN BASES"
DULCE

In this second episode of season three, we beat a path to one of the most hotly debated conspiracies in the field of UFO research: underground bases. In particular, we went out to investigate the lingering conspiracy, often told by self-claimed witnesses and those who knew them, about a research facility buried deep inside a mesa in Dulce, New Mexico, on the Apache reservation. It was there, incredibly, witnesses described horrendous and bizarre research that was conducted by extraterrestrial scientists and their human counterparts in hybridizing a new species of humanized ETs. And if that sounds scary enough, imagine hearing stories of an actual firefight between the ETs and U.S. military personnel in which there were scores of human fatalities. How the base was constructed in the Archuleta Mesa on the Jicarilla Apache reservation, what apparatus was used to hollow out an entire mesa, who lives in that underground facility, and what the local residents see and have been talking about for fifty years—these were the mysteries we sought to unravel.

Could we get inside a heretofore secret facility and find out its purpose? Was there a way for the *UFO Hunters* to uncover some of the stories of how the U.S. government managed to carve out underground cities before the eyes of its citizens without causing a stir on the surface? And do we still use a network of underground tunnels today and if we do, who are its beneficiaries? This was what we tried to find out as we set off to the hills of northern New Mexico on a search that would reveal a photograph that would bring our little show to the attention of the United States Senate where a fundamental change to Title 18 of the federal criminal code, was in the offing.

THE STORY

The Greenbrier

The guests at the Greenbrier, an elegant five-star hotel resort just outside White Sulphur Springs in rural West Virginia, might have watched in fascination in 1959 as the fleets of vans crewed by maintenance workers in white coveralls busied themselves on the hotel grounds ostensibly installing televisions in the suites. Guests might have wondered why television installation men took so long to finish the job and why the occasional dump truck could be seen slowly making its way across the resort's grounds. At the same time other construction crews were at work building an entire new wing of the hotel. And then, after the maintenance crews and construction apparatus disappeared and things seemed to return to normal, no one thought about all that activity until a 1992 *Washington Post* article by reporter Ted Gun revealed that right under the noses of hotel guests, the United States government, under the rubric of a project known as Project Greek Island, had actually constructed a nuclear-hardened bunker the hotel guests where obliviously enjoying the resort. It was a bunker that operated from 1962 to 1992 to shelter members of the United States Congress during the height of the Cold War, in the event of what President Eisenhower and most of our military leaders feared could be a nuclear attack that would destroy the functions of the U.S. government.

But President Eisenhower waged peace for eight years, President Kennedy stared down and then bargained with Nikita Khrushchev over his missiles in Cuba and ours in Turkey, President Nixon opened the door to the People's Republic of China, and presidents Reagan and Bush persuaded Mikhail Gorbachev to allow the Berlin Wall to come down and with it the end of the Soviet Union. After the collapse of the USSR, Project Greek Island became an artifact that was ultimately commercialized into a tourist attraction.

The Archuleta Mesa

Members of the Jicarilla Apache reservation tribal police might have been perplexed by all the reports of UFOs hovering over the mesa. At least one member of the tribal police was even more perplexed by the long line of black vans leaving the mesa very early in the predawn darkness and heading down the road toward Albuquerque. He often thought about stopping the convoy, maybe for a taillight that was broken or a minor traffic infraction that would allow him to take a peek inside one of the vans. His curiosity was piqued even more when one evening, at the base of the mesa, he saw what he thought was a coyote scrambling through the brush, but when he looked at it more closely, to his shock, the coyote had the head of a rabbit. What was going on in the *Alice in Wonderland* world beneath the Archuleta Mesa?

The story of the Dulce Base has been around for decades. As we learned from interviews with researchers like John Lear and John Rhodes, Dulce is reputed to be an underground laboratory staffed by humans and ETs working on different subterranean levels with humans on the upper-most levels, humans and ETs on the middle to lower levels, and ETs only on the lowest levels. Reputed to be something like a chamber of horrors in which human abductees are dissected and their organs and DNA stored for hybridization purposes, the technology to facilitate these experiments is mostly alien technology. For a variety of reasons, depending upon the source you're listening to, humans are cooperating with the aliens because of the technology we're receiving and because there is huge corporate money behind this.

The technology to build a complex of this nature has certainly been around since the 1950s. The concept itself, as we learned from the

Greenbrier, was to shield sensitive facilities underground so that in the event of a nuclear war, these facilities could still function. Thus, it would have been straightforward to utilize the large drilling machines with nuclear-heated drill tips to burrow into the mesa, melt the rock and dirt into a tunnel, and hollow out the mesa. All this was done in secret, of course, on an isolated part of a Native American reservation where the residents could watch silently but say nothing. In many ways, it was the perfect location with the perfect cover.

There were a number of people who tried to penetrate this cover or, once inside, blow the whistle. One of those was a former security guard at the base named Thomas E. Castello. He, reportedly, fled the base and the horrors he had witnessed with photos of some of the facilities and the human bodies that had been dissected and floating in large vats. He was sheltered after he left by the Jicarilla Apache for a short period of time and then, again, reportedly, left the United States for Europe. Sketches based on those photos have been widely circulated among various Dulce researchers.

Another person who reported on activities at the base was Paul Bennewitz, who reported on what was called an alien firefight. As the story goes, there was a dispute between the human scientists and the ET scientists that became threatening. This conflict broke out on the lowest, ET-only level in which human military personnel were not allowed. And the restriction against the human military was so stringent that their very presence amounted to nothing less than a declaration of war. Thus, when they broke in to protect the human scientists a firefight broke out that Paul Bennewitz said people had witnessed. Ultimately, Bennewitz became a victim of a disinformation campaign.

The other person who told the story of the Dulce Base was Phil Schneider, who had trained to be a geological and structural engineer. He has explained that as early as 1954, President Eisenhower entered into an agreement at Holloman Air Force Base with an ET species under which agreement the aliens would be allowed to take cows and test the way their embryos could be implanted in human subjects. This expanded to a large hybridization program underground at Dulce, New

Mexico, the underground facility with seven levels where only large Grey aliens were allowed at the lowest level. Schneider said that the fire-fight at Dulce between humans and aliens began at this lowest level when a human security officer entered a lecture given by a large Grey to human scientists. He was carrying a sidearm in his belt. Weapons were strictly prohibited in the presence of the Greys, and the security officer was killed as soon as he entered the area by the large Grey. All of this, Schneider said, was witnessed on security monitors by other security personnel, who entered the area with weapons and were killed instantly along with the human scientists. The incident was ultimately ruled an accident or misunderstanding, but has gone into UFO lore and has been repeated by many Dulce aficionados.

Schneider, Bennewitz, and Castello all talked about human-animal hybrid experiments and animal-to-animal hybridization in the various biogenetics labs at Dulce. They reported mutilated cattle, strange types of embryos stored in test tube–like enclosures, and vats of human body parts. Other individuals who claimed to be witnesses talked about having been abducted for medical experimentation purposes at Dulce and then escaping. If any of this is true, it is an incredible story. However, it is a story that cried out for some evidence, whether the evidence comes from witnesses not involved with the Dulce base or any piece of extrinsic physical evidence. And it was in search of this evidence and the background stories from witnesses that we set out to find when we embarked on this segment of our underground alien bases episode.

THE EPISODE

Pat, Kevin, and I began a discussion about a theory that purported that the United States was host to hundreds of underground bases, facilities that housed everything from strategic nuclear-hardened military bases (such as the one depicted in the movie *War Games*), to bases that housed government facilities that could operate in times of war, to bases where secret scientific experiments were taking place, including experiments involving extraterrestrials. This, I introduced to Pat and Kevin, was central to the legend of a major underground facility within the Archuleta Mesa in an area called Dulce, where there were ventilation pipes coming out of the mesa itself. What are ventilation pipes supposed to be doing if they are rising out of high desert sand and scrub? It makes absolutely no sense unless something is underneath that mesa.

"The only explanation," Pat said, "would be some sort of facility inside the hill." And Kevin said that if there were an underground base at Dulce there would have to be some sort of massive infrastructure supporting the facility and that the construction itself would have required the removal of the dirt from the site. There would have to have been a sophisticated ventilation system, a water management system, a sewer and drainage system, and a power system. "If this is a government facility, I'm sure they could have hidden a lot of it, but some of it will have to be apparent." And Pat agreed, adding that he knew for a fact that the United States has underground military bases that were built to protect and house the government and the military in the event of a nuclear attack. "But whether or not aliens are involved," he speculated, "in Dulce, that remains to be seen."

For Kevin's part, he said he wasn't even sure there was a base there and argued that the first thing that had to be shown was any evidence there was a base underground or anywhere in Dulce. If there is evidence of a base, he said, then he would move to the next stage, which was to determine what might have been going on there. I suggested that after he heard the stories from the people who lived there, I would enjoy hearing his opinion. "After you hear what folks have seen there, your minds may be open to the possibility that something very sinister is going on," I said. Pat simply shook his head.

At Dulce, we rendezvoused with former police officer Ken Storch, a UFO investigator who had visited Dulce on prior occasions and who had personally interviewed individuals, including a police officer, about the so-called firefight at Dulce. He was adamant that, in his words, "Something strange was going on at Dulce, New Mexico." We also met with Ken's research partner Bob, an undercover operative and former police officer—let's call him "Bob X"—and he said that, "Dulce was the ultimate undercover operation." Both of them believed, from their own investigations and multiple visits to the area, that something eerily disturbing was going on there.

One of the first questions we asked, as we met at a roadside location in the looming shadow of the Archuleta Mesa, was what got Ken and Bob interested in the Dulce story in the first place. Ken explained that they had first read about it in the Dulce papers he'd gotten from a retired United States Air Force colonel, which described the existence and the goings-on at a facility buried under the mesa. These papers, which first surfaced in the 1980s, documented the levels of experimentation taking place at that secret base. They also talked about a firefight at that facility.

"In 1979," Bob began, "the Greys took over our scientists. Delta Force, CIA, FBI, the security force in place in the mountain itself, went in to get the scientists and a firefight occurred. From sixty-two to seventy-two bodies were pulled out of there." Ken Storch added, "At our very first trip down here, we were contacted by a Jicarilla police officer." About which Bob said, "Out of my peripheral vision, I see a squad car pull up. The officer says to me, 'What are you looking at?' I said, 'The Archuleta Mesa.' Then I just bluntly looked at him and asked, 'Were you here in '79 when they dragged the bodies out of the mesa?' He looks me dead in the face and says, 'Yes, but we're not allowed to talk about it.'"

You could hear Kevin's exclamation of wonderment. "This is bizarre," he said. "An officer admitting to seeing bodies removed from this supposed firefight. But he's forbidden to talk about it. So there might be something to this. But still it's secondhand and it's just a story."

"What role does Archuleta Mesa play in all of this?" Pat asked our guests.

"The only thing we can think of," Ken said, "is that it's in a remote area and it's only accessible from certain points. There is a section up there thirty yards wide two to three hundred yards long where the tops of the trees are clipped off. And they're all lying in one direction. The first story that we got was it was a flying saucer from Area 51 that was reverse engineered that crashed. The second version was that it was an F-16 that crashed. We were unable to find out anything about that crash, who the pilot was, what happened to him, or anything."

Bob said that it was his experience that all of sudden, you ask a question and you get steered in one direction. Then you ask another follow-up question and you get steered in another direction. "Then you hit a brick wall."

Ken, who had logged many years as a homicide detective, said that the worst thing a detective could do was to take the evidence and lead it. He said, "What you have to do is you have to follow the trail. And you have to have an open mind and you have to be objective as you go down that path." Essentially, the evidence has to lead the investigator, not the other way around. As the celebrated homicide detective Bob Keppel, one of the "supercops" in the Atlanta Child Murders and Ted Bundy investigations, once said, police who come up with a preconceived notion of the case based on a smattering of evidence can easily go down the wrong path and neglect other information that would steer them in the right direction. The best approach is the Sherlock Holmes approach, eliminate what you can based on the evidence and investigate what's left (*The Riverman: Ted Bundy and I Hunt for the Green River Killer*, 1995, 2005).

In that vein, Kevin Cook said he was impressed by what Ken and Bob said but that there was still nothing definitive that proved there was an underground base at Dulce and nothing that proved ETs were there. We had to get to the top of the mesa, he said, "and maybe then I could get a better idea of what's happening at Dulce." And we drove off to find other local witnesses to events taking place around the mesa.

One witness, Troy Vincent, a member of the Jicarilla Apache nation, told us that based on what he had seen with his own eyes, he honestly believed there was a UFO base at the mesa. We wanted to know what, exactly he had seen and whether he could describe it for us in detail. He said, "At the front gate, as you're coming in, I saw this big old flying craft hovering. And it was probably about three or four football field lengths and round. As I stood there, all I could see was the bottom of the disk and the bottom of it, I could see the reflection from the Dulce lights shining against it. I thought it was going to hit the mesa, but it barely grazed the mesa. It flew over top of the mesa."

Kevin wanted to know if Troy believed the UFO originated from inside the mesa. "We already know," Troy said, "that there's a UFO base here." This astounded Kevin, who said it was amazing that the Jicarilla simply accepted that there was a UFO base on their own reservation. "This is a good sign," Kevin said, "for starting off our investigation."

There was a lot of ground to cover to get up to speed on the nature of Dulce. One of the most important researchers was the celebrated test pilot and CIA pilot John Lear, who had helped expose the secrets behind Area 51. I took off for Las Vegas to meet with John Lear while Pat and Kevin stayed in Dulce to interview more witnesses.

John Lear and I met at his house where I asked him to tell us how the entire story of Dulce, in all of its weirdness, began. Lear, who had been our guest on the Area 51 episode, said, "I met a woman named Ann West, who told me that she knew a security officer there named Thomas Castello. Supposedly he escaped from the Dulce Base with seven minutes of videotape and twenty-five black-and-white photos, and about a hundred pages of information revealing what was going on there. Castello contacted Ann West, who was a friend of his, and told her that he wanted her to bury this information. 'I'll contact you every four months,' he said, and 'if I miss two meetings in a row, then I want you to take that information and expose what's going on there.' When she was shown the photos before he put them in the box, he asked her to make some drawings. And these," John Lear said as he opened up a folder and spread papers across his desk, "are the original drawings that she made."

The drawings were stunning: what looked like human embryos in flasks or test tubes, human body parts floating in vats, and sketches of a strange factorylike facility. I asked John what he believed was going on there.

"There are seven levels," he said. "Levels of different experiments going on. Wombs submerged in yellow liquid that looks thicker than water. Dozens of creatures in each womb. You can't even count the tanks. Creatures have three fingers, two toes, not human."

What we believed from photographs that people had talked about, Lear confirmed for us: there is genetic experimentation going on with human beings. There are aliens living at Dulce and we are working with the aliens at Dulce. With this information from John Lear, I went back to Dulce with some of the history I had gotten, including the paperwork from John Lear, to meet back up with Pat and Kevin to continue our investigation. I particularly wanted to know who was in charge at Dulce. I explained to Kevin and Pat what Lear had told me and showed them the papers and sketches that Lear had given me. It was time for them to weigh in.

Both Pat and Kevin were highly skeptical. "Are you serious about this?" Pat said. "Looks like slabs of meat floating in a vat of liquid," Kevin said. I told both of them, "This is what John Lear told me and the sketches he gave me." And I showed them the humanoid figure in the flask. "Look at the human embryo in the flask. This is what he said was happening."

But Pat was far from moved, asking whether this constituted proof that an underground base existed at Dulce or whether the whole thing was just made up. And Kevin, pointing out the window of our camper, asked, "Are you telling us that right out here inside this mesa all this stuff is going on?" And that was absolutely what I was saying, based upon what John Lear had told me. But there were more witnesses to interview. Next up was John Rhodes, the repository of all information circulating not only about Dulce, but about the technology that enabled Dulce to be built and the technology that, he has said in the past, created a vast network of tunnels under the North American continent connecting both coasts and allowing scientists and military personnel with the highest security clearances to travel from base to base undetected from the outside. Sounds just like science fiction, but John Rhodes said he had proof from his own encounters with security personnel that it was true.

"The base is underneath Archuleta Mesa," Rhodes began. "And supposedly it consists of seven levels, each level increasing in security as you descend to the bottom. The information that was provided to us by Thomas Castello gave us very complex floor plans that had been drawn out." He showed us a diagram of the inner structure that featured a central hub. The hub, he said, was central security that connected with each level of the base from the top to the lower levels.

"At level two, you enter the first serious security checkpoint. They strip you down, take your clothing, weigh your body, and take biometric scans of you. Just in case you're trying to smuggle something out of the facility, they will know exactly what you weigh and what they've clocked in as your initial scan. If you try to smuggle something out, they already have your exact weight. If you are carrying something in your stomach, they have the initial biometric scan." And when Kevin commented on the seriousness of the security, Rhodes said that those in charge of the facility were frightened that the public might find out that human beings were being subjected to severe experimentation and involuntary genetic research, most of it beyond painful.

"At level three there is the computer bank area where they have the complete command and control of the facility, communications and intelligence." That level, Kevin said, doesn't sound especially dark. He asked where the dark stuff was located.

"It starts getting more interesting at level four," Rhodes said. "Here's where they get some of the more exotic research. They've studied the human aura, all aspects of telepathy, hypnosis, dreams." At this point Pat finally had to speak up because this was stretching his sense of credibility. "Wait a minute," he said. "Are you saying that this involves extraterrestrials? This may be where I have to draw the line."

"Both extraterrestrials and humans," Rhodes said. Then describing level six, Rhodes said that they call it "Nightmare Hall." At this level, "You have aliens experimenting on humans, humans experimenting on aliens, and they feel you can sacrifice the one for the many. Nobody's safe. This is where all the genetic experimentation is going on, where they fuse animals and humans together." John Rhodes was confirming for us exactly what Thomas Castello had told Ann West, who told John Lear, and what Lear had said to me.

Pat continued to argue that there was absolutely no proof of this fantastic story. The images Rhodes and I had shown him, he said, were only sketches, not actual photographs. But when it came to genetic hybridization, John Rhodes persisted, reminding us that back in 2003, photographs began circulating of a mouse with a human ear growing out of its back. And Pat agreed that he had remembered seeing that. "Remember," Rhodes said, "the military- and pharmaceutical-industrial complex is about thirty to forty years beyond what we know they're doing." The photo of the mouse with a human ear growing out of its back, a photo he displayed, proved that. "At the time when these photos of the mouse came out, this complex was successfully fusing humans and animals together. It was a precursor to what we're seeing now." Kevin weighed in, acknowledging that there might be some medical benefit of growing a human ear on a mouse. "But that was very different from aliens performing genetic experiments on humans."

Rhodes continued, "Human test subjects are housed on level five and then taken in on level six for experiments. Then they're transported to level seven. This is the horrific area. Guards like Thomas Castello said they have the cages there and were told not to talk to anybody. These were half men, half other animals."

"Who's doing these experiments?" Pat asked.

"Reptillian humanoid beings, the small Greys," Rhodes said. And at this point it was almost too much for Pat, who enumerated the species Rhodes was describing. "You're saying there are reptilians, small Greys, and human beings inside the structure engaged in some sort of activity in which they're willingly helping to perform experiments on other humans? That is a nightmare." I was surprised at Pat's shock over humans performing experiments on other humans, which types of experiments have been going on since before World War I. And we only have to think about the medical experiments at Nazi concentration camps and the experimentation on humans by Dr. Josef Mengele, not to mention experiments on the human brain sponsored by the CIA. But Pat said he was only trying to separate fantasy from reality. Rhodes continued.

"When you absorb all of the Dulce information, do you dare consider doing research on mice when if you use a human being, you could advance your research by thirty years?"

Kevin was trying to separate all the threads of this story. Before even getting to aliens and descriptions of genetic experiments on humans, he asked, "I just want to consider whether there really is a base at Dulce before we get to what goes on there."

Rhodes told him, "Back in 1972, the lead physicist for the Rand Corporation told the *L.A. Times* that the government had the technology to excavate tunnels across the United States and put maglev trains through those tunnels that were capable of reaching speeds of ten to fourteen thousand miles an hour. This is not science fiction. We have the capability to do it." And he showed us actual United States patents from Los Alamos National Laboratory describing thermonuclear boring machines that melt through rock, "just like you're taking a knife through butter." He explained that even though people believe that rock is so hard you have to break it down, it's not true. "We've been misled to believe that when it comes to tunneling."

Of course, there are millions of patents for machines that are created on paper but never manufactured. A patent, even though it is not easy to get, does not mean that the patent applicant has to roll it off a truck to demonstrate its functionality to the patent review officer from the U.S. Patent and Trademark Office. As an engineer, Kevin knew this. He said that for all the patents on paper, very few of them make it into production and a lot of them don't even work after they've been manufactured. Accordingly, he asked, "Is there anything that says these are real functioning boring machines?"

"I went to Bechtel, in Las Vegas, Nevada," Rhodes said. "And I put 'subterranean' into their computer system, which is what they call one of these." And he displayed the photo of the boring machine. "And I found images of the subterranean being tested at Los Alamos. The actual boring tips get superheated and they melt through solid rock. There's no excavation of materials that are needed. The rock is penetrated, cracks, and is lifted into molten glass all the way around the tunnel as a lining. In the early 1970s there were plans for a network of underground tube shuttles. There are two underground tube systems leading out from the base across the continent." And he confirmed for Pat that this underground network of tube tunnels was an actual reality. But Pat said he needed photographic evidence and more witness testimony and some physical evidence supporting this story that any of what Rhodes described was really going on.

Were there aliens at Dulce? As one of our witnesses, an older woman, said she was walking near the mesa on the reservation, when "Something touched me on the back. It had a big head and big eyes. It was those people." Her story was indeed compelling, but, as investigators of exotic stories, not just aliens, we had to look at other possibilities that might explain what was taking place at Dulce, if, indeed, there was any base there at all. And that was why our next guest was renowned Dulce researcher, Norio Hayakawa, who could provide alternate theories about the Dulce facility and the activities conducted there.

"In 1990," Norio began, "I brought a Japanese television crew right here in Dulce. We wanted to know what was going on. And, strangely enough, we were arrested and detained by the police chief. We asked him why we were detained and he didn't want to tell us anything. We asked him about the Dulce Base and he said he didn't want to talk about it. He didn't confirm or deny anything."

One has to ask, why was Norio and his television crew arrested and detained? Why was there no explanation for the arrest? What were the authorities trying to hide?

"The whole Dulce rumors started in the midseventies," Norio continued. "Started when cattle mutilations started taking place in this area and then later on rumors started circulating around that there is an alien base." But was this alien rumor part of the cover-up at Dulce?

"There is something going on here," Norio said. "The sightings and the cattle mutilations are facts." But whether there were extraterrestrials and human-alien hybrid experiments going on underground at Dulce, he said, goes beyond the facts that had so far been established. It was the cattle mutilations that had piqued Norio's interest. Why was the Dulce area so plagued with cattle mutilations? And for a possible answer to that, we sought retired New Mexico State Police officer, Gabe Valdez, who had become an important part of the Dulce story. Gabe had investigated cattle mutilations back in the eighties and nineties in which cattle, seemingly otherwise healthy, were killed and soft tissue was excised from their bodies. We were hoping that Gabe would share whatever he learned from his law enforcement investigations with us.

"In my profession," Gabe Valdez began, "you have to focus on the physical evidence. And the physical evidence that we found doesn't come from outer space. We found gas masks, monitoring instruments, radar apparatus, and helicopter equipment." All of which evidence made Kevin exuberant that we had finally uncovered a conventional tangible source of evidence about what might be happening at Dulce, and all of this from a New Mexico state trooper. No aliens, no ETs, only very terrestrial stuff. "This is a story from Dulce," Kevin said, "that I can get behind."

"What I found out," Gabe continued, "was that they were coming and marking the cattle ahead of time and then they'd hit them with a tranquilizer and then they'd take the lymph nodes out of them." The lymph node extractions were consistent in every mutilation case, Gabe confirmed. "Then they would take more stuff out to try to confuse people," he said. Pat asked whether the cows were killed and then savaged by coyotes or other predators. Gabe smiled a knowing smile, and said, "Coyotes don't wear gas masks."

Pat asked whether law enforcement officials were ever able to figure out what the cattle mutilation research was all about.

"We suspect that it's not disclosable," Gabe said, suddenly turning very serious. And we wondered, if it's not the extraterrestrials, but us, who was it that Gabe could not disclose? Was it the military, big business, big pharm? Was this some unknown shadow government organization? And we pressed, asking who would be keeping this a secret?

"Because of consequences," Gabe said. The consequences would be too dangerous for people if the truth behind the activities at Dulce were disclosed. "We had taken a lot of pictures of helicopters hovering over the area," he continued, and opened up his attaché case from which he withdrew a series of photos depicting helicopters with strange markings or no markings at all, one of which was only taken ten days earlier. That meant the activity, whatever it was, was still going on. "If the aliens are so advanced in their technology," Gabe said, "why would they leave so much evidence behind?"

Could witnesses have confused the unmarked helicopters with UFOs? We had to keep searching for more evidence because we had two alternate and mutually exclusive explanations, both of which were as startling as they were disturbing. Either extraterrestrials were staffing a scientific research center where they were hybridizing human beings with other species or there was a completely terrestrial entity, military or industrial, conducting experiments on human DNA that required them to excise the lymph nodes from tranquilized cattle that belonged to ranchers, cattle they ultimately killed.

"We came upon a helicopter over a cow lying on the side of the road," Gabe continued. "They hadn't done the whole process." He pulled another large photo out of his attaché case. "This fetus was inside the womb of a mutilated cow. It was not a complete cow fetus. Some part of it was." And we were looking at a photo of a bovine fetus with a human head and a human hand. Kevin was startled. He had never seen anything like this before, and asked what it was.

Gabe Valdez had given us a whole new approach to the Dulce story concerning the cattle mutilations he'd investigated. Far from researching UFOs per se, Gabe had pursued the taking and willful destruction of personal property and the disposal of that property on public roads. This was a criminal activity and certainly within the purview of any law enforcement agency. His investigation told him these were not extraterrestrials at all, but that he actually saw military-style helicopters over these mutilation sites. We asked Gabe about these mutilation sites and what was the most anomalous evidence he had uncovered during his investigation.

"They mutilated this animal about forty miles east of here and we came upon the aircraft while they were overhead. They did not complete the full mutilation process. And they left the fetus inside the animal." He was restating what he had shared with us earlier, only this time in greater detail. And when Pat asked whether it was a cow fetus, Gabe replied, "No. It looked like a human monkey. It had no bones in its head. It was all full of water. The fetus was about forty-two inches long. But something went wrong with it, whatever it was."

I asked whether Gabe thought that mutilated cow might have been used as an incubation chamber for a cloned creature.

"Exactly," he said.

And all we could say as we looked at the photo of the creature stretched out on what looked like an examination table for forensic analysis was, "My God."

"The front part of this is the head," Gabe said, "and the skin was open when we found it." Gabe pointed to two dots on the head and said that they were the eyes. "We really had to pull the skin back in order to see them. And look at the ear. It's an ear of a human."

"What happened to the fetus?" Pat asked.

"We took it to be analyzed," Gabe said. "It was very confusing to the veterinarian. The vet identified the eyes as belonging to a human being." And Gabe confirmed again that this looked like some crazy genetic experiment gone wrong, or, in Kevin's words, "This is madness."

Pat and I got into it over the nature of natural deformity versus intelligently designed hybrids with Pat saying that there are animals born with extra legs just like human beings can be born with deformed limbs. But, I stressed to Pat that it was one thing for there to be a natural deformity within the species as opposed to a fetus that had the body of one species, in this case a calf, and the head, hand, and ear of a human. This photo was not that of a deformed creature, but an artificially created entity, for what purpose, Gabe Valdez would not disclose. While Pat struggled with himself over the nature of what he called a "monstrosity," Kevin moved on to an assumption that if the creature we saw in the photo was a creation of something happening at Dulce, then there had to be some sort of a facility there. But where was it and how could we find any independent evidence of it?

We drove to the base of the mesa where we met with our archeological consultant, Garth Baldwin, to discuss the geological makeup of the mesa to see if it were even possible for an underground base to have been constructed there. We explained to him that within the mesa there was reputed to be an entire multilevel sophisticated biological engineering facility. Was that possible? What kind of rock formations are here and what kind of engineering would it take to build such a base inside the hill? From a construction and archeological perspective, what would the builders be dealing with?

"On the mountain," Garth told us, "you would find maybe one foot of soil and underneath would be hard bedrock. On the upper level you can see basalt, which is much too fragmentary for anything but supporting fence posts. But is also much too fragmentary to be ground out and support an entire interior multilevel structure. But below the top level, there are layers of basalt that are much more structurally sound. And sandstone's below that." He said that if you were constructing something in the interior, "You would have to start at the bottom of the mesa where there's a stable strata of rock they could get into."

"Let's say," Pat began. "You were hired by the government to design and build an underground base. Would there be any reason for you to pick Archuleta Mesa?"

"It's a mesa," Garth explained. "So you know you have a starting point where the stratigraphic layers of rock are so strong you've got a structure to begin with."

We gave Garth the specifications for the base. The base could extend up to 4.8 miles, John Rhodes had told us; this was the diameter of the base. "That would fit within the structure of the mesa," Garth said.

"It's conceivable that they're coming in through tunnels and drilling into the mesa so that they're drilling out the area for the base from the bottom up," Kevin said.

Garth almost demurred at first then said, "If that technology were true, then that would be possible. The human species has such a knowledge of mining and structural engineering that I'm not surprised by anything our engineers can do." Simply stated, if the technology were true, then construction of such a base inside the mesa would have been possible. John Rhodes had shown us that the technology did exist, had been patented, and that construction companies had utilized it. And that, at least, satisfied Kevin's skepticism about the possibility of such a structure.

Next up, riding a snowcat up to the top of the mesa where the team could look around for any indications that there was something inside the mountain. The team took with them one of our Jicarilla Apache guides who had been to the top of the mesa before and had told us of stories others reported of vent shafts going deep into the interior of the mesa. Folks who felt around the opening of these vent shafts for the flow of air had told him that at times, they could hear the groans of human beings from deep inside the mesa. And now Pat and Kevin were at the summit where Kevin believed that he might finally learn the truth about what might be underneath his feet.

Pat asked our guide Richard Vigil what he thought of the mesa and the legends he had heard.

"There's a lot of things flying in the sky around here," he said. "But I don't talk about them. I keep it to myself. There are a lot of people around here who think the same thing. If I left the reservation with these stories, people would think I'm nuts."

Pat asked what specifically Richard had seen atop the mesa.

"Me and one of my cousins," Richard said, "we were walking along the edge and we spotted a hole right on this side." And he pointed to a spot in the side of the mesa right over the ridgeline. "I hear things like it's a vent or something like that."

The top of the mesa is ringed with electronic towers, transmitters, and cell phone towers as well as a power station. All of which is strange for a simple hill in the middle of nowhere. The amount of electronics atop the mesa and the story of the mysterious vent prompted Kevin to scan the area with our FLIR camera to pick up any heat signatures emanating from underneath the mesa.

While Kevin scanned the area, trying to pick up anomalous air currents, Pat pressed Richard more to talk about some of the stories he'd heard, especially, the stories about the underground tunneling system that the Jicarilla believed ran through the area. And Richard pointed to a line running south across the valley and into an adjoining hill about fourteen miles away that he said housed a tunnel. But when Pat asked Richard to show him some more tunnel locations or shafts into the mesa, Richard said that he couldn't take them to any. He was too wary about showing them but he revealed that there were two more tunnels on the other side of the hill and other holes into the mesa itself. When Pat asked him if there was any way Richard could take him to the holes, Richard said, "I'm not gonna go there." Thus, the mystery remained because the people, who lived with it, were very wary and not about to reveal the mesa's secrets.

Everyone we had talked to in the area said they had seen UFOs, and plenty of them. But whether they were flying in the area because of what was going on under the mesa or because witnesses were mistaking the helicopters Gabe Valdez had described, we couldn't tell. All we heard was that there were UFOs, strange-looking animals, and strange "little people," also called "shadow people," who sometimes visited the reservation.

Yet, although Gabe and Norio were clear that there were no ETs at Dulce, another witness, Darren Mitchell Gray, a member of the Jicarilla Apache tribe, told us that he was riding in a bus with schoolchildren, when all of them just about freaked out when they saw a flying disk. "The kids were screaming. The little girls were rushing to the head of the bus and they were holding on to the cloak of the priest. I couldn't believe my eyes. I was looking at a flying disk. I saw a UFO coming from the area of Archuleta Mesa." And another witness testified that "Something had come over the car. Three red lights in a triangular shape."

He told us that he had seen what could only have been a UFO flying over the Jicarilla Apache reservation.

We saw some wild things at Dulce and were told some hair-raising stories. But, having heard the different sides of the Dulce story, Kevin was still unconvinced that an entire underground facility could be constructed without raising the interest of those working and recreating on the surface. How could the excavation of a secret facility take place in plain sight of those living above it? And for that answer, akin to a proof of concept, we traveled to the site of just such a facility, constructed during the Cold War as part of President Eisenhower's plan to keep the United States government functioning in the event of a nuclear attack. That facility, whose existence was ultimately revealed in *The Washington Post*, is known as the Greenbrier.

THE GREENBRIER

This lavish White Sulphur Springs, West Virginia, resort, a 1913 throwback to a gilded age of opulence, is hardly the place for a secret bunker. This is what Kevin Cook remarked upon as our car pulled up to the classically Georgian-style entrance. Imagine a heavily fortified, self-sufficient, but harshly bland series of concrete chambers constructed under *Downton Abbey* while the Crawleys and their service staff went through their days above ground in complete oblivious insouciance.

As our tour guide, Linda Walls, remarked as we met her at the entrance, "The best way to keep a secret is to hide it in plain sight."

Dating the foundation of the resort to 1778, even before the Treaty of Paris that ended the Revolutionary War, Linda said that the resort had a tremendous history. The construction of the actual bunker began in 1958 and was completed in 1961, Linda told Kevin. The bunker is over 112,000 square feet and is lodged underneath the West Virginia wing of the resort. Walking us through the main foyer and adjoining halls of the resort, Linda led us through the wing to a decorated false wall, camouflaging a huge, heavy door, which was the entrance to the bunker. "Behind this wall, you'll be amazed at what you'll see," she said as Pat Uskert folded back the wall to reveal an eighteen-ton metal door. We turned the large wheel that rolled back the police-type bars that bolted into the wall and, voilà, the bunker was accessible. It was like entering a time capsule, a machine transporting us back to the stomach-crunching fear of the Cold War and the threat that a powerful explosion of light from a nuclear warhead and an incinerating fireball generating a mushroom cloud of radioactive dust would change the world forever.

"Once the decision was made to seal the bunker from the outside," Linda explained, "those inside would have had to rely on a sixty-day supply of food, a forty-two-day supply of diesel fuel, and a limited supply of oxygen." To have even known about this facility, one would had to have reached a top-security clearance. However, every day, hotel guests at Greenbrier walked past the camouflaged vault doors to visit the conference center in the West Virginia Wing, and they never knew they sere standing over a top-secret government facility. In fact, the entrance room to the bunker was also used as an exhibit center. Linda explained that thousands of visitors to conferences had actually stood in a part of the bunker without realizing the facility's true purpose. It was simply a conference center for things like medical exhibits or book exhibits that could have been sealed off from the rest of the world when the alarm sounded that the Soviets had gone into missile-launch mode or that their nuclear heavy bombers were heading over the Bering Straits, which was the fear during the 1962 Cuban Missile Crisis.

"When the time came to seal the bunker," Linda explained, "this conference center where we are standing would have been divided into twenty-four offices for the support staff of Congress." Inside the bunker there were also hospitals, dormitories, and even a crematorium.

"How was it possible that this place was constructed without hotel guests and hotel staff knowing about it?" Pat asked.

Linda said that she was working at the resort while the bunker was still a secret, but had heard rumors about it from other members of the staff. Asked whether she had ever seen anyone looking suspicious walking toward the exhibit center portion of the bunker, Linda explained that she and others did have questions about some of the television repair workers. That was the cover. The television repair crews were actually building out the bunker facility.

"We now know that the television repair crews were spending eighty-five percent of their time working on shelter management," Linda said.

Kevin made the obvious connection between Greenbrier and Dulce, conceding that if the government could construct this entire bunker facility in plain sight at a resort frequented by guests from Washington and the suburbs, it was conceivable that the Dulce facility could have been constructed on relatively inaccessible Jicarilla Apache reservation land.

We asked Linda when she first learned, for real, that the bunker existed under the Greenbrier.

"The day the article appeared in *The Washington Post*," she said.

On May 31, 1992, *The Post* broke the story of the existence of the bunker. But until that time no one knew that the Greenbrier resort was a cover for a bunker to house the legislature and their support staff during and in the aftermath of a nuclear attack. Linda said that the last government truck left the facility on July 31, 1995. This meant that not only was the Greenbrier bunker still functioning, but that it was likely, in fact almost certain, that other similar facilities were already functioning as bunkers in times of war. Just as important for our purposes, Greenbrier was the proof for the possibility of a Dulce facility in both the construction and operational phases. In fact, Kevin said, according to calculations he made, if the Greenbrier facility was over 112,000 square feet, Dulce could have been over 300,000 square feet. And it could have taken over a decade to build without even a hint of activity in the outside world, particularly because it was on an Apache nation reservation. The people who built Dulce, if, in fact, it was built, could have constructed it for a variety of reasons, not necessarily to house

ETs and human scientists. And building it on reservation land meant that no one would question it, and even if someone did, he or she would be told to shut up about it. Even our own guide, Richard Vigil, would not show Pat the holes leading into the interior of the mesa. He was that cautious.

BILL'S BLOG

By the end of this episode, we'd established proof of concept of underground secret facilities. It only takes one facility to establish that. We'd spoken to a number of self-described eyewitnesses who said they saw UFOs hovering over the Archuleta Mesa. We spoke to people and eyewitnesses who described cattle mutilations and had actually seen, and photographed, black helicopters over the carcasses of mutilated cows. On a separate occasion when I visited the mesa, a black helicopter hovered over our small team and, hours later, Gabe Valdez telephoned our guide Richard Vigil to ask if we enjoyed the trek to the top. When I asked how Gabe knew we were there, he said that the helicopter hovering over the mesa had photographed our presence. Why? What are they trying to hide and who are "they"?

We saw an actual photograph of the strangest kind of entity I had ever seen in my entire life, a fetus in the womb of a mutilated cow. But it's not a bovine fetus. What was it? Is there some exotic genetic experimentation going on at Archuleta? Is there an interbreeding of species going on and incubation inside cows, which is why they're mutilating these cattle and using UFOs as a cover story? If you don't believe that all this can go on under the very eyes of an entire population, pay a visit to the Greenbrier, a completely undisclosed secret underground base constructed before the eyes of a very well-heeled clientele. Greenbrier proves that these types of underground bases are not only a possibility but an absolute reality.

If the Greenbrier served as proof for the possible construction of Dulce, we were still left with the question of why. Were people like John Rhodes and John Lear correct in their revelations about the stories told by Ann West and Thomas Castello? Were the descriptions of strange craft by members of the Jicarilla Apache nation conclusive proof of UFO activity over the area? Or, as I suspected, was there an even darker explanation for all the phenomena people had observed?

Later in the third season of *UFO Hunters*, we visited Bucks County, Pennsylvania, to investigate the sightings over Philadelphia and its suburbs, including Hunterdon County, New Jersey. We met with Nancy Talbot from BLT laboratories, where I had the chance to ask her about Dulce. She explained that you didn't need extraterrestrials to figure out what might have been the main purpose of a facility such as Dulce. She explained further that bovine serum is very close to human serum and, in fact, solutions based on bovine serum had been used to culture human ovum. To that point, a fugitive Dr. Josef Mengele, on the run in the 1950s through South America from Nazi hunters, once bragged to his patients in a small Brazilian community that he had the ability to grow human twins in the wombs of cows. We believe this might mean that cows themselves could have been used as incubation units for types of human hybrids, perhaps to grow organs specific to certain DNA types for organ replacement. Just imagine what that would mean to the military, to industry, to big pharmaceutical companies: an almost endless supply of genetically specific organ replacements for those who could afford it. All you need is the right kind of cow and the best medical insurance.

Nancy Talbot warned us that our exposure of the human-bovine fetus had stirred up some real discontent. Just a few years earlier, President George W. Bush had railed against human cloning and human-animal interbreeding in his 2006 State of the Union address. In 2009, after our March broadcast of the Dulce episode, senators Sam Brownback and Mary Landrieu, from Kansas and Louisiana, respectively, introduced a bipartisan bill to ban human-animal hybrids. Was this a result of our Dulce episode's revelation of a human-bovine fetus? Nancy Talbot had warned us that we had stepped on some very big toes, which were not necessarily the toes of extraterrestrials, assuming they had toes. And weeks after that warning, my sartorial CIA friend took me patiently and quietly aside on the shores of the Long Island Sound and, although smiling, explained in very specific terms that although we could hunt down UFOs to our hearts' content; tickle the perimeters of Area 51, triggering Humvee headlight responses from the camo-dude guards posted inside; describe ten-thousand-year-old alien artifacts buried beneath the ancient hall of records under the Sphinx; demonstrate with the evidentiary precision of a Perry Mason that the Orfordness Lighthouse could not have possibly been the source of the moving light in Rendlesham Forest, we could never, ever, at our own peril, get between an industry and its money.

It was a lesson we would soon learn.

OUR REVELS NOW ARE ENDED

U p until the inception of *UFO Hunters* most UFO-themed reality shows followed a set formula. In the first part of the show, bring on the experts, the graybeards, the researchers, maybe a witnesses or two, and assert the reality of UFOs. Then, in the latter parts of an episode, bring on the debunkers, sneering skeptics laughing at assertions of the ufologists. Then bring on the narrator, a voice of calm mediation often repeating the claims of both sides and providing the viewer with the calm reassurance that this case has two sides, but, until we have more proof, there is really nothing here, just entertainment, you can go home now. When we began the setup for episodes of *UFO Hunters*, we used a different approach. Rather than leave an unchallenged assertion that we were trying to prove UFOs were real, we started from the opposite end of the argument, focusing on the small details of the argument to see if the argument logically held any substance. We also looked for whatever evidence we could find that would either support or refute an argument. Sometimes we found that we could conclusively disprove a debunker assertion. We debunked the debunkers. Other times we approached the same forensic analysis to show that although an event might have been real, such as the 1897

Aurora UFO crash mystery, it likely was not a UFO at all. Other times, we let the evidence simply speak for itself by applying what we called the "plausibility test." Was it plausible that a debunker argument was logical or was the argument so implausible that a UFO explanation had greater plausibility? And this approach stood us in very good stead with viewers.

We also used the approach described by Sir Arthur Conan Doyle in his Sherlock Holmes stories. We evaluated every argument we could about a specific case and then sought to eliminate it conclusively. If we could eliminate it, it was gone. If we could not, then it stood further investigation until we hit a brick wall. Whatever remained was part of the mix. Most UFO debunkers start from the premise that extraordinary claims of UFOs require extraordinary evidentiary proof. But that's simply not true because they're starting from the premise that UFOs or ETs don't exist. It's a prejudged argument. As Sherlock himself, the world's greatest detective, albeit fictional, said in A Study in Scarlet, "It is a capital mistake to theorize before you have all the evidence. It biases the judgment." And this is exactly what most debunkers do and what we on UFO Hunters did not do. We reasoned backward by evaluating the major debunker arguments of a case on the basis of evidence and eliminated them if they didn't stand up to evidentiary scrutiny. Again, as Sherlock Holmes said in The Sign of the Four, "Eliminate all other factors, and the one which remains must be the truth." This became our mantra.

Here are some examples:

In the "UFO Before Roswell," our first televised episode, we sought to find any evidence that Harold Dahl actually saw a UFO that dropped molten slag on his boat, and that the B-25 Mitchell bomber crashed because it was carrying UFO debris from the Maury Island incident. Historical records told us that Harold Dahl eventually recanted his UFO story after he was visited by FBI agents following up on the crash. The Dahl story itself was not made public until after the Kenneth Arnold sighting, days later, was made public, and that Kenneth Arnold himself was hired by Ray Palmer, who had been contacted by Dahl's partner Fred Crissman, to investigate Dahl's story. Kenneth Arnold failed to find any evidence to support Dahl's story. However, because Army Air Force officer Lieutenant Frank Brown had investigated Kenneth Arnold and found him to be of high credibility and because Kenneth Arnold had contacted Frank Brown about the Dahl story, Frank Brown and Captain William Davidson flew a B-25 to Washington to investigate on behalf of the Army Air Force. Although Ray Palmer had sent the slag that Dahl claimed came from a UFO to a lab in Chicago, where no anomalous material was found, Davidson and Brown agreed to fly a box of the slag back to California for further analysis. Ultimately, the B-25 crashed in flames over Kelso, Washington, killing both Davidson and Brown. The cause of the crash was rumored to be the UFO material they carried. Our task was to untangle this story and establish what facts we could beyond the rumors.

We established that there was no extant physical evidence of any UFO material. The slag we found was simply that, residue from a smelting facility on Puget Sound. The Kelso crash site did exist and we found aircraft wreckage there. We also found the B-25 crash reports filed by the two noncommissioned officers that were part of the crew on Captain Davidson's B-25, whom Captain Davidson had ordered to parachute out from the plane when it caught fire. They did, and lived to file their reports, which, explained that because Davidson and Brown knew the plane was going down, they, heroically and in the best tradition of our military pilots, refused to parachute out and steered the doomed B-25 away from populated areas where the crash would cause innocent people on the ground to suffer injury and damage. They stayed with the ship, navigating it as it burned toward a desolate area where it crashed, killing both of them. Why did it crash?

From the crash reports we understood that a fire had broken out in the bomb bay where the cereal carton of slag was being stored. We knew from the crash reports that the fire spread to the wing. What caused the fire? To test out a causality theory, we took the slag we had collected from the beach at Maury Island and placed it near a circuit breaker panel that our effects producer had constructed to re-create a circuit breaker panel that might have been in the bomb bay of the B-25. Would the heavily ferrous slag override the breaker and instead of allowing it to break the circuit, jump the circuit, overload the electrical system, and cause an electrical fire? Would the aluminum alloy, once heated and oxidized, cause a large fire to break out so as to compromise the airworthiness of the plane?

Our experiment showed that this was a possibility; the ferrous material we set by our breaker panel caused an electrical fire. Our experiment with an aluminum sample showed that it would ignite explosively. We showed that what the tech sergeants reported was likely caused by the slag itself. Thus, although there was no UFO that we could determine, we did determine that it was the material that Davidson and Brown were transporting that caused the fire that resulted in the crash. Forensic analysis untangled the mysteries of the Kelso crash even though there was likely not a UFO. And in the very end we located Frank Brown's great-nephew, explained why his great-uncle had flown the B-25 to Washington, and provided him with our explanation of the crash. Our first episode didn't find the UFO, however we did find the likely cause of the crash and, in a moment that gratified all of us, brought closure, after sixty years, to the great-nephew of a heroic pilot and his captain. How great was that?

One more example and that's it, lest we find ourselves on a Möbius strip of endless repetition. The hotly debated RAF Bentwaters incident, revisited over the years since December 1980, when it first took place and was plumbed and plumbed again by generations of UFO researchers. At the end of the day, one issue hung out there. What was the light in Rendlesham Forest that U.S. Air Force security personnel and Deputy Base Commander Charles Halt saw? If they saw, as the debunkers argued, the beam from the nearby Orfordness Lighthouse as it swept across the land, then so much for the vaunted UFO. If it had been impossible for Colonel Halt and his team to have mistaken the Orfordness light for what they saw, then the debunker claims failed. What was it?

We walked through the entire story at RAF Bentwaters and through

Rendlesham Forest with the now retired Charles Halt. We ascertained that the military personnel at RAF Bentwaters knew exactly what the Orfordness beam looked like because they could see it from the runway. They'd seen it countless times. Then we retraced Halt's path through the forest to the open clearing at a farmhouse where he said his team saw the light, that had led them through the forest, came to rest and was self-illuminated so brilliantly that it looked like the windows of the farmhouse were aflame because of the reflection. The debunkers said that Halt and his team were still looking at the Orfordness beam reflecting from the farmhouse windows. Was it the beam or was it something else that reflected in the clearing? Okay, what would Sherlock Holmes do? First, he'd go to the lighthouse to see exactly where the beam would fall. Which is what we did.

The lighthouse keeper on the edge of the North Sea was Richard Seaman, who led us up the winding stairs to the light itself, where we saw that where the beam would track across the land there was a metal bar. He explained that the metal bar prevented the beam from playing across the forest and especially into the clearing where the farmhouse was. A moment of dispositive conclusiveness, but we needed more. After ascertaining that the light would have been prevented physically from playing across the forest, we headed back to the clearing where we met Charles Halt, who helped us plot out in the clearing exactly where the illuminated object was whose light reflected in the farmhouse windows. Then we plotted the location of the Orfordness Lighthouse. We took GPS waypoints for every position. Then, back at our effect producer's studio, we constructed a scale model of the forest, the clearing, the farmhouse, the object in the clearing that had led Halt through the forest, the position of Halt and his team, and laid out the direction of the lighthouse beam. John Tindall, our effects producer, set up a laser-pointer beam to mimic the beam from the lighthouse. Then, illuminating the entire board, he showed that the lighthouse beam, the bar across it preventing it from playing across the land notwithstanding, could not possibly have done a U-turn so as to reflect into the farmhouse windows. It was physically impossible. And thus we debunked the debunkers once again and showed that their primary explanation for the light in the forest was completely without merit, conclusively disposing of their arguments.

In addition to *UFO Hunters* being a snapshot in time, the series also marked the evolution of reality television itself from the very staid documentary presentations of *UFO Files* to the organic interactions among the principal characters more akin to *Ice Road Truckers, American Pickers,* and, even in some respects, to *Duck Dynasty.* You can see this over the three seasons as we tried different ways to engage an audience into suspending their disbelief so as to consider something so unbelievable as to challenge their very concept of reality. But in so doing, *UFO Hunters* was ultimately a television show, a succession of media moments.

Media itself is a form of a distortion field because it puts a frame around something so as to elevate from everyday reality into a degree of art. Television is art in a closed field, the stuff that dreams are made on, modifying reality to squeeze it through a camera lens. The camera itself is the first frame around reality and the television monitor or computer monitor is the next frame, turning raw reality into art simply by isolating it by enclosing it in a frame. Thus, series like *UFO Hunters, UFO Files,* and *Ancient Aliens* are heightened depictions of reality, distorted by the very act of filming, broadcasting, and viewing.

As an example of how television itself creates artifice even when documenting something ostensibly true, consider this. We began in season one by filming with only one camera until the Stephenville lights episode at the end of the season. Using only one camera meant that each element of a scene had to be filmed separately and then edited together. It also meant that each setup for a new show in the same segment meant cutting the scene, repositioning the camera on a different subject, be it a character, or a long shot or group shot, and then repositioning for another setup even in the same scene. Thus, Pat would be talking to Vincent Thirkettle in the Bentwaters episode and we wanted to capture the two of them talking, a close-up of Thirkettle talking, a reaction close-up shot of Pat, and Pat's next question to Thirkettle, then a two-shot from a distance. This was a completely artificial form of reality because sequential setups created a noncontinuity that had to be re-created into a continuous scene in the postproduction editing bays. Similarly in the Mexico's Roswell episode when we were interviewing our multiple guests in the Coyame desert, the single camera had to move from place to place in the same scene to capture movement, conversations, reaction shots, and close-ups, all of which were edited together in post. This, too, was a re-creation of reality.

When we started using two cameras, A camera might be filming the two or three shots of Pat, Ted, or Kevin, or me sharing information, while B camera would focus on a close-up of one of us either reacting or talking. It made for a faster shoot and, believe it or not, less artifice because what was being captured on tape was closer to the actuality of what was being depicted in the production cut even though the entire episode had been edited in post. Interestingly, when one of our viewers wrote to me that he could no longer watch the show because of what I had explained in a blog post that just the necessity of filming something that was not like filming a baseball game made for an artificial depiction of reality—video as art—I tried to explain to him that television itself was a form of artifice even when presenting something real. *UFO Hunters* was not raw news footage, but a sequence of images that, through art, conveyed what we saw as the truth. Hence, in a Keatsian universe, artifice was truth. Thus, *UFO Hunters* was not fiction even though the process of television production itself goes beyond journalism into a place where the reality itself is enhanced. We tried, in our own limited way, to achieve through revelation of what we discovered a moment of catharsis, where the heightened reality of television emblazoned a moment of truth about the reality we were depicting so as to bring the viewer to an appreciation and understanding of his or her own place in the universe.

Like the experience of Dave Bowman in *2001: A Space Odyssey,* we sought to bring our audience to the event horizon of their own collective childhood's end. It was an understanding not just to play out the possibility that we are not alone in the universe, but, like Dave in his final descent into the home world of the obelisk, to understand that in a universe of enormous possibilities:

We have met ET and it is us.

memory metal and, 52–54
Roswell incident and, 26–29, 31–32,
34–40, 45, 50–54, 56–57, 61, 63, 298
Army Corps of Engineers, U.S., 79
Arnold, Kenneth, 338–39
art, 289
giant triangles and, 102–3
Phoenix lights and, 130–31
television-created artifice and, 342–43
Aryanism, 147, 170–75, 179
A-10s, 117, 120
Atlanta Child Murders, 317
Aurora UFO crash, 109, 338
Auschwitz, 171, 190
Austria, 172
Autec episode, 88
Aviation Week & Space Technology, 120,
129–30, 201, 227
Avrocar, 193, 195

B

Bad Solsburg, 189–90
Baldwin, Garth:
Dulce Base and, 327–28
Needles incident and, 151, 153–55
Southaven Park incident and, 267–68
ballistic missiles, 147, 169, 182, 197, 269,
278, 311–12, 331
ball lightning, 219
balloons:
fire, 31, 36
giant triangles and, 93
helium, 78–79
memory metal and, 55
metal-clad, 99
Morristown lights and, 84–86, 90
physical appearance of, 37, 51
Project Mogul and, 26, 28, 33–34, 38,
46, 51–53, 55
Roswell incident and, 26, 28, 30,
32–34, 36–39, 46, 51–53, 55, 57
Tinley Park lights and, 67, 71, 76,
78–81, 84
weather, 26, 30, 32–33, 36–38, 46, 51,
55, 57
Balthaser, Dennis, 39, 43–44
Barbaresco, John, 127–28
Barnett, Barney, 44, 48–49
Barwood, Francis Emma:

Phoenix lights and, 121–23, 136, 138–40
Symington's news conferences and,
122–23
Bat Cave, 49
Bechtel, 322–23
Beck, Chip, 277
Bell Laboratories, 42
Bellport, N.Y., 244, 251
Bennewitz, Paul, 313–14
Berlin, 143, 169, 173, 181, 184
Berlin Wall, 312
Berne, Eric, 190
Bible, 282, 289
binoculars, 116, 258
birdlike artifacts:
in giant triangles, 93, 102–4, 107–8,
110, 112–13
model of, 104, 107–8, 110, 112–13
physical appearance of, 102, 107
Birnes, Nancy, 18, 61
Bittner, Robert, 159
black budget programs:
Phoenix lights and, 119–20, 124, 130
Schratt and, 192, 194
Black Forest, 177
Black Panthers, 200, 234, 241
Blanchard, William, 28–30, 35, 38–40
Blavatsky, Helena Petrovna, 170–71
blimps, 129–30
Blonder, Steven, 125–27
BLT laboratories, 335
Blue Book, Project:
Heflin and, 208–9, 214–16
McDonald and, 202, 207, 232
RB-47 and, 226, 232
Tinley Park lights and, 80
Zamora and, 217, 219–20
Bob X (undercover operative), 316–17
Boeing 737s, 78
Boston, Mass., 19, 238
Boyd, Alpha, 58–59
brains, 322
belief systems and, 21
Star Child Skull and, 291–92, 294,
296–97, 309
Braun, Wernher von, 195–97
ETs and, 174
Nazi UFOs and, 191–92, 195
Brazel, Mac, 35, 37–38, 47